ACTION RESEARCH

ACTION RESEARCH

Fourth Edition

Ernest T. Stringer
Curtin University of Technology

Los Angeles | London | New Delhi
Singapore | Washington DC

Los Angeles | London | New Delhi
Singapore | Washington DC

FOR INFORMATION:

SAGE Publications, Inc.
2455 Teller Road
Thousand Oaks, California 91320
E-mail: order@sagepub.com

SAGE Publications Ltd.
1 Oliver's Yard
55 City Road
London EC1Y 1SP
United Kingdom

SAGE Publications India Pvt. Ltd.
B 1/I 1 Mohan Cooperative Industrial Area
Mathura Road, New Delhi 110 044
India

SAGE Publications Asia-Pacific Pte. Ltd.
3 Church Street
#10-04 Samsung Hub
Singapore 049483

Copyright © 2014 by SAGE Publications, Inc.

Printed in the United States of America

Library of Congress Cataloging-in-Publication Data

Stringer, Ernest T.
Action research / Ernest T. Stringer, Curtin University of Technology.

pages cm
Includes bibliographical references and index.

ISBN 978-1-4522-0508-3 (pbk.) — ISBN 978-1-4833-0183-9 (web pdf)
1. Human services—Research. 2. Action research. I. Title.

HV11.S835 2014
361—dc23   2013013952

This book is printed on acid-free paper.

Acquisitions Editor: Helen Salmon
Assistant Editor: Kalie Koscielak
Editorial Assistant: Kaitlin Perry
Production Editor: Libby Larson
Copy Editor: Mark Bast
Typesetter: C&M Digitals (P) Ltd.
Proofreader: Bonnie Moore
Indexer: Maria Sosnowski
Cover Designer: Candice Harman
Marketing Manager: Nicole Elliott

SFI® Certified Sourcing
www.sfiprogram.org
SFI-00453

SFI label applies to text stock

14 15 16 17 10 9 8 7 6 5 4 3 2

CONTENTS

Foreword   **x**
Egon G. Guba

Preface   **xv**

About the Author   **xxii**

1. **Research in Professional and Public Life**   **1**
   The Purposes and Applications of Action Research:
       Who Does Action Research, and Why Do They Do It?   1
           Action Research: Systematic Processes of Inquiry   5
   Making a Difference: Practical, Solutions-Oriented Inquiry   10
   Participatory Approaches to Inquiry   14
   The Role of the Researcher   20
   Working Principles   23
       Relationships   24
       Communication   26
       Participation   28
       Inclusion   31

2. **The Theory Behind the Practice**   **36**
   The Theoretical Foundations of Action Research   36
   The Place of Theory in Action Research   37
   The Theory Behind the Practice   40
   "But It's Not Scientific": The Question of Legitimacy   41
   Power, Control, and Subordination   45
   Understanding Power and Control: Postmodern Perspectives   47
   Action Research: The Next Generation   54
   Giving Voice: Representing People's Experience   57
   Changing Work and Social Practices: "Scripts" for Policies,
       Plans, and Procedures   59
   What We Learn From the Literature   64
   In the Company of Friends   68

3. Setting the Stage: Planning a Research Process   **73**

Designing Effective Research   73

Seeking Consensus: Designing Meaningful Research   75

Entering the Field: Building a Picture   76

    Establishing Contact   76

    Sampling: Identifying Stakeholding Groups   77

    Sampling: Identifying Key People   79

    Establishing a Role   81

    Agenda   82

    Stance   82

    Position   82

Mapping the Context: Constructing a Preliminary Picture   85

Ethics in Action Research   88

    Formal Ethics Approval: Internal Review Boards

        and Agency Procedures   91

Checking for Rigor   91

    Credibility   92

    Transferability   93

    Dependability   94

    Confirmability   94

Sociable Research Processes   94

Collaborative Design: A Foundation for Effective Research   96

4. Look: Gathering Data   **99**

Focusing: Framing the Research Question   99

Gathering Data: Acquiring Information   101

Sources of Information   103

Interviews: Guided Reflection   105

    Semistructured Questioning Procedures   106

    Field Notes: Applying the Verbatim Principle   110

    Tape Recorders   110

Focus Groups   111

Participant Observation   113

Documents, Records, and Reports   115

Visual Media   116

    Photographs and Videos   116

Surveys   118

Reviewing the Literature: Evidence From Research Studies   120

Gathering Statistical Information—How Many . . .?   122

Extended Understanding: Descriptive Analysis   123

	Alternative 1: Working Ethnographically—Collaborative	
	Descriptive Accounts	124
	Alternative 2: Six Questions—Why, What,	
	How, Who, Where, When	124
	Alternative 3: Community Profile	125
	Meetings: Group Processes for Collaborative Inquiry	127
	Preliminary Meetings	127
	Organizing Meetings	128
5.	**Think: Reflection and Analysis**	**135**
	Interpretation: Developing Understanding	136
	Analysis and Interpretation Phase I: Distilling the Data	139
	Categorizing and Coding	139
	Analyzing Key Experiences, Epiphanic Events,	
	or Critical Incidents	144
	Case Example: Facilitating Workshops	145
	Analysis and Interpretation Phase II: Enriching the Analysis	147
	Frameworks for Enriching the Analysis	148
	Alternative 1: Interpretive Questions—Why, What,	
	How, Who, Where, When	148
	Alternative 2: Organizational Review	150
	Alternative 3: Concept Mapping	152
	Alternative 4: Problem Analysis—Antecedents and	
	Consequences	155
	Writing Reports Collaboratively	157
	Organizing Meetings	157
	Procedures for Analysis	157
	Constructing Reports	159
	Participatory Visual Methods: Presentations	
	and Performances	160
	Conclusion	163
6.	**Act: Action Plans—Implementing Sustainable Solutions**	**166**
	Constructing Action Plans	166
	Planning	168
	Identifying Priorities for Action	168
	Constructing Action Plans	169
	Quality Check	173
	Implementing	175
	Supporting	175
	Modeling	178

	Linking	179
	Reviewing	180
	Evaluating	182
	Conclusion	183
7.	**Strategic Planning**	**187**
	Managing Sustainable Change	187
	Managing Processes of Change and Development	189
	Strategic Planning	191
	A Unifying Vision	192
	Operational Statements: Enacting the Vision	194
	Action Plans	195
	Reviewing the Plans	196
	Political Dimensions	196
	Budgeting and Financial Planning	198
	Guiding the Research Process	200
	Principles in Operation	200
	Appropriate Language	201
	Making Decisions	202
	Support and Monitoring	203
	Evaluating	204
	Steps to Evaluation	204
	Celebrating	207
8.	**Reports: Informing Stakeholders**	**210**
	The Purpose of Reporting	210
	Constructing General Reports	210
	Formal Reports	211
	Giving Voice: Reporting in Action Research	212
	Reports, Theses, and Dissertations	214
	Structure of a Report	217
	Section 1: Introduction—Focus and Framing	218
	Section 2: Review of the Literature	218
	Section 3: Methodology	219
	Section 4: Research Outcomes or Findings	223
	Section 5: Conclusion—Discussion of Findings	225
	Giving Voice: Alternative Report Structures	227
9.	**Action Research and the Internet**	**231**
	Social Media and Online Collaborative Tools	231
	Blogs	231
	Twitter	233

Facebook	234
Second Life	235
Skype	236
ooVoo	237
Google Docs	237
Dropbox	237
Wiki	238
Cloud Storage	239
PhotoVoice	239
Action Research Websites	240
General	240
Education	241
Community Development and Community Organizations	242
Disabilities	243
Health	244
Project Management and Evaluation	246
Gender Issues	246
Youth	246
Appendix: Case Examples of Formal Reports	**247**
Transitions: The Experiences of Older Women From Hospital to Home	**247**
Transitions: Experiences of Older People From Hospital to Home—Progress Report	**258**
A New Mathematics Curriculum	**264**
Understanding the "Understanding": Preliminary Findings on Aboriginal Perspectives on Engagement With Governments	**277**
Milyirrtjarra Kuurl Mirrka Palyalpayi (Making Good Food at Warburton School)	**287**
References	**293**
Index	**299**

FOREWORD

I was recently asked, in another context, to speculate on the future of educational research in the event it was to change in a direction that I hoped it would. My response was that I hoped *all* research that might properly be called human inquiry would exhibit three characteristics: decentralization, deregulation, and cooperativeness in execution. I believe that this book describes a mode of inquiry that fits all of these specifications.

By *decentralization* I meant to indicate a movement away from efforts to uncover generalizable "truths" toward a new emphasis on local context. The hiatus between theory and practice has been remarked on too often to require repetition here. The reason for that hiatus, I have long asserted, lies in the gap between general laws and specific applications; such laws can have, at best, only probabilistic implications for specific cases. The fact, for example, that 80% of patients presenting a given set of symptoms are likely to have lung cancer does not imply that a particular patient with those symptoms ought to immediately be rushed into surgery.

We have witnessed, over the past half century or so, determined efforts to find general solutions to social problems, be they low pupil achievement, drug abuse, alcoholism, AIDS, or other challenges. The cost to national economies has been prodigious, and there is precious little to show for it, little "bang for the buck," as some folks are wont to say. It ought to be apparent by now that generalized, one-size-fits-all solutions do not work. The devil (or God, if you prefer) is in the details. Without intimate knowledge of local context, one cannot hope to devise solutions to local problems. *All* problems are de facto local; inquiry must be decentralized to the local context.

By *deregulation* I meant to indicate a movement away from the restrictive conventional rules of the research game, the overweening concern with validity, reliability, objectivity, and generalizability. I have argued elsewhere that these methodological criteria can have meaning only within a paradigm of inquiry that is defined in the conventional way and, specifically, based on the premise of concrete, tangible reality. However useful the premise of such a reality may be in the physical sciences (and history has shown it to be useful there indeed), it is simply irrelevant in the arena of human inquiry, for in that arena there is no tangible reality; everything that social inquirers study depends on mental constructions and mental interpretations. Thus the usual distinction between ontology (the nature of reality) and epistemology (how one comes to know that reality) collapses: Inquirers do not "discover" knowledge by watching nature do its thing from behind a one-way mirror; rather, it is literally created by the interaction of inquirers with the "object" (construct) into which they have inquired. Whatever may be the criteria for research quality in this new arena, the conventional criteria clearly do not fit.

By *cooperativeness in execution* I meant to indicate a style of inquiry in which there is no functional distinction between the researcher and the researched "subjects" (in conventional parlance). They are all defined as participants, and they all have equal footing in determining what questions will be asked, what information will be analyzed, and how conclusions and courses of action will be determined. These participants, sometimes called stakeholders or local members, may include some with special training in inquiry, but if so, these specialists have no privilege in determining how the study will go; *all* participants share the perquisites of privilege. I insist on this joint approach both because local stakeholders are the only extant experts on local culture, beliefs, and practices and because moral considerations require that local perspectives be honored.

The reader will quickly see, I am sure, that this book conforms to these stipulations exceptionally well. On the matter of decentralization, Dr. Stringer takes issue with "applied scientific expertise" aimed at "eradicat[ing] [a] problem by applying some intervention at an individual or programmatic level" (Chapter 1). He argues that there is evidence to suggest that "centralized policies and programs generated by 'experts' have limited success" in overcoming problems. His proposal for action research returns the focus of inquiry to the local context.

On the matter of deregulation, Dr. Stringer asserts, in a previous edition, that "formal research operates at a distance from the everyday lives of practitioners, and largely fails to penetrate the experienced reality of their day-to-day work. The objective and generalizable knowledge embodied in social and behavioral research often is irrelevant to the conflicts [they] encounter" (Chapter 1). He opts instead for the resurgence of action research, which is fundamentally different from the classic approach of defining variables and generating, through hypotheses and tests, explanations for why people behave as they do. That action research may not conform to conventional criteria of research rigor is much less important than the fact that it takes a more democratic, empowering, and humanizing approach; assists locals in extending their own understanding of their situations; and helps them to resolve the problems they see as important.

On the matter of cooperativeness in execution, Dr. Stringer calls for a form of inquiry that represents a "moral intertwining" of all participants, including, of course, the inquirer. The major concerns that occupy the attention of all but the most ardently conservative investigators—empowerment, democracy, equity, liberation, freedom from oppression, and life enhancement—are central to action research. Ethics and morality are inscribed as essential features of human inquiry—not simply as standards to be met in the interest of humanity but as standards that determine the very nature of study outcomes. Values cannot be separated from the core of an inquiry by the simple expedient of claiming objectivity, for findings are literally created by the inquiry process. And that process is permeated by values at every step.

Now, all of this has a very theoretical sound, and that lack of grounding is one of the major difficulties that has accompanied calls for new approaches and new paradigms. However important theoretical justifications may be, they have little value if their implications are not translated into forms useful to the *practitioners* of this nontraditional social research. It is this urgent need to which this book responds and, in my opinion, responds very well. Let me mention several of its features that commend it for this purpose:

- The language of the book is eminently accessible to practitioners who may be unfamiliar with typical research parlance. This is clearly not a book written solely for professional researchers; it is within the grasp of any reasonably literate reader. There is no arcane language to confuse the unwary.

- Every procedure described is accompanied by step-by-step instructions. The professional researcher may find these instructions unnecessarily detailed, but the novice will surely appreciate being helped at each juncture. And even the professional will find the details useful precisely because the approach differs so dramatically from what is normally found in a research methods text.

• The book is written to be useful to a wide variety of audiences, including but not limited to teachers, health workers, social workers, community workers, counselors, and many other lay workers and professionals. But to say that a book is intended to be useful for this or that audience has little meaning unless those audience members can find themselves represented in examples and depicted in situations. This aim is well met in this volume.

• The representations made by the author are illustrated throughout by personal anecdotes. Indeed, the inclusion of these anecdotes is perhaps the most useful feature of the book, because it makes clear to the reader that the author is speaking from a wealth of personal experience. He has not only "talked the talk" but also "walked the walk." The reader can have confidence that every assertion has been validated in a real-life situation and that every procedure recommended has been found to work in some real-world instance. And precisely because the author makes plain that his background is not essentially dissimilar from the reader's, the reader will find these anecdotes confidence building. What is being proposed is not only possible for an expert but also possible for an everyday reader. And if it can work with a cultural group as different from "typical" Westerners as are Australian Aboriginals, it can probably work in just about any cultural setting.

It is not only the practitioner of action research with whom Dr. Stringer is concerned, however; he is equally interested in persuading the more conservative academic of the soundness of his proposals. Accordingly, he includes a final chapter that sets the whole in a proper theoretical context. His reflections address the question of the legitimacy of his proposed approach in order to secure for it a wider acceptance, discuss the issues of power and control, and set action research in the context of the postmodern position. The skeptic and the critic may or may not find his arguments persuasive, but, if taken seriously, these arguments raise important questions about which each reader will have to satisfy himself or herself. And the novice may take comfort in the fact that rational arguments do exist for the practice of a kind of inquiry that many practitioners have intuitively felt to be right (for them) but about which they have felt insecure on the grounds of rigor or objectivity. There is indeed more in heaven and earth than has been dreamed of in the received philosophy.

—Egon G. Guba

IN MEMORIAM: EGON G. GUBA

Once in a while we come upon people who make a significant difference in our lives. Egon was one of those people for me. His gentle friendship, insistent mentoring, and keen intellect provided the impetus to write this, my first book. Initially rejected by the publishers, it is now in its fourth edition and a tribute to the man who helped me frame and shape my rough ideas into a form that now provides a resource for people around the world.

The legacy of Egon's contribution to the world of research and evaluation will last through the ages as people construct and support their research scaffold on the foundation he, with his wife, Yvonna, laid down in recent decades. Thank you, Egon Guba, for the wonderful gift you gave to us all.

PREFACE

THE PURPOSE OF THIS BOOK

This book has been written for those workers, both professional and non-professional, who provide services to people in community, organizational, or institutional contexts. It speaks to teachers, health professionals, social workers, community and youth workers, businesspeople, planners, and a whole range of other people in teaching, service delivery, or managerial roles. Its purpose is to provide a set of research tools that will enable people to deal effectively with many of the problems that confront them as they perform their work. I attempt to provide clear guidelines to enable novice practitioner researchers to move comfortably through a process of inquiry that provides effective solutions to significant problems in their work lives. The "biographical bulletins" that punctuate the text are designed to clarify meaning and to increase understanding of relevant facets of research processes.

THE ROLE OF THE RESEARCHER

A common approach to action research envisages processes of inquiry based on a practitioner's reflections on his or her professional practices. It has been clear to me for many years that while reflection on practice is an important ingredient in any context, when practitioners remain locked into their own perceptions and interpretations of a situation, they fail to take into account the varied worldviews and life experiences of the people with whom they work. They can fail to understand fundamental dynamics that determine the ways their clients, students, patients, or customers will behave or respond in any given circumstance. Action research as presented in this text works from an assumption that all people affected by or having an effect on an issue should be involved in the processes of inquiry.

In these circumstances the task of the practitioner researcher is to provide guidance and support to other participants or stakeholders in the research process. I therefore speak throughout this book to those who coordinate or facilitate inquiry as research facilitators. For ease and clarity, I often shorten this to researchers or facilitators. Practitioners may accept the role of researcher, therefore, when they enact research processes with groups of other stakeholders—students, clients, administrators, and so on. Ultimately, however, all participants in the research process should rightfully be called researchers insofar as they engage in deliberate processes of inquiry or investigation with the intent of extending their understanding of a situation or a problem.

In many situations, the demands of professional or community life prevent practitioners from taking such an active leadership role, and these practitioners may call on the services of outside consultants to perform coordinating, facilitating functions. In such cases, the consultants can accept the role designated in this book as researchers or research facilitators.

FOURTH EDITION

Previous editions of this text were largely derived from my experience in a variety of Australian contexts. Much of my initial writing was based on work with Aboriginal community groups and organizations and with government departments, business, and industry. In recent decades, however, I have extended my experience through work in numerous sites in the United States, East Timor, Singapore, the United Kingdom, Europe, South Africa, and more recently in the remote Ngaanyatjarra Lands in the desert areas of Western Australia. Here, a group of Aboriginal women have demonstrated how action research can enhance the strength and resilience of even the most marginalized peoples. In these circumstances I have been able to verify my faith in the processes incorporated into this book, engaging in projects that enable people from diverse social, cultural, and economic backgrounds to work strongly and productively on issues affecting their lives. As I write this edition at Cornell University Public Service Center I continue to be astonished by the wide range of community-based activities generated by and with staff of the center that enrich the experience of both faculty and students.

I have attempted to integrate the flavor of some of this wide-ranging work into this text, but limitations of space prevent a full exploration. Suffice it to say that I continue to find the process of unleashing the energy and potential of the people to be both humbling and fulfilling. I have watched in admiration as a small neighborhood group in New Mexico engaged in a delightfully effective action research project in their local school and have been filled with awe at the emerging power of the people of East Timor as they rebuilt a school system devastated by departing occupying forces. I have been amazed at the way Aboriginal women have transformed a small breakfast program into a more extensive community development program that incorporated a community and regional catering service, production of school learning materials, and development of learning activities with students. The desire to "tell the story" of their work took them to conferences and government departments, far out of the comfort zone of their small desert communities into alien city environments, where they stunned audiences with the simplicity and power of their presentations.

So it is "ordinary people" who give me the most satisfaction, as I watch them grow in skill and power as they accomplish wonderful outcomes through the systematic application of the research processes outlined in this book. But I am also impressed with people in positions of power and authority who, given the opportunity, provide the support and resources to accomplish these ends. Recently I wrote a small biography for an action research association in which I described the meaning that action research has given to me:

> Action research is more than a process, to me. It's a passion. . . . I have been constantly reassured that the wisdom of the people, and the knowledge they have of their own situation provides a much better basis for action than ideas that come from my own experience. I have been gratified by the deeply purposeful work in which people have engaged, delighted in the very practical, immediate outcomes they achieve, and heartened by the sense of empowerment that comes to them in the process. It is the energy and enthusiasm that results from these participatory processes that continues to inspire me.

My hope for you as you read this edition is that you will also come to be inspired, heartened, and gratified through engaging the potential of the people with whom you work through the systematic and soulful application of action research.

STRUCTURE OF THE BOOK

This book provides a resource for practitioners at all levels, to assist them in their efforts to conduct inquiry and to hone their investigative skills so that they will formulate effective solutions to the deep-rooted problems that detract from the quality of their professional lives. In the chapters that follow, I present an approach to inquiry that assists them to systematically explore real-life problems they experience in their work contexts and to formulate effective and sustainable solutions that enhance the lives of the people they serve.

Chapter 1 reviews the nature of research and provides an overview of action research. It includes a discussion of the basic values inherent in this approach to research and suggests professional, organizational, and community contexts where action research might be appropriately applied. The chapter also presents a basic routine—look, think, act—that serves as a framework to guide the research process. It presents a clear description of the role of the researcher and introduces the reader to the working principles of action research.

Chapter 2 presents the theoretical foundations of action research, assisting the reader to understand why it is carried out in the manner suggested in these pages. In doing so it provides an understanding of the ways in which action research is grounded in philosophical and theoretical developments that charter the multifaceted terrain of research in the social world.

Chapter 3 presents processes for designing an effective action research process. It includes the preliminary activity required to ensure that an adequate sample of people is included in the research and outlines processes for establishing initial contact with them. The chapter also maps out procedures for ensuring that research is carried out ethically and rigorously.

Chapter 4 focuses on data gathering—ways of gathering information that assist research participants in increasing their understanding of the issue they investigate. The chapter provides techniques for gathering and recording data—observation, interviews, surveys, document searches, and so on.

Chapter 5 provides a description of the process through which stakeholders interpret or analyze the data. It presents two major processes for distilling qualitative information to identify key features and elements that enable participants to develop insightful understandings of the issue investigated.

Chapter 6 presents procedures that enable participants to formulate practical solutions to their problems. Three phases of activity are described: planning, in which priorities are set and tasks defined; implementing, the supporting, modeling, and linking activity that enables participants to accomplish their tasks; and evaluating, through which participants review their progress.

Chapter 7 focuses on more complex processes for developing sustainable solutions to the deep-seated problems often contained within large organizations, government agencies, business corporations, and community contexts. This chapter provides an orientation to strategic planning processes and organizational arrangements for implementing activities and evaluating outcomes.

Chapter 8 suggests ways of organizing and formulating formal reports. It contrasts ways of organizing experimental scientific reports with structures appropriate for interpretive action research and then presents a more detailed approach to formulation of the latter. Although this style of reporting is relevant to formal reports required in bureaucratic settings and funding agencies, it is particularly suited to academic reports required for university theses and dissertations.

Chapter 9 acknowledges a changing world, where social media has become a central part of social life, providing the means to communicate with a broad range of people locally, regionally, nationally, and globally. It provides an introduction to some of the more common forms of social media, as well as an introduction to some of the resources available on the Internet. Instructors responsible for delivery of courses using this text might well consider covering this chapter early in the course, making use of social media to facilitate communication between participants and sharing of materials.

The appendix provides examples of reports from four action research projects.

ACKNOWLEDGMENTS

In previous editions of this book I have acknowledged many of the people who have contributed to its development. My debt to them continues, and the number of people who continue to participate in the development of ideas likewise proliferates. My first forays into the research literature, initiated by my good friend Geoff Mills, eventually moved me to write the first edition of this volume under the wonderful guidance of Egon Guba. Seven books later, I am still refining my understanding of action research and find myself both nurtured and challenged by my interactions with colleagues, friends, students, and my family. Similarly, I find that my contributions as an editorial board member of the *Action Research Journal* and my time as president of the Action Learning, Action Research Association extended my understanding and capacity to engage in effective action research.

More recently, the youth and energy of Ros Beadle have provided me with an enriched understanding of the potential of social media and multimedia in action research, and the reemergence of my good friend Anthony Kelly has regrounded me in a developmental approach that seeks to build the human potential that is part of any social or community context. The staff of the Public Service Center have likewise contributed greatly to my work at Cornell University, and I particularly thank Leonardo Vargas Mendez, Amy Somchanhmavong, and Leslie Montanye for providing a home for me in Ithaca. My time here was also enriched by continuing conversations with David Greenwood and Shelley Feldman and many other faculty with whom I came into contact. I thank all those with whom I have interacted in these contexts, as they provide the rich diversity of relationship and perspective that nurtures my professional and community life.

Centrally, though, I acknowledge the strongly supportive role provided by my partner, wife, companion, and friend Rosalie Dwyer, who continues to nurture the creative spirit within me. Her thoughtful comments, active encouragement, detailed scrutiny, and constant companionship provided the personal and spiritual energy that sustained me through the process of writing and editing.

Finally, I would like to acknowledge the fine work of the editorial team at Sage who continue to provide the detailed support required to engage the extended processes of writing, editing, and producing this book. Thank you most especially to Helen Salmon and Kaitlin Perry in editorial, Libby Larson in production, copy editor Mark Bast, and Nicole Elliott in marketing.

SAGE and the author gratefully acknowledge the feedback from the following reviewers: Erik Juergensmeyer of Fort Lewis College; Pamela L. Clark of Plymouth State University; Louis H. Berry of the University of Pittsburgh; Hollyce Giles of Guilford College; and Susan T. Dinnocenti of Sacred Heart University.

COMMUNITY-BASED ACTION RESEARCH

Where previous editions of this book have referred to *community-based action research,* this edition uses the simpler term *action research.* In my understanding of action research, to be effective the processes of inquiry must always be participatory and seek to establish a sense of community among participants. Community based, in the sense of establishing a "common unity" of purpose and perspective, is inherent in all aspects of investigation. Through working together, establishing an understanding of each other's experience and perspective, we establish the basis for truly effective outcomes, with head, heart, and hand.

Community is not a place. It is a state of mind.

ABOUT THE AUTHOR

After an early career as a primary teacher and school principal, Ernest T. Stringer was a lecturer in education at Curtin University of Technology in Western Australia. From the mid-80s, based at Curtin's Centre for Aboriginal Studies, he worked collaboratively with Aboriginal staff and community people to develop a wide variety of innovative and highly successful education and community development programs and services. His work with government departments, community-based agencies, business corporations, and local governments assisted them to work more effectively with Aboriginal people. In recent years, as visiting professor at the University of New Mexico and Texas A&M University and as visiting fellow at Cornell University, he taught research methods courses and/or engaged in projects with African American and Hispanic community and neighborhood groups. As a UNICEF consultant he recently engaged in a major project to increase parent participation in East Timor schools. He is author of *Action Research* (Sage, 2007); *Action Research in Education* (Pearson, 2008); *Action Research in Health* (with Bill Genat; Pearson, 2004); and *Action Research in Human Services* (with Rosalie Dwyer; Pearson, 2005). Until recently, he was a member of the editorial board of the *Action Research Journal* and past president of the Action Learning, Action Research Association (ALARA).

1

RESEARCH IN PROFESSIONAL AND PUBLIC LIFE[1]

THE PURPOSES AND APPLICATIONS OF ACTION RESEARCH: WHO DOES ACTION RESEARCH, AND WHY DO THEY DO IT?

Action research is a systematic approach to investigation that enables people to find effective solutions to problems they confront in their everyday lives. Unlike experimental or quantitative research that looks for generalizable explanations related to a small number of variables, action research seeks to engage the complex dynamics involved in any social context. It uses continuing cycles of investigation designed to reveal effective solutions to issues and problems experienced in specific situations and localized settings, providing the means by which people in schools, businesses, community agencies and organizations, and health and human services may increase the effectiveness and efficiency of their work. In doing so it also seeks to build a body of knowledge that enhances professional and community practices and works to increase the well-being of the people involved.

For many people, professional and service occupations—teaching, social work, health care, psychology, youth work, and so on—provide appealing avenues of employment. These occupations have the potential to provide meaningful and fulfilling work that is intrinsically rewarding. Increasingly, however, people in these sectors find their work to be more demanding and less satisfying. They often struggle to balance growing demands on their time and energy as their workloads continue to expand, and they are routinely confronted by problems rarely encountered 20 or 30 years ago.

The pressures experienced in professional practice reflect tensions in contemporary society. The complex influences that impinge on people's everyday social lives provide a fertile seedbed for a proliferating host of family, community, and institutional problems. Professional practitioners and agency workers are increasingly held accountable for solutions to problems that have their roots in the deeply complex interaction between the experiences of people and the realities of their social lives: stress, unemployment, family breakdown, alienation, behavioral problems, violence, poverty, discrimination, conflict, and so forth.

Although adequately prepared to deal with the technical requirements of their daily work, practitioners often face recurrent crises outside the scope of their professional expertise. Teachers face children disturbed by conflict in their homes and communities, youth workers encounter resentful and alienated teenagers, health workers confront people apparently unconcerned about life-threatening lifestyles and social habits, and social and welfare workers are strained past their capacity to deal with the impossible caseloads spawned by increasing poverty and alienation.

There is an expectation in social life that trained professionals, applying scientifically derived expertise, will provide answers to the proliferating problems that confront people in their personal and public lives. Community responses to crises that arise from drug abuse, crime, violence, school absenteeism, and so on invariably revolve around the use of a social worker, youth worker, counselor, or similar type of service provider whose task it is to eradicate the problem by applying some intervention at an individual or programmatic level. These responses have failed to diminish growing social problems that have multiplied much faster than human and financial resources available to deal with them. Moreover, evidence suggests that centralized policies and programs generated by "experts" have limited success in resolving these problems. The billions of dollars invested in social programs have failed to stem the tide of alienation and disaffection that characterize many areas of social life in modern industrial nations.

If there are answers to these proliferating social problems, it is likely that centralized policies will need to be complemented by the creative action of those closest to their sources—the service professionals, agency workers, students, clients, communities, and families who face the issues on a daily basis. Centralized policies, programs, and services, I suggest, should allow practitioners to engage the human potential of all people who contribute to the complex dynamics of the contexts in which they work. Policies and programs should not dictate specific actions and procedures but instead should provide the resources to enable effective action appropriate to particular places. The daily work of practitioners often provides many opportunities for them to acquire valuable insights into people's social worlds and to assist them in formulating effective solutions to problems that permeate their lives.

We therefore need to change our vision of service professionals and administrators from mechanic or technician to facilitator and creative investigator. This new vision rejects the mindless application of standardized practices across all settings and contexts and instead advocates the use of contextually relevant procedures formulated by inquiring and resourceful practitioners. The pages that follow describe some of the ways professional and community workers can hone their investigative skills, engage in systematic approaches to inquiry, and formulate effective and sustainable solutions to the deep-rooted problems that diminish the quality of professional life. This volume presents an approach to inquiry that seeks not only to enrich professional practice but also to enhance the lives of those involved.

As a young teacher, I had the rare experience of being transferred from the relative security of a suburban classroom to a primary school in a remote desert region of Western Australia. My task was to provide education for the children of the Aboriginal people who, at this time, still lived as they had for millennia, moving through the land in small family groups, hunting for their food, and sleeping in leaf shelters. On my first day in class, I was confronted by a wall of silence that effectively prevented any possibility of teaching. The children refused to respond verbally to any of my queries or comments, hanging their heads, averting their eyes, and sometimes responding so softly that I was unable to hear what they said. In these discomfiting circumstances, I was unable to work through any of the customary routines and activities that had constituted my professional repertoire in the city. Lessons were abbreviated, disjointed, and seemingly pointless, and my professional pride took a distinct jolt as an ineffective reading lesson followed an inarticulate math period, preceding the monotony of my singular voice through social studies.

The silence of the children in the classroom was in marked contrast to their happy chatter as we walked through the surrounding bush that afternoon, my failing spirits leading me to present an impromptu natural science "lesson." In this and following lessons, the children taught me a great deal about the living bushland that was their natural home—the small

(Continued)

(Continued)

animals and birds that, though unseen by my city-bred eyes, were every-where; the plants, fruits, roots, and berries that were edible; the places where water could be found (precious commodity in this desert environ-ment); and how to survive when the weather was very hot. My "teachers" were a mine of information, and they revelled in the opportunities to demonstrate to me their knowledge about the environment and their skill in being able to move so easily in what I saw as a hostile setting.

I discovered that I was able to make use of this knowledge and interest in the classroom, fashioning a range of learning activities related to literacy, mathematics, social science, and natural science. In small ways I was thus able to accommodate my approach to teaching in this unique educational environment, but the experience endowed me with an understanding that the regular routines of teaching were unsuited to my current circumstances. All the taken-for-granted assumptions of my professional life rang hollow as I struggled to understand the nature of the problems that confronted me and to formulate appropriate educational experiences for this vibrant, inde-pendent, and sometimes fractious group of students. Texts, curricula, teaching materials, learning activities, classroom organization, speech, interactional styles, and all other facets of classroom life became subjects of inquiry and investigation as I sought to resolve the constant stream of issues and prob-lems that emerged in this environment. To be an effective teacher, I discov-ered that it was necessary to modify and adapt my regular professional routines and practices to fit the lives of the children.

The legacy of that experience has remained with me. Although I have long since left school classrooms behind, the lessons I learned there still pervade all my work. I engage all professional, organizational, and community contexts with a deep sense of my need to explore and understand the situation. An attitude of inquiry enables me to engage, examine, explore, formulate answers, and devise responses to deal more effectively with each context I engage—and the diverse experiences and perspectives of the people within it.

In these situations, I now cast myself as a research facilitator, working with and supporting people to engage in systematic investigation that leads to clarity and understanding for us all and to provide the basis for effective action. In many places in the United States, Canada, Australia, East Timor, and Singapore I use techniques and procedures that can be fruitfully applied to the day-to-day work of people in schools, organiza-tions, and community settings. I am now a practitioner–researcher.[2]

As becomes evident in the following sections, action research is not merely a tool for applying a standardized set of procedures to professional, organizational, or community life, nor a "job" intended as the provenance of trained researchers. Neither is it a superficial set of routines that legitimate any set of social or professional practices. Far from providing a set of fixed prescriptions to be applied in any context, action research provides a flexible and practical set of procedures that are systematic, cyclical, solutions oriented, and participatory, providing the means to devise sustainable improvements in practice that enhance the lives and well-being of all participants.

Action Research: Systematic Processes of Inquiry

Research is systematic and rigorous inquiry or investigation that enables people to understand the nature of problematic events or phenomena. Research can be characterized by the following:

- A *focus* on a problem or issue to be investigated
- A systematic *process of inquiry*
- Development of *explanations* that lead to increased understanding

Research can be visualized as nothing more than a natural extension of the activities in which we engage every day of our lives. Even for simple problems— Where are my blue socks? Why did the cake burn?—we ask questions that enable us to analyze the situation more carefully. (I wore my blue socks yesterday; I probably put them with the laundry. Perhaps I overheated the oven, or maybe I left the cake in the oven longer than I should.) Tentative analysis enables us to understand the nature of the problem and to work toward a potential solution. (I looked in the laundry, and the socks were there. Next time I baked a cake, I lowered the temperature of the oven and did not burn the cake.) All research is an extension of these day-to-day inquiries and involves procedures that require people to move past their day-to-day understandings to engage more precise and rigorous forms of description, observation, and explanation. The meticulous association of what is observed and what is explained provides explanations whose power and efficacy exceeds those used in people's day-to-day lives. Experimental and survey research (sometime called quantitative research) is intended to provide generalizable explanations that provide the basis for predicting and controlling events and phenomena through rigorous application of numerically based hypothesis-testing procedures.

As becomes evident in the next chapter, however, although procedures for these types of investigation have been highly successful in predicting and controlling phenomena in the physical world, they are much more problematic in the social world. Research in the social world requires quite a different set of assumptions and procedures.

Action research therefore is based on the proposition that generalized solutions, plans, or programs may not fit all contexts or groups to whom they are applied and that the purpose of inquiry is to find an appropriate solution for the particular dynamics at work in a local situation. A lesson plan, a care plan, or a self-management plan that fits the lifeworld of a middle-class suburban client group may be only tangentially relevant in poor rural or urban environments or for people whose cultural lives differ significantly from the people who devised them. Generalized solutions must be modified and adapted in order to fit the context in which they are used.

In most fields of human activity—teaching, health care, social work, business, industry, and so on, there is often a need to modify and adapt processes to suit the particular people and conditions operating in their context. Around the world continuing reports testify to the fact that service professionals continue to have difficulty in working effectively with people whose social lives differ considerably from their own. The routine practices, plans, and processes that comprise their regular ways of working are ineffective, and they fail to accomplish outcomes required of their work. Their resulting stress and frustration is often mirrored in the antagonism or apathy of their clients and the continuing reports of failure of agencies to make headway in dealing with seemingly intractable social problems.

In these arenas, action research provides the means to systematically investigate and design more effective solutions to the complex array of issues at work in any social setting. The primary purpose of action research is to provide the means for people to engage in systematic inquiry and investigation to design an appropriate way of accomplishing a desired goal and to evaluate its effectiveness. As will become evident, however, practitioners do not engage this work in isolation. An assumption of action research is that those who have previously been designated as subjects or clients should participate directly in the research. Action research works on the assumption that all people who affect or are affected by the issue investigated should be included in the processes of inquiry. Professional practitioners, as research facilitators, engage their communities of interest in careful and systematic explorations that, in very direct ways, enable them to resolve complex issues in their individual, group, community, or organizational life and in so doing, to improve the quality of their lives.

As a graduate student, I was excited by the possibilities of experimental and survey research. Here, I thought, were the means for obtaining answers to the significant social problems that concerned me. By careful measurement of critical variables related to the problem under investigation and precise definition and measurement of the relationship between them, it would be possible to describe the genesis of the problem and take appropriate steps to resolve it. The major task was simply to identify the key variables and measure and analyze them using appropriate statistical techniques. It would then be possible to predict the ways people would behave or perform in particular circumstances and to take remedial action.

In my attempts to understand the reason for low achievement levels of minority students, I set out to map the variables that had impacts on their school performance, with the intent of first defining and then measuring the extent of the relationships between the factors that related to their academic performance. I equipped myself for the task by taking many courses in descriptive and inferential statistics and experimental and survey research methods, while concomitantly immersing myself in the voluminous and burgeoning research literature that spoke to these issues.

My disenchantment with this approach to inquiry came through courses in anthropology and sociology, which awakened me to a relativistic social universe. It was a perspective that revealed a world far different from the mechanistic, soulless vision that, at that time, was favored by scientists. For me, the new paradigm encompassed social spheres composed of the changing lives of people as they created and re-created their realities according to systems of meaning inherent in their differing situations. The social world, I discovered, was not static and mechanistic but dynamic and changing, encapsulated by and redefined continuously by the symbolic systems of thought and language through which human beings fashion their physical and social universe.

The transformation of my thought was dramatic. I realized that I, as an impartial, objective observer, could never hope to define, discover, or measure the worlds of meaning that embodied human behavior in any social setting; that any hypothesis or explanation I formulated at a distance from those worlds of meanings could bear little meaningful relationship to the actions and activities of the people who inhabited them; and that any interpretation of their behavior that failed to take into account the ways in which participants defined and described their situations must necessarily fail as an explanatory system.

(Continued)

(Continued)

Through rigorous exploration and inquiry, I had acquired a new vision of the world, a new way of comprehending the complexity that surrounded me, and, in doing so, reconfigured my relationship with the people I proposed to study. Far from defining and describing the variables that explained the nature of their existence and generating explanations about why they behaved as they did, I was now cast in a position of ignorance in relation to those who had previously been potential subjects of study. Only through them, the cultural experts in their own settings, could I acquire the information that would enable me to understand how they behaved as they did. A new "researcher" emerged, one for whom participatory processes became an essential feature of any process of investigation.

Action research is a collaborative approach to inquiry or investigation that provides people with the means to take systematic action to resolve specific problems. Action research is not a panacea for all ills and does not resolve all problems but provides a means for people to more clearly understand their situations and to formulate effective solutions to problems they face. The basic action research routine provides a simple yet powerful framework—Look, Think, Act (see Box 1.1)—that enables people to commence their inquiries in a straightforward manner and build greater detail into procedures as the complexity of issues increases. The terms in parentheses in Box 1.1 show how the phases of the routine relate to traditional research practices.

Box 1.1   A Basic Action Research Routine

In relation to a specified issue or problem

Look

- Gather relevant information (Gather data)
- Describe the situation (Define and describe)

Think

- Explore and analyze: What is happening here? (Analyze)
- Interpret and explain: How or why are things as they are? (Theorize)

Act

- Plan: Define a course of action based on analysis and interpretation.
- Implement: Implement the plan.
- Evaluate: Assess the effectiveness of actions taken.

The Look, Think, Act routine is but one of a number of ways in which action research is envisaged. Kemmis and McTaggart (1999), for instance, present action research as a spiral of activity: plan, act, observe, reflect. Different formulations of action research reflect the diverse ways in which the same set of activities may be described, although the processes they delineate are similar. There are, after all, many ways of cutting a cake.

Although the Look, Think, Act routine is presented in a linear format throughout this book, it should be read as a continually recycling set of activities. As participants work through each of the major stages, they explore the details of their activities through a constant process of observation, reflection, and action. At the completion of each set of activities, they review (look again), reflect (reanalyze), and re-act (modify their actions). These cycles can sometimes be framed as phases of a research process so that planning, implementing, and evaluating, for instance, can be seen as cycles of a project (see Figure 1.1). As experience shows, action research is not a neat, orderly activity

Figure 1.1   Action Research Interacting Spiral

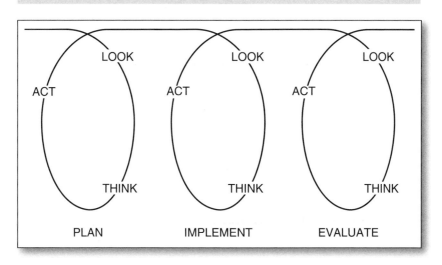

that allows participants to proceed step by step to the end of the process. People will find themselves working backward through the routines, repeating processes, revising procedures, rethinking interpretations, leapfrogging steps or stages, and sometimes making radical changes in direction. The steps and cycles of an action research process, however, provide a compass or map that assists participants to track their progress, wherever and however they proceed.

In practice, therefore, action research can be a complex process. The routines presented in this book, however, can be visualized as a road map providing guidance to those who follow this less traveled way. Although there may be many routes to a destination, and although destinations may change, travelers on the journey will be able to maintain a clear idea of their location and the direction in which they are heading.

The procedures that follow are likely to be ineffective, however, unless enacted in ways that take into account the social, cultural, interactional, and emotional factors that affect all human activity. "The medium is the message!" As will become evident in the next chapter, the implicit values and underlying assumptions embedded in action research provide a set of guiding principles that can facilitate a democratic, liberating, and life-enhancing approach to research.

MAKING A DIFFERENCE: PRACTICAL, SOLUTIONS-ORIENTED INQUIRY

A colleague approached me after listening to my report on one of the action research projects in which I had been involved. "You know," she said, "the difference with your work is that you expect something to actually happen as a result of your research activities."

My colleague's statement characterizes, for me, one of the significant differences between action research and traditional research. Traditionally, research projects are complete when a report has been written and recommendations presented to the contracting agency or published in an academic journal. An action research project can have these organizational or academic outcomes, and also provide the basis for rich and profound theorizing and basic knowledge production, but its primary purpose is as a practical tool for developing solutions to problems experienced by stakeholders in the context. If an action research project does not *make a difference,* in a specific way, for practitioners or their clients, then it has failed to achieve its objective. The analogue of hypothesis testing in action research is some form of change or development tested by its ability to move toward the resolution of the problem under study.

Action research has been employed successfully in schools, hospitals, health clinics, community agencies, government departments, rural communities, urban and suburban organizations, churches, youth clubs, ethnic groups, extension services, and many other settings. It has been used with factory workers, agency staff, school students, youth groups, young mothers, senior citizens, poor people, persons who are unemployed, community groups, people with disabilities or illness, and so on. Action research has been successfully facilitated by welfare workers, social workers, community workers, teachers, nurses, doctors, managers and administrators, urban and community planners, and agency workers in a wide range of social contexts.

The ability of ordinary people to engage in complex organizational work usually deemed the province of professionals has been demonstrated many times. One of the most striking examples I have seen was a community school set up by an Aboriginal group in a remote region of Australia. Weary of sending their young children 150 miles away to the nearest town for schooling, members of the community asked a young teacher to assist them in developing their own school. Untrained for this specialized task, she nevertheless worked with members of the community for some months to build the school from the ground up. Together, they formulated the curriculum and timetable, acquired teaching materials and equipment, secured funding, learned how to satisfy legal and bureaucratic requirements, and built a large, grass-covered hut for a school building. When this small school commenced operation, all classes were taught in one room, with community members helping to teach academic subjects, art, music, and language. The cultural style of the classroom was distinctively Aboriginal, with children happily and busily interacting in small groups, their work supervised by community members and the non-Aboriginal teacher. It was the most successful Aboriginal school I have seen in regard to the enthusiasm and engagement of the children and the sense of energy and excitement that typified the school's operation. Most striking, however, was the sense that community members considered it to be their school and the degree to which they continued, through an extended

(Continued)

(Continued)

period, to invest their meager financial resources and considerable time and energy in its operation.

Since I saw that school in operation I have come across many other contexts, including those in the United States, where teachers collaborated with their students, parent groups, and colleagues to make deepseated changes in their schools and classrooms. I have seen striking work in an urban classroom, a successful school comprised largely of Hispanic high school dropouts, and transformative processes enacted by a neighborhood group in an elementary school in a poor, largely Hispanic community. What I initially saw in rural and remote Australian contexts seems to have applications in many diverse contexts.

The following chapters present a set of routines intended to provide guidance for practitioners who wish to engage in action research. Readers may use this approach to inquiry to do several things:

- Enhance everyday work practices by
  - Reviewing goals and procedures (What things are we doing? How are we doing them?)
  - Evaluating effectiveness (To what extent are we achieving our objectives? How effective is our work?)
  - Planning activities and strategies (What needs to be done? How do we get it done?)
- Resolve specific problems and crises by
  - Defining the problem
  - Exploring its context
  - Analyzing its component parts
  - Developing strategies for its resolution
- Develop special projects and programs by
  - Planning
  - Implementing
  - Evaluating

Health professionals, for example, may wish to investigate and remediate poor health conditions or practices (e.g., smoking, drinking, low birth weight, or inappropriate medication) with a particular community group and to develop appropriate remedial strategies. School teachers may investigate strategies for dealing with low student achievement levels, poor attendance, student disinterest, or disruptive behavior. School principals may formulate programs for increasing community participation in their schools. Welfare workers may seek to act on the prevalence of child abuse or neglect among client groups. Community workers may wish to develop programs and projects to deal with the problems of neighborhood youth. Those involved in business may use action research procedures to improve organizational efficiency or effectiveness or to work more effectively with client groups. All will benefit from the use of procedures that enable them to explore systematically the conditions that operate in their specific contexts and that help them develop practical actions for dealing effectively with the problems that confront them. Box 1.2 indicates just some of the ways in which action research processes can be used to enhance common practices in a variety of professional fields.

Box 1.2   Applications of Action Research

Education	Health Care	Social Work
School improvement	Care plans	Child protection plans
Curriculum development	Case management	Program development
Evaluation	Health promotion	Assessment and evaluation
Instructional processes	Community projects	Youth programs
Class projects	Evaluation	Parenting programs
Special programs	Service development	Community development
Community engagement		

(Continued)

(Continued)

Organizations	Community Planning	Business & Commerce
Organizational change	Urban planning projects	Strategic planning
Review		Action plans
Planning	Neighborhood planning	Business plans
Budgeting		Marketing
Project development	Housing development	Product development
Program development	Youth services	Production processes
Human resource development	Resources and facilities	Operational efficiencies
	Community initiatives	Organizational review
	Community skills audit	
	Funding	

PARTICIPATORY APPROACHES TO INQUIRY

As an evolving approach to inquiry, action research envisages a collaborative approach to investigation that seeks to engage "subjects" as equal and full participants in the research process. A fundamental premise of participatory action research is that it commences with an interest in the problems of a group, a community, or an organization. Its purpose is to assist people to extend their understanding of their situation and to resolve significant issues or problems that confront them. Put another way, action research provides a model for enacting local, action-oriented approaches to inquiry, applying small-scale theorizing to specific problems in specific situations (Denzin & Lincoln, 1994).

Action research is always enacted in accordance with an explicit set of social values. In contemporary democratic social contexts, it is seen as a process of inquiry that has the following characteristics:

- It is *democratic,* enabling the participation of all people.
- It is *equitable,* acknowledging people's equality of worth.

- It is *liberating,* providing freedom from oppressive, debilitating conditions.
- It is life *enhancing,* enabling the expression of people's full human potential.

Action research works on the assumption, therefore, that all stakeholders—those whose lives are affected by the problem under study—should be engaged in the processes of investigation. Stakeholders participate in a process of rigorous inquiry, acquiring information (collecting data) and reflecting on that information (analyzing) to transform their understanding about the nature of the problem under investigation (theorizing). This new set of understandings is then applied to plans for resolution of the problem (action), which, in turn, provides the context for testing hypotheses derived from group theorizing (evaluation).

Collaborative exploration helps practitioners, agency workers, client groups, students, and other stakeholding parties to develop increasingly sophisticated understandings of the problems and issues that confront them. As they rigorously explore and reflect on their situation together, they can repudiate social myths, misconceptions, and misrepresentations and formulate more constructive analyses of their situation. By sharing their diverse knowledge and experience—expert, professional, and lay—stakeholders can create solutions to their problems and, in the process, improve the quality of their community life.

The role of the research facilitator, in this context, becomes more facilitative and less directive. Knowledge acquisition or production proceeds as a collective process, engaging people who have previously been the "subjects" of research in the process of defining and redefining the corpus of understanding on which their community or organizational life is based. As they collectively investigate their own situation, stakeholders build a consensual vision of their lifeworld. Action research results not only in a collective vision but also in a sense of community. It operates at the intellectual level as well as at social, cultural, political, and emotional levels.

Action research therefore seeks to change the social, organizational, and personal dynamics of the research so that all who participate benefit from its outcomes. It is a collaborative approach to inquiry that seeks to build positive working relationships and productive communicative styles. Its intent is to provide a climate that enables disparate groups of people to work harmoniously and productively to achieve a set of goals. It is fundamentally a consensual approach to inquiry and works from the assumption that cooperation and consensus should be the primary orientation of research activity. It links groups that potentially are in conflict so that they may attain viable, sustainable, and effective solutions to problems that affect their work or community lives through dialogue and negotiation.

The payoffs for this approach to research are potentially enormous. Not only do research participants acquire the individual capacity to engage in systematic research that they can apply to other issues in other contexts, but they also build a supportive network of collaborative relationships that provides them with an ongoing resource. Solutions that emerge from the research process therefore become much more sustainable, enabling people to maintain the momentum of their activity over extended periods of time. Links established in one project may provide access to information and support that build the power of the people in many different ways.

There are many examples of the way this can operate. I've seen highly effective classrooms where teachers organized students into collaborative work groups to investigate ways to clearly define their learning goals and formulate strategies to accomplish them. I've seen community nurses engage people with chronic health conditions to assist them in establishing ways to live more comfortably and deal effectively with issues confronting them in their day-to-day lives. I've seen youth workers accomplish wonderfully effective programs for marginalized youth that have transformed the communities in which they lived. At the heart of all these activities has been a process of discovery involving the people themselves—clients, students, local youth groups, and so on. In each case the people acquired the capacity to become self-directed and self-sufficient, acquiring a supportive group of peers who could assist them and support them as they engaged the tasks before them.

The effect on the people themselves often has been quite dramatic. At the completion of one action research project, I asked the women in the participating neighborhood group about their experience. One burst out excitedly, "It was such an empowering experience!" As they explored this comment further, it was clear that the women had really appreciated that people had listened seriously to their viewpoints, that they had learned so much, and that they had been actively involved in the research. Originally this project was to have been carried out by research consultants, but with assistance from a local university professor, the members of the neighborhood group had engaged in a "survey" of parent and teacher perspectives on a school issue. The result not only provided the basis for ongoing developments within the school but provided members of the neighborhood group with the capacity and desire to apply their newfound knowledge to a project in a local high school. This was clearly a case where participants had built their capacity to engage in research, as well as increased the capability of the school to engage in much-needed changes to procedures for communicating with parents.

Building people's capacity to attain significant outcomes that are sustainable over time requires everyone concerned to take into account the impact of activities on all of the issues affecting their lives. It is not sufficient to try to "get the job done" if underlying conditions inhibit or prevent the work in which people are engaged. Too often we have come to accept the impersonal, mechanistic, and allegedly objective procedures common to many contexts as a necessary evil. We endure hierarchical and authoritarian modes of organization and control despite the sense of frustration, powerlessness, and stress frequently felt by practitioners, client groups, students, or others affected by underlying issues within the situation.

It is not difficult to understand why people often suffer deep-seated feelings of frustration. They feel that the centrally controlled programs and services they must institute cannot take into account the multitude of factors that impinge on people's lives. Professional practitioners often feel compelled to implement programs and services according to formally sanctioned practices and procedures, despite their ineffectiveness in achieving the goals they were designed to accomplish. Welfare services often maintain people in states of dependency, passive and irrelevant learning processes are common in many school systems, and medical practices frequently maintain high levels of dependency on prescription drugs. All are symptomatic of underlying disorders embedded in generally accepted practices in our social institutions, agencies, and organizations.

In my professional life, I have often seen programs that isolate people from their families or communities. I have seen services that demean the recipients and organizations and agencies that operate according to rules and regulations that are shamelessly insensitive to the cultures of their clients. I have seen young children isolated from their families for months, sometimes years at a time, in order to be given a "good education." I have seen police fail to act on violence against women because the women were drunk. I have seen millions of dollars wasted on training programs that were purportedly designed to serve community needs but that failed to reach the people for whom they were formulated. I have seen health clinics that were incapable of serving rural community needs because they operated according to practices common in city hospitals. In one community, I was shown the boys' and girls' hostels for high school children, isolated from each other by the length of the town, with the girls' hostel protected by a barbed-wire fence. The administrator who showed me these institutions was proud that "we haven't had an illegitimate pregnancy in years" and seemed unaware of the potential for enormous damage to family and community life inherent in the situation.

The list goes on and on, reflecting the failure of centrally controlled social, educational, health, welfare, and community services to adapt and adjust their operations to the social, cultural, and political realities of the specific locations where they operated. I grieve for the people who have been damaged in the process, including those workers who have become hardened to the plight of the client groups they serve.

I have seen other situations, however, in which administrators, professional practitioners, and workers engaged the energy and potential of the people they served to develop highly effective programs and services. I have seen women's groups that provided for significant needs within their communities, police initiatives that greatly enhanced the peace-keeping mission of the department, and health programs that greatly reduced the incidence of trachoma. I have also seen education and training programs traditionally shunned by marginalized groups become so successful that they were unable to accommodate the numbers of people requesting entry. I have also applauded community youth programs that were able to unite hostile community factions to diminish the problems of young people in their town. I rejoice in them. They have in common a developmental process that maximized the participation of the people they served.

I have written elsewhere of the success of an independent school started by the community in which it operated. It stands in stark contrast to another school I visited. The principal, hired by an outside agency, proudly related the story of the new high school he had set up. With little assistance or support, he had organized the renovation of the school building, bought the furniture and equipment, designed the curriculum, and hired the teachers. "I have only one major problem," he confided. "I can't get the parents to show any interest."

As practitioners develop programs and services, therefore, or seek to solve problems that threaten the efficacy of services for which they are responsible, they need to take into account the impacts of those developments and solutions on the lives of the people they serve. Tony Kelly and Russell Gluck (1979) proposed that programs be evaluated not only according to their technical or functional worth but also according to their impact on people's social and emotional lives. Their evaluative criteria investigate the effects of our research activities on

- *Pride:* people's feelings of self-worth
- *Dignity:* people's feelings of autonomy, independence, and competence
- *Identity:* people's affirmation of social identities (woman, worker, Hispanic)
- *Control:* people's feelings of control over resources, decisions, actions, events, and activities
- *Responsibility:* people's ability to be accountable for their own actions
- *Unity:* the solidarity of groups of which people are members
- *Place:* places where people feel at ease
- *Location:* people's attachment to locales to which they have important historical, cultural, or social ties

These concepts echo features described by Egon Guba and Yvonna Lincoln (1989) in their book *Fourth Generation Evaluation.* Their hermeneutic dialectic process, or meaning-making dialogue, requires interactions that respect people's dignity, integrity, and privacy through

- Full participatory involvement
- Political parity of those involved
- Consensual, informed, sophisticated joint construction

- Conceptual parity
- Refusal to treat individuals as subjects or objects of study

These principles are consonant with those presented by Gustavsen (2001), who outlines the conditions required for a "democratic dialogue," and with Habermas's (1984) concept of "communicative action." The implicit assumption in these ideas is that procedural matters that directly affect the quality of people's lives need to be taken into account, not only for humanitarian or ethical reasons but also for underlying pragmatic purposes. As Guba and Lincoln put it so succinctly, attention to these properties is likely to "unleash energy, stimulate creativity, instill pride, build commitment, prompt the taking of responsibility, and evoke a sense of investment and ownership" (1989, p. 227).

THE ROLE OF THE RESEARCHER

The assumptions delineated earlier dramatically change the role of the person traditionally called "the researcher." The primary aim of researchers has been to be as unobtrusive as possible in order to not influence the outcomes of their investigations. Action research, however, requires researchers to actively participate in the research process, not as an expert who *does* research *on* people but as a resource person. He or she becomes a facilitator or consultant who acts as a catalyst to assist stakeholders to define their problems clearly and to monitor and support their activity as they work toward effective resolution of the issues that provide the focus of their investigations. Titles such as *facilitator, associate,* and *consultant* are more appropriate in action research than *director, chief,* or *head,* which are common to more hierarchical operations. The language signals the nature of relationships and the orientation of the research.

A group of community workers characterized their community-based work in this way (Kickett, McCauley, & Stringer, 1986, p. 5):

- You are there as a *catalyst.*
- Your role is not to impose but to *stimulate people* to change. This is done by addressing issues that concern them *now.*
- The essence of the work is *process—the way things are done—*rather than the result achieved.
- The key is to enable people to develop their own analysis of their issues.

- Start where people are, not where someone else thinks they are or ought to be.
- Help people to analyze their situation, consider findings, plan how to keep what they want, and change what they do not like.
- Enable people to examine several courses of action and the probable results or consequences of each option. After a plan has been selected it is the worker's role to *assist in implementing* the plan by raising issues and possible weaknesses and by helping to locate resources.
- The worker is not an advocate for the group for which he or she works.
- The worker does not focus only on solutions to problems but on *human development.* The responsibility for a project's success lies with the people.

This "bottom-up" or grassroots orientation uses stakeholding groups as the primary focus of attention and the source of decision making. It is an approach that requires research facilitators to work in close collaboration with stakeholders and to formulate "flat" organizational structures that put decision-making power in stakeholders' hands.

The approach differs from the authoritarian manner that is, unfortunately, all too common in institutional and organizational life. People in positions of power tend to assume that, being organizationally superior, they have superior knowledge. We have all experienced or observed the authoritarian teacher, administrator, director, social worker, or expert who is feared or mistrusted by clients and organizational inferiors, the autocrat who demands that work be carried out according to his or her dictates. This type of tyranny represents the extreme end of a spectrum of authority but is, to a greater or lesser extent, embedded in the hierarchical operations of many institutions and organizations. Such authority is based on the premise that managers, administrators, policy makers, or "representatives," because of their knowledge of the big picture, are best able to make decisions for client groups and constituencies.

In many situations, this expectation runs contrary to the lived experience of the people. "Experts" are usually trained in narrow areas and often cannot understand the intricacies and complexities of people's lives. "Representatives" often speak for only one group in a constituency and reflect perspectives and interests of that group alone. Moreover, many of the procedures used to try to broaden inputs from constituent groups are so flawed as to be of little value. Surveys, for instance, are usually limited in scope and are frequently riddled with the agendas, interests, and perspectives of the people who commission or construct them. Further, consultation processes frequently occur under conditions that inhibit the participation of many constituent groups.

A colleague referred to community consultation techniques used by government agencies in his state as processes of "insultation." People usually were asked to attend meetings in places such as schools, public offices, libraries, or upscale hotels, venues that were either inaccessible to people who lacked private transportation or socially or culturally alien to them. Meetings often were held at times or under conditions that prevented the attendance of women with children, employed people, poor people, and members of minority groups. The processes of consultation tended to be dominated by those who happened to have no work or home responsibilities or who had the personal resources to make themselves available at times suited to the institution or the bureaucracy.

I have been present at many meetings at which "representatives" have been asked to provide information that was intended to be used as the basis for significant changes to community life. In one instance, I attended a community consultation meeting with senior politicians and government bureaucrats who wished to gain input on government policy initiatives. It was held at a time when most people in that town were unavailable, so that two vocal young women with little standing in the community became the focus of the consultative process. The only other participants were retired people who were given little information about the nature of the processes in which they were involved and appeared to be puzzled by the discussions that took place.

The politicians and bureaucrats who flew into town about noon flew out fewer than three hours later, apparently happy with their "community consultation." I have little doubt that any action that resulted from that visit was not well received by people in the community. They almost certainly would have been insulted by the paucity of the consultation process and would have perceived any actions as the imposition of outside authority on their lives.

In many situations, people tend to react negatively to authoritarian processes. Having been subject to the well-intentioned but often misguided attentions of people in official positions, they protect themselves in the only ways available to them. Thus, when outside authority is imposed on their lives, they often respond with

> *Aggression,* directed at those who are perceived as controlling their lives
>
> *Apathy,* which sucks away their vitality and leaves them with feelings of hopelessness or helplessness
>
> *Avoidance,* which isolates them from the source of authoritarian control

When working with people, we as practitioners need to create the conditions that will mobilize their energy, engage their enthusiasm, and generate activity that can be productively applied to the resolution of issues and problems that concern them.

WORKING PRINCIPLES

Within business and industry it is now widely recognized that participatory approaches to treatment, teaching, and management are much more effective ways of accomplishing productive and effective outcomes. Participatory processes require a quite different approach to work than commonly accepted in the past. As indicated earlier, we require a set of practices that take into account the human and social dimensions of the context. No longer can we act as though we are dealing with an insensate machine; now we must acknowledge and take account of people's active, creative, willful, and potentially fractious response to any situation. We need to acquire practices, processes, and skills that enable us to work effectively in this more dynamic situation. The principles outlined in the following paragraphs, therefore, signal some of the issues and factors that need to be taken into account in order to accomplish truly effective outcomes to the sometimes complex and deep-seated problems that affect people's lives.

Action research seeks to develop and maintain social and personal interactions that are nonexploitative and enhance the social and emotional lives of all people who participate. It is organized and conducted in ways that are conducive to the formation of a *community of inquiry*—the "common unity" of all participants—and that strengthen the democratic, equitable, liberating, and life-enhancing qualities of social life. The principles delineated in the following sections—relationships, communication, participation, and inclusion—can help practitioners to formulate activities sensitive to the key elements of this mode of research.

Relationships

The type, nature, and quality of relationships in any social setting have direct impacts on the quality of people's experience and, through that, the quality of outcomes of any human enterprise. Action research has a primary interest, therefore, in establishing and maintaining positive working relationships (see Box 1.3).

Box 1.3   Relationships in Action Research

Relationships in action research should

- Promote feelings of equality for all people involved
- Maintain harmony
- Avoid conflicts, where possible
- Resolve conflicts that arise, openly and dialogically
- Accept people as they are, not as some people think they ought to be
- Encourage personal, cooperative relationships, rather than impersonal, competitive, conflictual, or authoritarian relationships
- Be sensitive to people's feelings

Key concepts: equality, harmony, acceptance, cooperation, sensitivity

---

A new manager was appointed to supervise the work of a group of social workers with whom I was acquainted. Having little experience in the work of these experienced practitioners, and being ambitious, this manager set out to impress her superiors with her efficiency and effectiveness. She embarked on projects that her staff considered inappropriate and put great pressure on them to work in ways that she perceived to be efficient. In the process, she tried to have them act in ways that were contrary to their previously effective work routines and constantly referred to her superior, the director, when they disputed her direction.

Within a short time, work conditions deteriorated dramatically. The social workers struggled to maintain their operation and, in the process, experienced great frustration and stress to the extent that they started to experience both physical and emotional problems. One staff member took a series of extended leaves, another began visits to a psychiatrist, and another transferred to a different section, her position being filled by a series of temporary workers. Eventually, the manager, also under stress, left the agency, and the entire section was disbanded.

This situation is, unfortunately, not an isolated one. Practitioners who have worked in organizational or institutional settings for any length of time will find the scenario all too familiar.

The force of this type of event is to sensitize us to the need to be consciously aware of the nature of relationships in our everyday professional lives. It suggests the need to reject styles of interaction that emphasize status and power and to move to more consensual modes of operation. It implies the need to develop cooperative approaches to work and harmonious relations between and among people and to reject the aggressive, impersonal, and manipulative relations characteristic of many bureaucratic systems. It emphasizes collegial relationships, rather than those based on hierarchy, and leadership roles that help and support people rather than direct and control them.

When we seek to organize any set of activities within an organizational or community setting, we need to examine the type, nature, and quality of relationships among clients, practitioners, administrators, and other stakeholders. At the base of a productive set of relationships is people's ability to feel that their ideas and agendas are acknowledged and that they can make worthwhile contributions to the common enterprise. This, ultimately, is at the core of the processes of a democratic society.

I am reminded of one of the really fine school principals with whom I served. He was, to me, a leader in the fullest sense of the word. Knowledgeable and skillful, he provided me, as a young teacher, with suggestions for ways to improve my teaching that did not imply that I was not already a capable teacher, suggesting or indicating the areas of weakness

(Continued)

(Continued)

in my teaching without making me feel put down; he enhanced my feelings of competence and worth by praising my strengths. He was "Dick" to us teachers much of the time but became "Mr. Filmer" when the occasion warranted our serious attention, or in the more formal moments of ritualized school activities. The words *gentleman* and *scholar* in their best older senses come to my mind. He was a leader of stature and capability who still provides me with the touchstones by which I evaluate my relationships with colleagues, students, and clients. I still cherish the memory of the time I spent with Dick Filmer.

Communication

Action research requires all participants to engage in communication that facilitates the development of harmonious relationships and the effective attainment of group or organizational objectives (see Box 1.4). German scholar Jurgen Habermas (1979) suggests that positive change originates from communicative action that provides people with the capacity to work productively with each other. His formulation of the "ideal speech situation" suggests four fundamental conditions for communication to be effective:

- *Understanding:* The receiver can understand what is being communicated.
- *Truth:* The information is accurate and is not a fabrication.
- *Sincerity:* The communicator is sincere in his or her attempts to communicate and has no hidden agendas.
- *Appropriateness:* The manner, style, and form of communication are appropriate to the people, setting, and activity.

Institutional and bureaucratic arenas, because of the nature of their organization and operation, provide many examples in which these conditions are not met. Understanding, for instance, is often inhibited by the use of jargon, complex language, or esoteric subject matter. Professional workers sometimes use technical language that clients either cannot understand or cannot relate to their experience. Academics frequently speak in an idiom that mystifies practitioners and laypersons alike. In these instances, understanding is limited, and communication is faulty.

Manipulation through the use of distorted information or failure to make covert agendas explicit is so common that it is often accepted as an unfortunate but necessary part of social, organizational, and political life. Damage to communicative action through untruthfulness, however, often leads to more general problems. When people have been tricked or duped, they are frequently unable to continue to work harmoniously with those they feel have cheated them, and the chances of productive and effective work taking place are diminished accordingly.

Box 1.4   Communication in Action Research

In effective communication, one

- Listens attentively to people
- Accepts and acts on what they say
- Can be understood by everyone
- Is truthful and sincere
- Acts in socially and culturally appropriate ways
- Regularly advises others about what is happening

Key concepts: attentiveness, acceptance, understanding, truth, sincerity, appropriateness, openness

In many situations, communication is jeopardized when people feel that the manner or style of the communication is inappropriate or that the person involved is not the appropriate person. When a person from the majority culture speaks for the interests of a minority group in the absence of an appropriate spokesperson, when an administrator makes decisions about a program or service without consulting his or her staff, and when academic experts with little field experience are responsible for professional training, effective communication is difficult to achieve.

I once argued with one of my female colleagues about the need for members of minority groups to speak for themselves in public forums and to be in control of their own affairs. I was unable to make my point clearly until I asked the question, "Would it be right for a man to be head of the National Organization for Women?" with the implication that a man could control the affairs of that organization, represent the interests of women, and present papers on women's needs at conferences. She saw the point immediately.

Apart from these basic conditions of communication, however, the manner, style, and organization of communicative activity provide many cues and messages that can have significant impacts on people's feelings of well-being and their orientation to activities and agendas. When people feel acknowledged, accepted, and treated with respect, their feelings of worth are enhanced, and the possibility that they will contribute actively to the work of the group is maximized. Communication is key to the effective operation of any process of inquiry, providing the means to ensure that people are fully informed of events and activities and have all the information they need to accomplish their work together.

Participation

To the extent that people can participate in the process of exploring the nature and context of the problems that concern them, they have the opportunity to develop immediate and deeply relevant understandings of their situation and to be involved actively in the process of dealing with those problems. The task in these circumstances is to provide a climate that gives people the sense that they are in control of their own lives and that supports them as they take systematic action to improve their circumstances (see Box 1.5).

Box 1.5   Participation in Action Research

Participation is most effective when it

- Enables significant levels of active involvement
- Enables people to perform significant tasks
- Provides support for people as they learn to act for themselves
- Encourages plans and activities that people are able to accomplish themselves
- Deals personally with people rather than with their representatives or agents

Key concepts: involvement, performance, support, accomplishment, personalization

Until historically recent times, people were intimately involved in the production of goods and the delivery of services that were part of their day-to-day lives. The farms that surrounded villages provided employment as well as food and clothing, and storekeeper, smith, mason, and preacher were known to everyone who lived locally. Today, the large and centralized social systems characteristic of modern societies alienate people from those who provide for their well-being and from the decisions that affect their lives. People are increasingly subject to the faceless dictates of transnational corporations and state and federal agencies for their employment, health, education, and other aspects of community life.

Centralized control has the advantage of concentrating resources to foster large projects and programs—such as health and education systems—that have the capacity to improve or maintain the quality of life of large populations. The downside of centralized control is that those who determine the "texts" of these projects, programs, and services do so in ways that fit their own interests and agendas and the imperatives of their own social and cultural perspectives. A managerial and professional class dominates decision-making processes, often to the detriment of people from lower classes or cultural minorities. The decision makers determine how things will operate, who will benefit, under what circumstances, and according to which criteria, and services are provided by a professional elite that often has little understanding of the circumstances of the people they serve.

In such situations, there is often a tendency to standardize procedures and practices according to managerial or professional cultural imperatives, on the assumption that these fit the general population, notwithstanding that any large population will vary greatly according to the social groups that constitute it. Social identities related to class, ethnicity, race, religion, age, gender, locality, employment, and leisure activities will relate to divergent lifestyles, beliefs, customs, mores, morals, values, skills, knowledge, understanding, and behavioral propensities. When the social and cultural perspectives of a group diverge significantly from those necessary for the group to take advantage of the standardized procedures developed by central policy makers, problems are likely to occur.

Control always has been a significant factor in bureaucratic life, and supervisory roles increasingly are framed in control-oriented managerial terms. Although there is nothing necessarily problematic about framing leadership activity as management, the language of that discipline tends to reflect the ethos of the corporate world in which it was nurtured. There is a tendency to incorporate the values and agendas of the corporate world—with its emphasis on profit, production, and control—into all areas of social, educational, and welfare life, to frame projects according to economic or technical agendas, for instance, while social, cultural, emotional, and spiritual issues fade into obscurity.

Professional practitioners are currently becoming more aware of the limitations of that expertise, however, and there is an increasing tendency to engage clients, patients, consumers, and students in decision-making processes. We have also become more sensitive to the view that an army of experts is unlikely to be able to meet people's needs if the people themselves remain merely passive recipients of services. As practitioners in many fields now realize, unless people come to understand procedures and practices by participating in their development, any program or service is likely to have limited effects on their lives. Patients who fail to maintain appropriate health practices, passive and disinterested students, recalcitrant welfare recipients, disorderly youth, and families in crisis will often not respond to the authoritative dictates of the "experts" whose task it is to "solve" their problems.

A colleague of mine once had the task of presenting training programs on alcohol and drug abuse. Most of the participants were enrolled under court order, as part of their sentences for drug- or alcohol-related offenses. The program, which included information about the physical and psychological effects of alcohol and other drugs, was presented to an audience that was, from my colleague's accounts, almost completely unreceptive. "You could tell that they didn't want to be there and that they wouldn't believe anything I said to them anyway," he commented. "It was a real waste."

I previously had been involved in a workshop given by a senior academic to a community group that had requested a program that would help them better understand the devastating effects of alcohol consumption. The workshop included exploration of a complex three-factor model of drinking behavior that taxed my intellectual capabilities and required considerable concentration on the part of the other participants. As the workshop progressed, they pointed out that the model was inadequate relative to some of the realities of their community life and suggested modifications that would improve it. All participants worked energetically throughout the afternoon, to the extent that the facilitator commented that he was able to cover more ground in that afternoon than he could in three weeks of course work with his postgraduate students. The energy, involvement, and motivation of the participants reflected their orientation to the processes of the workshop. It made sense from their perspective and spoke to issues that concerned them.

Action research seeks to engage people directly in formulating solutions to problems they confront in their community and organizational lives. It is the researcher's task to facilitate and support these activities, rather than to determine their direction. Leadership, in this instance, is defined according to its function of facilitating organizational and operational processes, rather than defining and controlling them. Active participation is the key to feelings of ownership that motivate people to invest their time and energy to help shape the nature and quality of the acts, activities, and behaviors in which they engage.

Inclusion

Action research seeks to enact an approach to inquiry that includes all relevant stakeholders in the process of investigation. It creates contexts that enable diverse groups to negotiate their agendas in an atmosphere of mutual trust and acceptance and to work toward effective solutions to problems that concern them (see Box 1.6).

Box 1.6   Inclusion in Action Research

Inclusion in action research involves

- Maximization of the involvement of all relevant individuals
- Inclusion of all groups affected
- Inclusion of all relevant issues—social, economic, cultural, political— rather than a focus on narrow administrative or political agendas
- Ensuring cooperation with other groups, agencies, and organizations
- Ensuring that all relevant groups benefit from activities

Key concepts: individuals, groups, issues, cooperation, benefit

---

A feature of modern life is the concentration of power in the hands of small groups of people. In public life, "representatives," "leaders," or "managers" are given decision-making power over large groups to enable them to control and organize activities. As a consequence, participation in the organizational lives of schools, health agencies, and other community institutions is often characterized by the dominance of middle-class professional groups and, particularly, administrative interests. Management is greatly affected by the need to play off the agendas of the various client groups and to deal with political machinations that often arise. In these circumstances, the desire for smoothly administered programs limits the extent to which administrators are willing to tolerate the intimate involvement of their diverse and sometimes antagonistic clients. Administrators therefore often focus decision-making processes on an inner circle of their staff or maintain control through truncated decision-making procedures. Committee membership is often carefully controlled to ensure that only restricted groups of people are involved, and meeting agendas are regulated judiciously.

In these circumstances, the voices of the most powerless groups tend to go unheard, their agendas ignored, and their needs unmet. Organizational procedures often operate according to administrative priorities and fail to accommodate the social and cultural imperatives that dominate people's lives. Problems proliferate as practitioners struggle to cope with escalating crises that result from the failure of programs and services to cater to client needs. Moreover, these pressures are sometimes exacerbated by political or community demands that "something be done." All too often, superficial solutions provide the semblance of immediate action but in effect can actually exacerbate the situation.

In recent years lawmakers in the United States enacted legislation that increases penalties for criminal offenses, responding to a growing chorus in the country to send young "criminals" to prison and to extend their sentences. In a country with the third highest rate of incarceration in the world, the likely outcome of these pressures will be to increase, rather than decrease, criminal activity. I remember the words of a friend of mine who, in his earlier years, had "done time" for a number of offenses. His time in prison had, apart from anything else, increased his criminal skills considerably. He had learned a number of ways to break into and start cars, how to break into stores and houses, how to dispose of stolen goods, and how to evade capture. The major outcome of his prison experience was an increase in the extent of his criminal skills and knowledge.

The potential payoff for opening up the processes of organizational life is enormous. Not only does it provide the possibility of increased human resources; it also creates conditions likely to lead to the formation of operational processes that are socially and culturally appropriate for diverse client groups. By including people in decisions about the programs and services that serve them, practitioners extend their knowledge base considerably and mobilize the resources of the community. Including more people in the process may seem to increase the possibilities for complexity and conflict, but it also enables practitioners to broaden their focus from one that seeks the immediate resolution of specific problems to more encompassing perspectives that have the potential to alleviate many interconnected problems.

REFLECTION AND ACTION

Introduction

The Reflection and Action section at the end of each chapter provides opportunities for readers to reflect on the issues presented and to engage in activities that assist them to "make sense"—to better understand—the content of the chapter. The activities are based on the assumption that we learn better by "doing" rather than just reading, thinking, talking, or listening. Individual readers may relate the issues to their own experience to ensure that they understand the concepts, procedures, and techniques described. The process of clarifying and understanding will be enhanced if they engage in conversations around these issues with friends, colleagues, or classmates.

The activities provide opportunities for readers to practice some of the techniques and procedures presented. Practice the activities suggested, reflect on what you have done, and have others observe you, if possible. The process of reflecting and obtaining feedback on your actions will be informative. The activities themselves are best applied to a real-life situation to which you have access. It can be your own workplace or a community context where you can spend time over a period of weeks. You will be asked to explore a simple issue or problem that you or others are experiencing in this place. If you cannot find such a place, then perform the learning activities as best you can, possibly in your own homes or with friends and neighbors. The learning activities are best enacted in a "strange" place, a place with which you are not terribly familiar but to which you have access. In these circumstances you may be less comfortable, but you will probably learn more about a process of investigation.

Reflection

Think about the following questions:

- What are the main features of action research?
- Can you describe how action research relates to other forms of research? How is it similar? How is it different?
- Think about a place you work or where you engage in significant activities (office, clinic, school, clubs, church, friendship groups). What are some of the issues and problems you or others experience in this context?
- From these issues or problems select one that you may be able to work on for the next few weeks, as you work your way through this book. Select one that is relatively simple and easy to investigate, as this is only a practice. Later you may wish to apply what you have learned to a more significant problem.
- How do the principles of action research fit this context? Will you need to change the way you, as researcher, interact with people? In what ways?
- How might you change the way you usually operate or interact with people—e.g., as manager, teacher, principal, health professional—in order to enact your researcher role?

Action

- As you explore the Reflection issues, keep a journal and record information about the place, issues or problem you wish to investigate, and issues related to carrying out these activities.
- Discuss these issues with a group of colleagues, classmates, or friends.
- You are about to engage in an action research process in this place. What does this mean? Discuss with colleagues, classmates, or friends.

NOTE

1. A box at the end of each chapter provides a summary of the material presented therein.

2. Throughout this book, I use my own experiences to illustrate points made in the text. These sections, *biographical bulletins*, are set off from the text with a different typeface.

Box 1.7   Research in Professional and Public Life

Purpose

To describe action research purposes and processes

Content

Research is a systematic approach to investigation and inquiry leading to increased understanding of issues and problems investigated.

Action research is solutions-oriented investigation leading to resolution of issues investigated.

A basic action research routine includes repeated cycles of investigation based on a Look, Think, Act routine:

Look: acquiring information

Think: reflecting on the information gathered

Act: planning practical steps toward resolution of the issue investigated

Applying participatory approaches to investigation stimulates feelings of pride, dignity, identity, control, responsibility, and unity.

Establishing the researcher as facilitator and catalyst, encouraging people to change by addressing issues that concern them.

Effective action research is accomplished by enacting a set of working principles that focus on

Relationships

Communication

Participation

Inclusiveness

2

THE THEORY BEHIND THE PRACTICE

THE THEORETICAL FOUNDATIONS OF ACTION RESEARCH

Chapter 1 alluded to the underlying philosophical stance of action research, revealing the emergence of the tradition and its relationship with other research paradigms. Fundamentally, action research is grounded in a qualitative research paradigm whose purpose is to gain greater clarity and understanding of a question, problem, or issue. Unlike quantitative research (sometimes referred to as experimental or positivistic research) based on the precise definition, measurement, and analysis of the relationship between a carefully defined set of variables, action research commences with a broadly defined question, problem, or issue. Investigations therefore seek initially to clarify the issue investigated and to reveal the way participants describe their actual experience of that issue—how things happen and how it affects them.

In these circumstances, action research is necessarily based on localized studies that focus on the need to understand *how* things are happening, rather than merely on *what* is happening, and to understand the ways that stakeholders—people concerned with the issue—perceive, interpret, and respond to events related to the issue investigated. This does not mean that quantitative information is necessarily excluded from a study, because it often provides significant information that needs to be incorporated into the study. This information can be included in the processes of meaning making that are essential to action research, but it does not form the central core of the processes of investigation.

This research stance acknowledges the limitations of the knowledge and understanding of the "expert" researcher and takes account of the experience and understanding of those centrally involved in the issue explored—the stakeholders. By so doing, researchers take into account a central reality of social life— that all social events are subject to ongoing construction and negotiation. By incorporating the perspectives and responses of key stakeholders as an integral part of the research process, a collaborative analysis of the situation provides the basis for deep-seated understandings that lead to effective remedial action.

Formally, then, action research, in its most effective forms, is phenomeno-logical (focusing on people's actual lived experience or reality), interpretive (focusing on their interpretation of acts and activities), and hermeneutic (focusing on how people make meaning of events in their lives). It provides the means by which stakeholders explore their experience, gain greater clarity and understanding of events and activities, and use those extended understandings to construct effective solutions to the problem(s) on which the study was focused.

These processes do not, however, occur in a socially neutral setting but are subject to deeply seated social and cultural forces taken into account through the participatory processes of investigation of action research. A more extensive exposition of these forces is provided in the final chapter of this text.

THE PLACE OF THEORY IN ACTION RESEARCH

The place of theory in action research is far from clear and differs from its place in experimental or quantitative research. For the latter, established theory "drives" the processes of inquiry, and the hypotheses to be tested are drawn from established theory. In effect, researchers say, "Given theory 'x,' what explains the problem we are investigating?" An educator seeking to understand why particular students are performing poorly may, on the basis of a preliminary study of a representative group of students, suggest that the answer most likely lies in "lack of student motivation" (or "delayed cognitive development" or "poorly devised learning strategies"). These preliminary hypotheses are drawn from theories of motivation (or cognitive development or learning theory), and the suggested explanation—the hypothesis—is then formulated and tested, using carefully designed research procedures. Failure to disconfirm the hypothesis gives credence to both the suggested explanation and the theory from which it is drawn. It should be noted that research in this mode does not "prove" something to be true or false and that any one study merely provides some evidence for accepting the research hypotheses, within the conditions stipulated in the research design.

The purpose of theory in action research, however, is somewhat different. Reason and Bradbury suggest (2001, p. 451) that "theory is used to bring more order to complex phenomena, with a goal of parsimonious description so that it is also of use to the community of inquiry." For them, a good interpretation—theory—is one that is more reasonable than others. And reasonableness can be tested in the community of inquiry. "A new theory enables us to 're-see' the world, or see through taken-for-granted conceptual categories that are oppressive or no longer helpful."

Earlier versions of action research assumed that there was a direct logical connection between theory and practice, but as Gustavsen (2001) points out, there can be no question of a direct relation. While theory can inform or influence practice, he suggests, "The link is a discursive one where ideas, notions, and elements from the theory can be considered in the development of practice but with no claims to being automatically applicable" (p. 18). "Theory," he goes on to suggest, "can inform a process of enlightenment and out of this process can emerge new practices."

There is another element to this relationship between theory and practice. The explanations and theories of the academic world often do not fit comfortably into people's everyday reality. The language, forms of propositional knowledge, and sometimes esoteric idiom of academic texts are frequently inaccessible to a professional or lay audience. Academic theories are embedded in a set of concepts, assumptions, and views of reality that make sense only within a particular social context—in this case, the discourses of the academic world.

Another reason why academic theory may not "make sense" to people is that *any* theory is just one in a wide set of possibilities for explaining or interpreting events in the social world. The particular lens through which we view the world will affect what we see. In astronomy, for instance, different "lenses" collect particular forms of light, particles, or energy. A lens designed to collect light in the infrared spectrum will show the same celestial object quite differently from a lens that collects X-ray or radio sources of information. So it is with social theory. Different theories will focus on different aspects of the situation and interpret the information according to the assumptions and orientations of the theory.

It is not that any theory is "wrong" or "right" but that it focuses on particular aspects of the situation and interprets them in particular ways. We might look at an event and "theorize" it in terms of colonialism, gender domination, racial politics, power relationships, personality, socially learned behavior, prejudice, or any number of other ways of describing and interpreting the situation.

One of the strengths of action research is that it accepts the diverse perspectives of different stakeholders—the "theory" each will hold to explain how and why events occur as they do—and finds ways of incorporating them into mutually acceptable ways of understanding events that enable them to work toward a resolution of the problem investigated. People from outside the research context who impose their own theories without having a deep understanding of the nature of events and the dynamics of the context are likely to either misrepresent or misinterpret the situation. They are, in effect, prejudging the situation on the basis of limited understandings, even though they may feel they can see *exactly* what is happening.

One of the tasks of action research, then, is to ensure that the ways that stakeholders describe and interpret events become the central focus of the research process. These different perspectives consequently become subjects of interaction and negotiation as people creatively explore ways of conceiving the situation that assist them in resolving a problem.

Having said that, however, it is not possible to enter a research process atheoretically. That is, each person involved, including research facilitators and professional practitioners, will have assumptions about appropriate ways of enacting research processes drawn from their own perspectives and values. The approach to research presented in this book, for instance, is based on assumptions articulated within the first chapters as "working principles." A fundamental assumption is that the procedures and processes of research work to ensure that power differentials do not undermine the need to clearly hear the voice of less powerful groups.

The theory, in this case, is a theory of *method* and provides clarity and understanding about the way participants enact processes of inquiry in order to achieve the practical and effective outcomes we desire. This type of theorizing we must do prior to and during the research to ensure that we can clearly articulate our purposes and processes. It is quite distinct from theories about the nature of events surrounding the particular issue on which a project focuses. Though academic theories may provide interesting interpretations of events, they are likely to distort and misinterpret the situation if they take precedence over stakeholder theories in practice. More relevant and effective theories emerge from the hermeneutic dialectic—meaning-making dialogues—between stakeholders, using the concepts, terminologies, and formulations that make sense to them. This does not mean that academic theories cannot enter the research arena, but it does mean that academic theories may become relevant only when stakeholder theories have been described and elaborated.

The following commentary, therefore, focuses on methodological theory— the theories that inform and clarify the nature of the action research processes presented in this book.

THE THEORY BEHIND THE PRACTICE

Action research starts, as does all research, with a problem to be solved or an issue to be resolved. Unlike positivistic science, however, its primary goal is not the production of an objective body of knowledge that can be generalized to large populations. Instead, its purpose is to build collaboratively constructed descriptions and interpretations of events that enable groups of people to formulate mutually acceptable solutions to their problems. Action research, however, recognizes the complexities of human interaction and takes into account the need to enact ways of working that protect or enhance the dignity and identities of all people involved. As indicated in other chapters, it is oriented toward ways of organizing and enacting professional and community life that are democratic, equitable, liberating, and life enhancing.

The approach to inquiry presented in this book may appear somewhat idealistic. Competitive social values, impersonal work practices, and authoritarian modes of control impose themselves as constant conditions of our work. Institutionalized practices—those commonly accepted as "the way things are done"—seem so pervasive and normal that we often cannot envisage other ways of working, even when those practices are ineffective or, in some cases, detrimental to our purposes.

> I once engaged in a study of classrooms by observing three primary school classes for a year. Although at that time I had been a classroom teacher for almost 10 years, the study dramatically changed my vision of schools. My discovery that children spent extended periods passively watching or listening resulted in a significant change in my perspective. As a classroom teacher, my vision of classrooms was one in which there was a constant and sometimes almost overwhelming flow of activity. I was astounded that young children were forced to cope with long periods of inactivity during which they were permitted only to watch and listen as the teacher interacted with other students. That experience changed my perception of classroom life quite fundamentally, so that I am now much more sensitive to the pervasive passivity of school life and to the need to engage students constantly in active learning processes.

The pressures of bureaucratic life, the limitations of resources, and the competitive push for career advancement consistently work against attempts to humanize and democratize research processes. Procedures that highlight the active participation of people in formulating and controlling research activities and events are hard to attain and difficult to maintain. When they can be achieved, however, they provide a powerful means of accomplishing any set of social or professional goals. The act of observing and reflecting on our own practices can be an enlightening experience, enabling us to see ourselves more clearly and to formulate more effective ways of working that enhance the lives of the people with whom we work. Collaborative processes not only generate a sense of purpose and energy but also provide the means for the accomplishment of goals and the solution of problems and produce conditions that enhance participants' personal, social, and professional lives.

"BUT IT'S NOT SCIENTIFIC": THE QUESTION OF LEGITIMACY

Although action research is gaining increased support in the professional community, it has yet to be accepted by many academic researchers as a legitimate form of inquiry. From time to time, practitioners who engage in action research will find themselves subject to the negative comments, sometimes quite vitriolic, of people who do not regard such work as genuine research because "it's not scientific." A recent proposal for a paper on action research that I submitted for presentation at a national educational research conference, for instance, was rejected after one reviewer commented, "There may be a place for this nonsense in AERA [American Education Research Association], but not, hopefully, in this [the research] division."

It may be worthwhile, therefore, to spend a little time here exploring issues related to action research, so that those who enact it may rest easy in the knowledge that despite such comments and questions, action research is a legitimate, authentic, and rigorous approach to inquiry. Fuller treatments of this debate are provided in a number of other books (e.g., Reason and Bradbury's *Handbook of Action Research* [2007], Denzin and Lincoln's *Handbook of Qualitative Research* [2011], and Lincoln and Guba's *Naturalistic Inquiry* [1985]), but an overview will at least provide a basic understanding of the nature of the issues to be addressed.

I have studied the issues related to the different forms of social research for many years. In that time, I have become aware that the field is sufficiently contentious to engage the attention of some of the world's leading scholars. The debate is far from concluded, although the weight of argument seems to suggest that what has traditionally been accepted as scientific research is but one of a number of legitimate approaches to academic and professional inquiry.

Whether action research is accepted as scientific depends on the way in which *science* is defined. Certainly it is, in one sense, rigorously empirical, insofar as it requires people to define clearly and observe the phenomena under investigation. Levin and Greenwood (2001, 2011) suggest that action research is emphatically scientific, though not in terms propounded by experimental or quantitative researchers. For them, "The nucleus of scientific activity is deliberative, democratic sensemaking among professional researchers and local stakeholders" (2001, p. 105). It is evident, however, that action research does not follow the carefully prescribed experimental procedures that have become inscribed as *scientific method.*

Experimental method, a traditional approach to scientific inquiry, seeks to test theories that purport to explain why or how the world is as it is. The ultimate aim is to derive lawlike statements that explain the nature of the world or reality. This methodology seeks to generate knowledge that is *objective* (not amenable to the subjective or authoritative judgments of people, organizations, or institutions) and *generalizable* (applicable to a wide variety of contexts). It must also be *reliable* (the results should be replicable by any person similarly placed) and *valid* (it should describe a *true* state of affairs). The laws of science seek to provide invariant forms of knowledge that enable us to predict future events on the basis of a preexisting set of conditions. In recent history, this ability to predict and therefore control many facets of the physical world has provided humanity with the ability to manipulate the environment to an unprecedented degree. The technological miracles of the modern world are a testament to the power of knowledge derived from the application of the scientific method.

The success of this form of scientific inquiry in the physical world, however, has not been mirrored in investigations of human behavior and the social

world. Except to the extent that humans are physical beings, scientific investigation has largely failed to provide a social equivalent of the comparatively
stable body of knowledge about the physical universe. A science of humanity,
social life, or individual behavior has failed to emerge within anthropology,
sociology, or psychology, despite the huge resources poured into research in
these disciplines in the past few decades. Human beings, it seems, are hard to
predict and difficult to control.

Two major factors account for the failure of the scientific method to provide a set of laws for human behavior and social life. First, scientific knowledge is now recognized to be much less stable, objective, and generalizable
than previously assumed and therefore is less secure as a basis for formulating
human action. Second, there is increasing acceptance of the fundamental difference between the nature of the social world and that of the physical world.
Although it has been relatively easy to accept the notion of a fixed reality that
could be *discovered* in the physical universe, the social universe is now recognized as a continually evolving cultural creation. Social reality exists as an
unstable and dynamic construction that is fabricated, maintained, and modified by people during their interaction with each other and their environments.
It operates according to systems of meaning embedded in each cultural context
and can be understood only superficially without reference to those meanings.
Investigation of the social and behavioral worlds cannot be operationalized in
scientific terms because the phenomena to be tested lack the stability required
by traditional scientific method. Humans are, to a large extent, what they
define themselves to be in any given situation.

So where does this leave those who wish to investigate human affairs in
order to provide knowledge that will "make a difference" to people's lives? In
the past, it has been accepted that "experts," or those authorized by credentials
that signal their access to scientific knowledge, should provide answers to
social problems. Researchers are becoming increasingly aware of the limitations of this perspective, however. Scientific knowledge is partial, incomplete,
and reductionist (i.e., it reduces phenomena to minute components), and while
it can contribute to an understanding of elements of the social world, in and of
itself it cannot provide a comprehensive explanation of events.

Professional practitioners, armed with a set of practices purportedly
derived from scientific theories about human behavior, often believe their
activities are based on objective knowledge. Though scientific knowledge
certainly contributes useful information, the routines and recipes that compose

professional practice are imbued with concepts, constructs, values, and perceptions derived from the particular social histories and cultural experiences of the individuals and groups that dominate professional and institutional arenas. They are also heavily influenced by the institutional imperatives of the organizational contexts within which practitioners work. As a result, programs and services often fail to provide for the real needs of the people, especially with marginalized or disempowered social groups. In some cases the failure to recognize the deep-seated disconnection of the service from the social reality of the people aggravates the problems the service was meant to remediate. Programs and services often deny the strengths that are an inherent part of their community and family lives, and welfare or educational services are often accompanied by degrees of implicit criticism and control that attack people's very humanity.

The strength and vitality of Aboriginal family and community lives, which I experience in a continuing way as I work in organizational and community contexts, is belied by the perspectives presented in the mass media. There is a tendency to focus on that minority of Aboriginal people who capture the sensationalizing gaze of the media, to generalize from that group to all Aboriginal people, and to fail to recognize and value the contributions of the many solid and hardworking persons who make up the majority of the Aboriginal community. Professionals tend to approach Aboriginal people with the intent of "helping" them or tend to believe them in need of "training." They talk of the "cultural deficits" of Aboriginal children and the need for Aboriginal people to learn "social skills" or to acquire "cultural capital." The ethnocentrism of this group of professionals would be merely annoying if it were not for the fact that many of them are in positions of power that permit them to have significant impacts on the lives of people for whom they have so little regard. Aboriginal people often find their lives controlled by experts and public servants who have little understanding of their social and cultural realities and are apt to act in ways that are inappropriate or demeaning from an Aboriginal perspective.

I have extended experience of similar dynamics in the United States, where Anglo or middle-class professionals fail to understand the deep social and cultural dynamics that affect the lives of their students and clients. African American, Hispanic, and Native American peoples continue to struggle against the tide of ethnocentrism that flows so strongly through the fabric of institutional life.

I am once again reminded of the words of Aboriginal social worker Lilla Watson as she spoke to a group of non-Aboriginal social workers: "If you've come to help me, you're wasting your time. But if you've come because your liberation is bound up with mine, then let us work together."

POWER, CONTROL, AND SUBORDINATION

One of the fictions of modern professional and organizational life is that scientifically based procedures will provide the means to achieve effective outcomes in any form of service—health, welfare, education, business, and so on. "Scientific" management processes purport to identify a "best practice" and formulate processes for applying it in precise detail. This is a continuing source of frustration for those whose duty it is to perform these services or to gain the outcomes stipulated by government departments and agencies, educational institutions, and health services for which they work. Centrally devised best practices rarely take into account the dynamic social and cultural forces that operate in diverse contexts in which professional practitioners work and therefore place them and their clients and students in untenable situations. These groups are subject to increasing levels of stress and disenchantment as restrictive legislative mandates and highly prescribed administrative controls attempt to dictate precisely the ways they enact their professional duties. Managers and administrators of programs and services are often subject to even greater stress, caught in the nexus of organizational imperatives, recalcitrant subordinates and clients, the complex reality of the social contexts they engage, and their personal needs for ego satisfaction and career advancement. Highly prescriptive plans provide little opportunity for managers and practitioners to adapt and adjust their work to the realities of the particular environments in which they operate and act to increase the levels of anxiety associated with their work.

The problem is, of course, that it is impossible to control human behavior with the rigor and precision demanded by the procedures of the physical sciences. The dynamism of social life and the creative and willful facets of human behavior prevent the high degrees of control embedded in scientific method and technological production. Attempts to impose the same type and extent of control in the delivery of human services have led to increasing levels of stress and alienation as practitioners struggle to provide necessary services within the boundaries of increasingly restrictive policies and procedural rules.

I rarely meet a friend or colleague who is "happy in the service" these days. Those who work in human service agencies or organizations as practitioners or managers frequently complain about the unrealistic demands and excessive numbers of directives that inhibit the effective accomplishment of their work. The complaints cover all fields, from social work, through education and health work, to community and youth work. The quality of professional life appears to be diminishing as demands for greater control and accountability increase.

How, then, are we to understand the events that make up our lives? Behavioral theorists, on the one hand, focus on the capabilities and characteristics of individuals and point to factors such as motivation, achievement need, intelligence, and cognition to explain people's behavior. Social theorists, on the other hand, tend to stress the large-scale forces—class, gender, race, and ethnicity—that influence social events. Marxist-oriented theorists, for instance, explain social events by the controlling and competitive relationships inherent in modern capitalist economic systems. The people who control the means of production, this genre of theory suggests, maintain systems of domination that reinforce the power and authority of those in positions of power at the expense of subordinate groups.

Although these theories are interesting and useful for some purposes, they are limited in their applicability to the problems experienced by people and social groups in their day-to-day lives. If we accept the economic determinism inherent in Marxist theory, for example, we are but puppets on the world stage, our lives ordered by the workings of the international economic order, our efforts to improve our lives essentially fruitless.

A recent genre of theory, known collectively as *postmodernism,* provides a distinctive way of envisioning the social world that enables us to understand human experience in different ways. Although modern perspectives of the world are bound to scientific visions of a fixed and knowable world, postmodernism questions the nature of social reality and the very processes by which we can come to know about it. Elements of postmodernism suggest that knowledge can no longer be accepted as an objective set of testable truths because it is produced by processes that are inherently "captured" by features of the social world it seeks to explain. Scientists, as products of particular historical and cultural experiences, will formulate explanations of the social world that derive from their own experiences and hence tend to validate their own perceptual universes.

From a postmodern perspective, attempts to order people's lives on the basis of scientific knowledge largely constitute an exercise in power. Knowledge, and the research that produces that knowledge, is as much about politics as it is about understanding. An understanding of what research is about is not just an exploration of method but an inquiry into the ways in which knowledge is produced and the benefits that accrue to people who control the processes of knowledge production.

> The theoretical discourse that follows is not presented as a description of "the" social world. It is articulated as one way of interpreting social experience and presents perspectives that seem to make sense from my viewpoint. In essence, I, as author, provide a framework of ideas as a rationale for action research. Those readers who find it unhelpful may choose to skip the next passage and formulate their own rationale for accepting or rejecting the approach to research that I advocate.

UNDERSTANDING POWER AND CONTROL: POSTMODERN PERSPECTIVES

Postmodernism derives much of its power from the way it deconstructs—that is, pulls apart for examination—mechanisms of knowledge production. Scientific rationality, a key feature of modern life, has itself become subject to forms of philosophical investigation that raise doubts about many of the taken-for-granted assumptions on which our understandings of the social and physical universe rest. An exploration of postmodern perspectives, therefore, assists us in extending our understanding of the frustrations experienced by practitioners as they work in social, community, and organizational contexts.

Michel Foucault's (1972) exploration of social life, for instance, reinforces the notion that there can be no objective truth, because there is an essential relationship between the ways in which knowledge is produced and the way power is exercised. Foucault's study of the development of modern institutional life led him to conclude that there is an intimate relation between the systems of knowledge—discourses—by which people arrange their lives and the techniques and practices through which social control and domination are exercised in local contexts. Humans are subject to oppression, Foucault suggests, not only because of the operation of large-scale systems of control and authority but also because of the normally accepted procedures, routines, and practices through which we enact our daily public and personal lives.

From a Foucaultian perspective, such institutional sites as schools, agency offices, hospitals, clinics, and youth centers might be viewed as examples of places where a dispersed and piecemeal organization of power is built up independent of any systematic strategy of domination. What happens in these contexts cannot be understood by focusing only on systemwide strategies of control. At each site, a professional elite, which includes administrators, researchers and teachers, social workers, nurses, doctors, and youth workers, defines the language and the discourse and, in doing so, builds a framework of meaning into the organization and operation of the system. Individual members of this elite exert control by contributing to the framing and maintenance of ordinary, commonly accepted practices, which are often enshrined in bureaucratic fiat, administrative procedure, or government regulation. The end point of this process is the accrual of "profit" or benefit to people in a position to define the "codes of knowledge" that form the basis for organizational life. Professional acceptance, employment, promotion, funding, and other forms of recognition provide a system of rewards for people able to influence or reinforce definitions inscribed in reports, regulations, rules, policies, procedures, curricula, texts, and professional literature.

Foucault (1972) contends that any large-scale analysis must be built from our understanding of the micropolitics of power at the local level. For him, any attempt to describe power at the level of the state or institution requires us to

conduct an ascending analysis of power, starting . . . from its infinitesimal mechanisms, which each have their own history, their own trajectory, their own techniques and tactics, and then see how these mechanisms of power have been—and continue to be—invested, colonized, utilized, involuted, transformed, displaced, extended, etc., by ever more general mechanisms and by forms of global domination. (p. 159)

If we accept Foucault's analysis, then many negative features of society are intimately related to the ways in which people organize and act out their everyday lives. Feelings of alienation, stress, and oppression are as much products of everyday, taken-for-granted ways of defining reality and enacting social life as they are the products of systems that are out of people's control. The means by which people are subjugated are found in the very "codes" and "discourses" used to organize and enact their day-to-day lives. Oppressive systems of domination and control are maintained not by autocratic processes but through the unconsciously accepted routine practices people use in their families, communities, and occupations.

Foucault suggests that the only way to eliminate this fascism in our heads is to explore and build on the open qualities of human discourse and thereby intervene in the way knowledge is constituted at the particular sites where a localized power discourse prevails. He maintains that people should cultivate and enhance planning and decision making at the local level, resisting techniques and practices that are oppressive in one way or another. Foucault (1984) instructs us to "develop action, thought and desires by proliferation, juxtaposition, and disjunction" and "to prefer what is positive and multiple, difference over uniformity, flows over unities, mobile arrangements over systems. Believe that what is productive is not sedentary but nomadic" (p. xiii). He suggests that we become more flexible in the ways we conceive and organize our activities to ensure that we incorporate diverse perspectives into our social and organizational lives.

The theme of control is also taken up by Fish (1980), who describes social life as "interpretive communities" made up of producers and consumers of particular types of knowledge or "texts." Within these communities, individuals or groups in positions of authority control what they consider to be valid knowledge. Classroom teachers, administrators, managers, social workers, health professionals, policy makers, and researchers are examples of "producers" who control the texts of social life in their professional domains. In organizing classrooms, writing curricula, defining the rules and procedures by which services operate, formulating policies, and so on, they control the boundaries within which particular interpretive communities operate. They have the power to dominate the ways in which things happen in their particular domains.

Fish's position is complemented by the work of Lyotard (1984), who casts doubt on the possibility of defining social and organizational life according to well-ordered, logical, and objective (read "scientific") systems of knowledge. He suggests that people live at the intersection of an indeterminate number of language games that, in their entirety, do not constitute a coherent or rational order, although each game operates under a logical set of rules. His vision of a social world atomized into flexible networks of language games suggests that each of us uses a number of games or codes depending on the context in which we are operating at any given time. There is a contradiction, Lyotard suggests, between the natural openness of social life and the rigidities with which institutions attempt to circumscribe what is and is not admissible within their boundaries.

Derrida's (1976) notion of the interweaving of discourses provides yet another perspective on the texts of social life. Derrida provides insight into the continuing tension between people in positions of control and their subordinates and clients. According to him, cultural life can be viewed as a series of texts that intersect with other texts through the processes of social interaction. In portraying written texts as cultural artifacts—that is, as human productions—Derrida suggests that both reader and writer interact on the basis of all they have previously encountered. Both author and reader participate separately in the production of meanings inscribed in and derived from that text, although neither can "master" the text—that is, control the meanings conveyed or received—in any ultimate sense. Writers tend to accept the authority to present reality or meaning in their own terms, but these meanings are deconstructed and reconstituted by readers according to their own experiences and interpretive frameworks.

In the context of organizational and institutional life, people such as administrators, teachers, social workers, and other practitioners who control the rules and procedures by which their subordinates, students, or clients work or live often fail to understand that each of the participants will understand those texts according to his or her own framework of understanding. Even when participants accept what is said or written, they may enact their interpretations of the text in ways that seem to conflict with the perspectives of the authors of the text. Much of the apparent recalcitrance or wrongheadedness of workers, students, and clients might be understood as merely misinterpretation.

There is an implicit ideological position in Derrida's writing. He suggests the need to find new ways of writing texts—rules, procedures, regulations, forms of organization, reports, plans, and so on—to minimize the power of people in positions of authority to impose their perceptions and interpretations. Thus he implies the need to structure organizations in ways that create greater opportunities for popular participation and a more democratic determination of the cultural values embedded in the procedures that govern people's lives. This also implies the need to enact knowledge-producing activities in ways that are more participatory and democratic, enabling the perspectives and agendas of client groups and students to be included in the development of programs that serve them.

Huyssens (1986) also speaks to these issues. He is critical of writers whose theorizing—systems of explanation—presumes to speak for others. He suggests that all groups have the right to speak for themselves, in their own voices, and to have those voices accepted as authentic and legitimate. The authenticity of these "other worlds" and "other voices" is an essential characteristic of the pluralistic stance of many postmodern writers. Huyssens's position has much in common with those of writers such as West (1989) and Unger (1987), who place a premium on the need to educate and be educated by struggling peoples. This stance reflects a movement within the postmodern tradition that shifts the focus of scholarship away from the "search for foundations and the quest for certainty" (West, 1989, p. 213) toward more utilitarian approaches to the production of knowledge.

West (1989) provides a compelling argument for a more pragmatic approach to our ways of understanding the social world. His notion of "prophetic pragmatism" points to the need for an explicitly political mode of cultural criticism. He suggests that philosophy—more generally, intellectual activity or scholarship—should foster methods of examining ordinary and everyday events that encourage a more creative democracy through critical intelligence and social action. He advocates ways of living and working together that provide greater opportunities for people to participate in activities that affect their lives. He urges philosophers—academics, researchers, experts, and professionals—to give up their search for the foundations of truth and the quest for certainty and to shift their energies to defining the social and communal conditions by which people can communicate more effectively and cooperate in the processes of acquiring knowledge and making decisions.

The underlying notion in West's (1989) work is not that philosophy and rational deliberation are irrelevant but that they need to be applied directly to the problems of the people. West's pragmatism reconceptualizes philosophy—and therefore research—as "a form of cultural criticism that attempts to transform linguistic, social, cultural and political traditions for the purposes of increasing the scope of individual development and democratic operation" (p. 230). He advocates fundamental economic, political, cultural, and individual transformation guided by the ideals of accountable power, small-scale associations, and individual liberty. This transformation can be attained, he implies, only through the reconstruction of the practices and preconceptions embedded in institutional life. On the political level, West acknowledges the need for solidarity with the "wretched of the earth," so that by educating and being educated by struggling peoples we will be able to relate the life of the mind to the collective life of the community.

West's emphasis on liberation links him, conceptually, with the German scholar Jurgen Habermas, who, although often not classified as postmodern, has provided important ideas that can assist us in understanding human social life. Habermas (1979) focuses on the need to rethink the cultural milieu in which people attempt to find meaning and satisfactory self-identity. He suggests that we clarify the nature of people's subjection and seek human emancipation from the threats of military conflict and dehumanized bureaucratic domination through more effective mechanisms of reflection and communication. Habermas proposes that the emphasis in institutional and organizational life on the factual, material, technical, and administrative neglects the web of intersubjective relations among people that makes possible freedom, harmony, and mutual dependence. His universal pragmatics attempt to delineate the basic conditions necessary for people to reach an understanding. The goal of "communicative action" is an interaction that terminates in "the intersubjective mutuality of reciprocal understanding, shared knowledge, mutual trust and accord with one another" (p. 3).

The general thrust of the ideas presented earlier is to question many of the basic assumptions on which modern social life is based. In general, these ideas are in opposition to rigidly defined work practices, hierarchical organizational structures, representation in place of participation, the isolation of sectors of activity based on high degrees of specialization, centralized decision making, and the production of social texts by experts or an organizational elite. Inversely, these perspectives suggest emphasis on the following:

- Popular and vernacular language and its meanings
- Pluralistic, organic strategies for development
- The coexistence and interpenetration of meaning systems
- The authenticity of "other worlds" and "other voices"
- Preference for what is multiple, for difference
- Flexibility and mobility of organizational arrangements
- Local creation of texts, techniques, and practices
- Production of knowledge through open discourses
- Flexibility in defining the work people will do
- Restructuring of relations of authority

Postmodern thought moves us, therefore, to examine the ordinary, every-day, taken-for-granted ways in which we organize and carry out our private, social, and professional activities. In the context of this book, it demands that we critically inspect the routines and recipes that have become accepted and commonplace ways of carrying out our professional, organizational, and institutional functions. By illuminating fundamental features of social life, postmodern writers provide us with an opportunity to explore social dimensions of our work and to think creatively about the possibilities for re-creating our professional lives.

The influence of postmodern perspectives now can be seen throughout the academic disciplines and in the professional literature. The editors of a previous edition of the *Handbook of Qualitative Research* (Denzin & Lincoln, 2005) suggest that "postpositivist inquirers of all perspectives and paradigms have joined in the collective struggle for a socially responsive, democratic, communitarian, moral and justice-promoting set of inquiry practices" (p. 1, 123). They further suggest, "The search for 'culturally sensitive' research approaches—approaches that are attuned to the specific cultural practices of various groups and that 'recognize ethnicity and position culture as central to the research process' (Tillman, 2002)—is already under way" (p. 1, 123). These suggestions stand alongside their advocacy of a new praxis deeply responsive and accountable to those it serves and a reimagined social science that calls for an engaged academic world that leaves the ivory tower and learns from experiences in community, organizational, and family settings (Levin & Greenwood, 2011). The next generation of research methods is emerging.

ACTION RESEARCH: THE NEXT GENERATION

This chapter focuses largely on the philosophical foundations of action research. I have presented arguments that seek to substantiate my assertion that it is a legitimate approach to research, despite procedures that vary from commonly accepted practices associated with scientific method. My intent has been not to show that scientific method is wrong or incorrect but to demonstrate that it sits alongside action research as one of a variety of authentic approaches to inquiry.

Even within action research, there is a place for some of the methods, procedures, and concepts usually associated with traditional science. Insofar as people live in a physical universe, traditional scientific research methods—sometimes unhelpfully labeled "quantitative" research—can provide much useful information. We can describe, for instance, the number of people involved in a setting and how they are distributed geographically, organizationally, and culturally. We can also enumerate the number and proportion of unemployed people, the number and types of dwellings, the age distribution of the population, and relationships among features such as gender, social class, race, educational attainment, employment, and poverty.

The meaning or significance of any of this information, however, can be determined only by the people who live the culture of the setting, who have the profound understanding that comes from extended immersion in the social and cultural life of that context. Numbers can never tell us what the information "means" or suggest actions to be taken.

I recently engaged in a conversation with a colleague regarding the utility of merely quantifying events. "Jim," I said, "if, over a period of 6 weeks, I read a local newspaper 40 times, have 120 meals, drink 30 bottles of beer, teach 24 classes, and punch the dean once, which event do you think will be most significant?" In this instance, it is easy to imagine which event is symbolically the most important. In many situations, however, outsiders, expert or otherwise, face grave risks in making judgments about the significance of events. Certainly, the number of times an event occurs is a poor indicator of its symbolic importance or the impact it is likely to have on people's lives.

Action research, therefore, ultimately focuses on events that are meaningful for stakeholders. It provides a process or context through which people can collectively clarify their problems and formulate new ways of envisioning their situations. In doing so, each participant's taken-for-granted cultural viewpoint is challenged and modified so that new systems of meaning emerge that can be incorporated in the texts—rules, regulations, practices, procedures, and policies—that govern our professional and community experience. We come closer to the reality of other people's experience and, in the process, increase the potential for creating truly effective services and programs that will enhance the lives of the people we serve.

This move to emphasize the perspectives and agendas of the client group rather than those of professional practitioners in the development and improvement of programs and services does not mean that simplistic, populist ideas current in mass culture provide the basis for service delivery or institutional practice. For instance, the McDonald's fast-food curriculum model would provide a rather unhealthy educational diet in schools. It does mean, however, that professionals take seriously the ideas and perspectives of those they serve, developing ways of working that implicitly honor the intelligence and integrity of the people with whom they work.

Recent theoretical debates have provided substantial recognition of the philosophical strength of this approach to inquiry. The working principles and values revealed in the first chapters of this book are given credence by Denzin's (1997) forward-thinking work, aptly subtitled *Ethnographic Practice for the Twenty-First Century.* He seeks to engage social scientific practices that "will move closer to a sacred, critically informed discourse about the moral, human universe" (p. xviii). Drawing from the work of Christians, Ferre, and Fackler (1993) and Lincoln (1995), he advocates approaches to inquiry that engage a feminist, communitarian moral ethic organized by the following assumptions:

- Community as ontologically and morally superior to persons
- Dialogical communication as the basis for moral community
- Transformation as the major goal of any ethical or occupational practice
- Commitment to the common good and to universal human solidarity
- A sacred conception of science that honors the ecological as well as the human

- A stress on human dignity, care, justice, and interpersonal respect
- A belief that those studied are active participants in collaborative research processes, with claims over any research materials produced in the research process

This perspective is consonant with an ethic of caring (Collins, 1991) that celebrates personal expressiveness, emotionality, and empathy; values individual uniqueness; and cherishes each person's dignity, grace, and courage. It is a model, in other words, that fits the intent and processes of action research. It emerges, philosophically, from *standpoint epistemologies,* that is, the ways of knowing and understanding implicit in the experience of particular social groups that challenge traditional approaches to social science. Standpoint epistemologies emerge from feminist theory contending that studies involving women should privilege women's lived experience and the standpoints, or perspectives, that experience brings to the ethnographic project. These perspectives challenge the notion of a single standpoint from which a final, overriding vision of the world can be written (Smith, 1989) and therefore question the ways traditional, patriarchal social science has been constructed. This dynamic extends to other interpretive communities and suggests that ethnic groups, people of color, gays, and so on draw on their group and individual experiences as the basis for texts that speak to the logic and cultures of these communities (Denzin, 1997).

Standpoint perspectives, therefore, advocate ways of formulating reports from the starting point of people's experience to provide a more accurate representation of reality, the production of local knowledge about the workings of the world (Denzin, 1989). Standpoint perspectives suggest the need to recover and bring value to knowledge suppressed by the existing texts and discourses of social science and by interpretations of people's lives that are inscribed in the apparatuses of the state, mass culture, and popular media.

Patricia Hill Collins's (1991) Afrocentric feminist epistemology, for instance, focuses on the primacy of concrete, lived experience; the use of dialogue in assessing knowledge claims; the ethic of caring; and the ethic of personal accountability. "This epistemology creates the conditions for an existential politics of empowerment that will allow African American women to actively confront racial, gender and class oppression in their daily lives" (p. 237). Trinh (1992) writes from an Asian perspective, challenging systems of domination that seek to impose an essential identity on a person and her experience. She advocates the production of texts that allow women to experience and assert their difference in relation to others and to assume the position of active speakers, listeners, readers, writers, and viewers.

Although standpoint perspectives relate particularly to the experience of marginalized groups, there is a more general point. They should sensitize writers to the need to resist impulses to formulate objective, generalizable accounts claiming to include the perspectives of all people. Reports need to incorporate and represent the perspectives and experiences of the diverse social groups affected by the events and phenomena studied to ensure that the standpoint of each group is presented as authentic and legitimate, rather than an aberration from a hypothetical norm.

Not so long ago, the human services agency in my state produced a carefully compiled child protection manual, complete with detailed procedures for evaluating events related to the well-being of children and formulating appropriate intervention strategies. A consultant had carefully prepared the manual, taking into account the latest information on child protection available in the literature and using intervention strategies deemed to be appropriate. The procedures, however, were inappropriate to the realities of Aboriginal family and community life, applying criteria for child care that were contrary to the values and conventions of Aboriginal communities and advocating interventions that were reminiscent of more repressive eras in Aboriginal history. Aboriginal staff of the agency went on strike in one region, forcing the agency to have the offending manual reviewed and modified to take Aboriginal cultural values into account.

GIVING VOICE: REPRESENTING PEOPLE'S EXPERIENCE

The desire to give voice to people is derived not from an abstract ideological or theoretical imperative but from the pragmatic focus of action research. Its intent is to provide a place for the perspectives of people who have previously been marginalized from opportunities to develop and operate policies, programs, and services—perspectives often concealed by the products of a typical research process. Research reports often mirror the style of "objective" scientific reports, providing dry, abstract renderings of ideas and events and masking the fact that they are the productions of a socially situated author who writes from his or her history of experience. The process often encapsulates events within the mystifying jargon of academic disciplines or buries them in the conceptual apparatuses of a bureaucracy.

Previous sections of this book have suggested alternative ways for action research participants to represent more effectively the outcomes of their research processes. The purpose of these alternatives is to ensure that accounts and reports capture the people's everyday, concrete, human experiences, allowing audiences to understand more clearly the realities of people's lives. The need for changes in reporting procedures is clearly presented in an increasing body of research literature (e.g., Berger Gluck & Patai, 1991; Bruner, 1990; Burnaford, Fischer, & Hobson, 1996; Lincoln & Tierney, 1996; Neumann & Peterson, 1997; Witherall & Noddings, 1991). These and many other authors explore ways of representing people's experience to more effectively grasp the many dimensions of life that formal, official reports often fail to reveal.

Denzin (1997) explores the underlying assumptions and principles of ethnographic writing and many of the dimensions of the reporting act. In so doing, he suggests that authors of official and academic reports might usefully employ technical processes used by journalists and fiction writers. He starts from the assumption that it is impossible to write objective accounts not ultimately inscribed with the perspectives and experiences of the author because of the interpretive processes inherent in data collection, analysis, and report writing. Drawing on a wide range of authors, he suggests that experiments in genre, voice, narrative, and interpretive style provide more effective ways of knowing—other ways of feeling our way into the experiences of others. Such writing, he suggests, reveals the meaning of events given by interacting individuals, focusing on experience deeply embedded in and derived from local cultural contexts that include homes, offices, schools, streets, factories, clinics, hotels, and so on. These accounts and reports recognize and represent the multiple interpretations of any event or phenomenon, yet also acknowledge the broader discourses inscribed or imprinted in people's local experiences—government policies, incipient racism, systems of privilege, imbalances of power based on social status, and so on.

Denzin works from the premise that the purpose of accounts derived from research processes is more than to record experience. Their goal, rather, is to provide the basis for transforming people's civic, public, and personal lives through the truths—the new ways of describing and interpreting events—revealed in the research process. Reports, therefore, must be more than impersonal, abstract accounts of "facts," which themselves are merely pieces of information acquired and interpreted selectively. They must be empathetic, evocative accounts that embody the significant experiences embedded in the taken-for-granted world of people's everyday lives. They must record the agonies, pains, tragedies, triumphs, actions, behaviors, and deeply felt emotions—love, pride, dignity, honor, hate, and envy—that constitute the real world of human experience.

In this context, the researcher–writer takes a different stance in the research and writing process. No longer "experts" capable of defining, describing, and interpreting the "facts" or "truth," researcher–writers position themselves toward writing processes that assist others in describing and interpreting their own experiences, sometimes acting as scribes for research participants or as coauthors or editors. The writer as scribe-for-the-other helps people give voice to their own interpretations of events, working with them to identify the key elements of their experience and shape them into a report.

CHANGING WORK AND SOCIAL PRACTICES: "SCRIPTS" FOR POLICIES, PLANS, AND PROCEDURES

Change is an intended outcome of action research: not the revolutionary changes envisioned by radical social theorists or political activists but more subtle transformations brought about by the development of new programs or modifications to existing procedures.[1] These developments and modifications, however, must necessarily be carefully planned and derived from the research processes to provide people with the means to more effectively deal with the problems investigated. The procedures presented in Chapters 6 and 7 suggest some ways of moving from reflection and theorizing to action. These moves need to be made more explicit so that the institutional imperatives of universities and bureaucracies do not inhibit the potential of the research process. There is a need to more overtly review the outcomes of research so they are presented in forms that may be applied directly to the texts that govern much of institutional life: the policies, plans, and procedures that dictate how programs and services are delivered to the people served by those institutions.

Experiments with forms of writing that more effectively capture people's experience, discussed in the previous section, are moves in the right direction, but they appear limited in their ability to provide tangible outcomes for those who participate in research. Academic research tends to focus on the production of written texts that reflect the imperatives of university life, and research reports often remain trapped within the walls of the university. They circulate within the texts and journals of the university and, even when enacted as performances, are presented as theatrical productions playing to audiences oriented toward institutional life. They do not penetrate the everyday lifeworld of homes, schools, clinics, offices, shops, and factories and are especially remote from marginalized peoples whose lives are often framed by oral traditions misrepresented by the forms of understanding presented in written texts.

Even approaches to research designed to be more sensitive to these dynamics are prone to processes of knowledge production that colonize the experience of others. Denzin's (1997) interpretive ethnography, for instance, seeks to produce evocative understandings through a variety of literary genres that perform or write of people's experience (see Chapter 5). Research products, such as reports, presentations, and performances, are taken from the locations of the study and used as generalized narratives for an audience unrelated to the research context. Those texts and performances are used largely by others to enable them to understand the experience of those written about and often place that experience in an etic (outsider) framework of generalized theory. Such theorizing tends to be macrofocused, incorporating broad concepts, such as power, class, gender, race, and so on, often providing no basis for action in people's daily lives. The terminology turns the focus away from people's lived experience toward more general social processes that they have little opportunity or hope of controlling. Critiques within this type of literary production usually focus on negative constructions of the situation, often framed within descriptions and explanations of macrosocial and cultural structures and treated as real entities, rather than as constructed ways of interpreting social phenomena.

These texts and performances are sometimes illuminating, providing understanding of the broader contexts within which people's lives are played out and revealing underlying forces of social life not evident existentially. They are, however, etic constructs that have the power to distort people's lived reality and misrepresent the existential experience of their everyday lives. They tend to be generalizing interpretations that focus on underlying elements of social life, such as power, race, and gender, rather than revealing the dynamic, interactive play of people and events as they work their way through their day-to-day lives. Dealing with macrostructures as they do, they often fail to provide the possibility for restorative action and run the risk, therefore, of becoming voyeuristic and disempowering.

The use of those types of production should, perhaps, not be underestimated, because they do provide useful ways of communicating evocative interpretations of social life that inform readers of social realities far removed from their own experiences. Action research, however, suggests the possibility of more socially responsive uses of research, providing the means for people to have a more direct impact on the significant issues that continue to detract from their social life and to make a tangible difference in the problems that diminish their lives. It reconceptualizes research as a participatory process that allows scholars—to follow West's (1989) dictum—to make their skills available for the purposes of the people.

Action research enacts localized, pragmatic approaches, investigating particular issues and problems in particular sites at particular moments in lives of interacting individuals and groups. Its purpose is to provide participants with new understandings of an issue they have defined as significant and the means for taking corrective action. The processes are necessarily participatory, enabling all people affected by the issue to have their voices heard and to be actively engaged in research activities. Action research suggests a move in emphasis from the creative texts of experimental interpretive ethnography toward the production of "practice scripts"— plans, procedures, and models derived from the final stages of action research that describe the actions people will take or the behaviors in which they will engage. Practice scripts—plans, procedures, and so on—also provide the means for people in professional or occupational roles to reformulate policies and practices to enable them to support the activities or changes in behavior of their clients, students, patients, or customers (see Box 2.1).

Box 2.1   An Action Research Framework

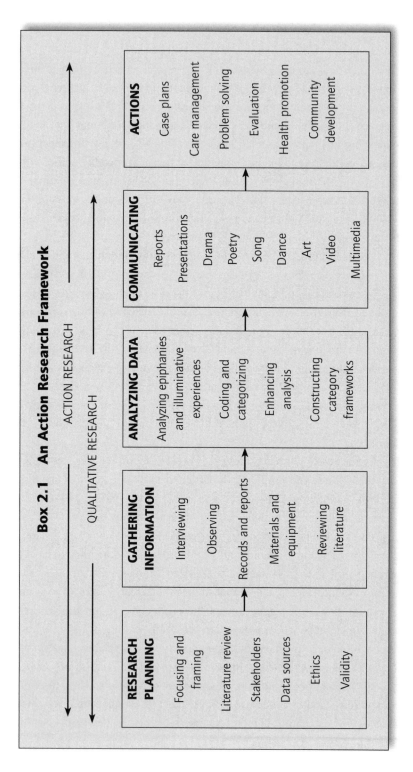

QUALITATIVE RESEARCH

ACTION RESEARCH

RESEARCH PLANNING

Focusing and framing

Literature review

Stakeholders

Data sources

Ethics

Validity

GATHERING INFORMATION

Interviewing

Observing

Records and reports

Materials and equipment

Reviewing literature

ANALYZING DATA

Analyzing epiphanies and illuminative experiences

Coding and categorizing

Enhancing analysis

Constructing category frameworks

COMMUNICATING

Reports

Presentations

Drama

Poetry

Song

Dance

Art

Video

Multimedia

ACTIONS

Case plans

Care management

Problem solving

Evaluation

Health promotion

Community development

Although academic research often seeks critique from within the constructs of the social sciences, critique in action research derives from the conjunction or clash of the diverse perspectives of individuals and groups participating, each perspective being challenged by the others. Critique is derived not from an etic, outsider interpretive framework but from the process of exploring and negotiating the perspectives emerging from the process of investigation. It uses concepts and terms from within the context, rather than those drawn from academic texts or bureaucratic discourses, and seeks constructions and interpretations of the issue that provides the basis for direct, tangible uses within the research context.

Change, the desired outcome of action research, therefore derives from the here-and-now ideas and concepts taken from the taken-for-granted life-world of the participants. It is based on the language, ideas, and concepts that make sense in their homes, offices, schools, factories, shops, clinics, centers, organizations, and institutions and are part of their everyday experience of family, community, work, professional, and commercial life. The products of research are not only written reports but also "practice scripts"—plans, procedures, models, maps, and so on—that provide the basis for reformulating practices, policies, programs, and services related to people's occupational or community life.

I am reminded of the long list of official policies, projects, programs, and institutional processes that have damaged the lives of minority peoples in Australia and the United States. I think of Dee Brown's *Bury My Heart at Wounded Knee* (1970) and Anna Haebich's *For Their Own Good* (1988), both of which depict the disastrous impact of official policies on the lives of indigenous peoples. I think of the way that I organized my classroom in an Aboriginal school, so that children were forced to sit with others with whom they had a taboo or avoidance relationship. I think of academics who, from the safety of their ivory tower, formulate research projects implicitly critical of professional practitioners. The list goes on. Last night, a good friend and I, musing over these dynamics, thought of the old saying that "the road to hell is paved with good intentions."

But I am also reminded of the great triumphs of those who worked with people so that they became the instruments of their own liberation. Great

(Continued)

(Continued)

leaders such as Mahatma Gandhi and Martin Luther King Jr. come to mind, but I am conscious of a flood of other local heroes with smaller accomplishments: the woman who established a play group to help young mothers come together to discuss their common issues—the genesis of a widespread network of play groups in my own state—and the psychiatrist who worked with parents and students in her local community to establish an independent school as a haven from a school ruled by an authoritarian principal. Fortunately, that list also goes on.

WHAT WE LEARN FROM THE LITERATURE

Historically, action research has been related to models of action research that sought to apply the tools of anthropology and other disciplines to the practical resolution of social problems (e.g., Goodenough, 1963; Lewin, 1946). Action research ultimately suffered a decline in favor because of its association with radical political activism in the 1960s. In the past two decades it has reemerged in response to both pragmatic and philosophical pressures and is now more broadly understood as "disciplined inquiry (research) which seeks focused efforts to improve the quality of people's organizational, community and family lives" (Calhoun, 1993, p. 62). Action research was also allied to the emergence of practitioner research (e.g., Anderson, Herr, & Nihlen, 2007), new paradigm research (Reason, 1988), and teacher research (e.g., Kincheloe, 1991). The approach to research suggested by action research is implied within the methodological frameworks of fourth-generation evaluation (Guba & Lincoln, 1989). Their dialogic, hermeneutic (meaning-making) approach to evaluation implies a more democratic, empowering, and humanizing approach to inquiry, which is the ideological basis for action research. Since that time there has been a proliferation of texts that speak to a wide range of audiences in professional, organizational, and community contexts (see following discussion), providing a rich resource that, over time, may transform the notion of research. Perhaps the best review of recent resources is provided by Bob Dick (2012), a testament to Bob's long history with and contribution to the field.

The literature on action research continues to expand significantly, with a wide range of books, journals, and social media providing information relevant to professional, organizational, and community contexts. The literature not only provides insight into approaches to action research but also presents many examples and case studies of the way people have applied it in different contexts. Since no one source can cover in detail all the issues that need to be addressed, the literature also assists us to extend our understanding through the ways that authors frame, explain, and describe action research. Different orientations and perspectives not only assist us to extend our understanding but also challenge the assumptions integral to any study or investigation. The particular way in which action research is framed in this text, for instance, is both challenged and informed by a number of other prominent authors in the field.

McNiff and Whitehead (2011), for instance, focus on self-study as an integral part of action research, suggesting that change must occur internally within the researcher—a change in the way people think and feel. Practitioners, they suggest, should not only commit seriously to improving their practice but in doing so give explanations of those improvements that make explicit the values and purposes that give meaning to their actions. These explanations take us past the everyday understandings and commonly accepted explanations and routines to develop "living theories" more closely grounded in the realities of the actual contexts within which people live and work. For them action research is about creating knowledge that enables people to find ways to improve their practice.

Coghlan and Brannick (2009) likewise characterize action research as an approach to inquiry that aims at taking action and creating knowledge and theory about action. Theirs is an integrative approach to research that incorporates three voices and audiences: first, second, and third persons. They suggest that research has traditionally focused on the third person. In a style reminiscent of McNiff and Whitehead, they present first-person research as a form of inquiry and practice one does on one's own, fostering an inquiry approach to his or her own life to act out of awareness of one's own basic assumptions, desires, intention, philosophy, and ways of relating to others. Second-person inquiry focuses on processes of working with others on issues of mutual concern, through face-to-face dialogue, conversation, and joint action. Third-person inquiry or practice aims at creating broader communities of inquiry, involving people beyond the direct second-person action, and is actualized through reporting, publishing, and extrapolating past the concrete to the general. Coghlan and Brannick refer to Reason and Marshall's (1987) notion of three audiences of research: me, us, and them. Their focus on organizations emphasizes the need for members of the system being studied to participate actively and collaboratively in the cyclical processes of investigation. Coghlan and Brannick suggest that defining characteristics of action research include research in action rather than about action; collaborative, democratic partnerships; research concurrent with action; a sequence of events; and an approach to problem solving.

Greenwood and Levin (2006), whose work is also particularly relevant to organizational contexts, present action research as "a set of collaborative ways of conducting research that simultaneously satisfies rigorous scientific requirements and promotes democratic social change" (p. 1). As with authors previously cited, they see action research as a process of generating knowledge and designing action, with local stakeholders and trained experts working together in a joint learning process. Action research, they suggest, centers on doing "with" rather than doing "for" stakeholders and credits local stakeholders with "the richness of experience and reflective possibilities that long experience living in complex situations brings with it" (2006, p. 1).

The sources just cited represent a small sample of publications with a similar orientation to that presented in this text. The field of action research is now served by many publications, websites, and social media that provide a rich body of resources for those intent on exploring the diversity of approaches to action research and the contexts in which it is applied.

A major source of information is found in academic journals that now include the *Action Research Journal,* an international, interdisciplinary journal providing a forum for the development of the theory and practice of action research; *ALAR—The Action Learning/Action Research Journal,* focusing largely on community contexts of action research; the *International Journal of Action Research,* providing a similar orientation to action research in online form; *Educational Action Research,* likewise providing an online service now encompassing professional areas other than education; and other online journals that include *Action Research International, AR Expeditions,* and the *Canadian Journal of Action Research.*

Reference resources for action research may be found in the canonical *Handbook of Action Research* (Reason & Bradbury, 2007), which explores the philosophical and theoretical underpinnings of action research as well as provides case studies from a number of fields; the forthcoming *Encyclopedia of Action Research* (Coghlan & Brydon-Miller, in press); and the *Sage Handbook of Educational Action Research* (Noffke & Somekh, 2009). Other general texts include those by McNiff and Whitehead (2009, 2011); Whitehead and McNiff (2006); and Fals-Borda and Rahman (1991); as well as an action research planner by Kemmis and McTaggart (1999). McTaggart (1997) describes the application of action research in an international context, while Heron (1997) provides a detailed and practical guide to cooperative inquiry, one of the many variants of the action research "family." Tyler (2006) and Reeb (2007) present community-focused approaches to action research, and Schmuck (2006) presents action research as a tool for social change.

Education is perhaps the most prolific source of action research resources, with a body of literature covering a wide range of educational issues. Some of this is in response to government-imposed testing regimes and provides rather simplistic procedures for using action research to seek out and test the "silver bullet" teaching techniques that will result in higher test scores. These appear to be largely futile, failing to engage the participatory and cyclical processes of inquiry that are the hallmark of standard approaches to action research. More sophisticated and effective approaches may be found, however, in a wide range of sources. Holly, Arhar, and Kasten (2008) show how action research can be used for curriculum purposes and incorporate case studies in classroom contexts. Mills (2013) positions action research as a fundamental component of teaching, alongside curriculum development, assessment, and classroom management, and Stringer (2004) applies action research more broadly to classroom teaching, student research, and work with families and communities. A nonexhaustive list of other reputable education sources includes Noffke and Stevenson (1995); McNiff, Lomax, and Whitehead (2003); Hendricks (2011); McNiff and Whitehead (2006); and Sagor (2004).

There is a considerable increase in resources for the health sciences, with offerings that now cover a number of professional fields and community contexts. Minkler and Wallerstein (2008), Winter and Munn-Giddings (2001), and Stringer and Genat (2004) present detailed procedures and case studies of action research in community and social care contexts. Hart and Bond (1995), Morton-Cooper (2000), and Koch and Kralich (2006) provide practical guidance for the use of action research in health care practice, and Benner (1994) provides a phenomenological perspective on research health issues consonant with action research. The increased interest in using action research in nursing is evident in the literature, which includes offerings from Bellman (2003); Bellman, Bywood, and Dale (2003); Williamson, Bellman, and Webster (2012); and Koshy, Koshy, and Waterman (2011), complementing an earlier contribution by Morton-Cooper (2000).

In other fields, Stringer and Dwyer (2005); French, Reynolds, and Swan (2001); Fortune, McCallion, and Briar-Lawson (2010); and Kagan, Burton, and Siddiquee (2008) present action research processes particularly relevant to social workers, therapists, psychologists, and other human service professionals. An increasing range of literature also focuses more generally on the conduct of action research in organizational settings, including offerings from Coghlan and Brannick (2009), McMurray and Pace (2006), and Whitehead and McNiff (2006).

These citations, however, provide only a sample of the literature on action research. It continues to proliferate and is complemented by an increasingly large array of websites and social media resources.

IN THE COMPANY OF FRIENDS

In this chapter, I have spoken of the dimension of power in research. For some, the move to empower people is seen as a set of divisive, confrontational interactions and activities that enable one person or group to wrest control from another. The communitarian ethic embedded in action research, however, suggests a more consensual approach to investigation requiring participants to enact the working principles discussed in Chapter 2. The position of the researcher changes from one of controller, advocate, or activist to one of facilitator. The researcher's role is not to push particular agendas but to neutralize power differentials in the setting so that the interests of the powerful do not take precedence over those of other participants. Interactions and activities must, however, allay the fears of people in positions of power, generating trust that enables them to feel sufficiently at ease to release some of their control over events. Their acquiescence is an essential feature of action research. They should feel that their institutional or organizational responsibilities, or their place and status in the context, are not threatened by the research activities.

Procedures must also generate trust within less powerful groups, so that groups are willing to participate in arenas in which previously they have been mistreated or demeaned. The reward for all groups is that they acquire ends or goals that otherwise would not have been possible for either, working by themselves.

The power-broker role of the researcher is exercised with the intent of facilitating change in the power dynamics of the situation. The result is not so much a transfer of power from one group to another—although that often occurs—as a change in the *nature* of power relations. Power is still exercised but in a different way. A teacher in a classroom does not relinquish the responsibility of facilitating students' education. The teacher can, however, choose to provide significant decision-making opportunities to students regarding the organization of the class, the curriculum, the timetable, and so on. Social workers and health professionals may similarly engage client groups in the process of formulating or restructuring the ways in which programs and services are organized and administered. This is not news for the business world, which has long recognized the need to take account of the experiences and perspectives of customers and clients.

Improved service delivery and problem resolution are not the only goals of these types of activities. Action research seeks to formulate ways of living and working together that enhance the life experiences of the participants. It provides ways of working that counter the impact of the current overemphasis on the technical and the bureaucratic and enables the formulation of procedures that take into account essentially human features—that speak to issues of emotion, value, and identity. To engage the more creative and caring features of human interaction increases the likelihood of greater "ownership" and more sustainable outcomes that have an enduring effect on people's work and community lives.

Ultimately, however, the routines of action research suggest ways of working that enable a harmonious and productive sense of social life. The end product is, if anything, peace of mind or the chance to participate in the pursuit of happiness. It is a movement away from competitive, power-driven, conflict-ridden organizational processes toward more cooperative, consensual ways of living.

A colleague once suggested that education could be defined as "the search for truth in the company of friends." Although "truth" may elude us, action research might, in a similar vein, be defined as "the search for understanding in the company of friends."

REFLECTION AND ACTION

Social theories seek to provide frameworks of concepts that assist us to develop a coherent understanding of the way people organize and live out their social lives. Over time, however, the complexity and diversity of social theory has threatened to undo this seemingly simple project. Complex theories, based in sometimes highly technical philosophical language, overlaid by multifaceted interpretive schema, seem not to provide a clear basis for understanding social life. While extended reading can assist in this process, the best way to build an understanding of theories of social life is to engage in dialogue on issues as they arise and in educational or professional settings to continue to extend the clarity that comes with a good set of theories. The following activities may assist in this process:

1. Reflect on the issues presented in this chapter.

2. Identify concepts or issues that you find most interesting or informative.

3. State how or why you find them interesting or informative. How are they meaningful for you?

4. Are there sections of the chapter that are uninformative or unclear or that do not seem relevant to your understanding of action research?

5. Are there other theoretical positions that might usefully have been included that would extend people's understanding of action research?

6. Summarize the main points made in this chapter. State the strengths and weaknesses of the chapter, from your perspective.

NOTE

1. The notion of a "script" is drawn from those used for plays or films. Not only does a script carefully define what takes place, but it also delineates what will be said and how things will be done.

Box 2.2   The Theory Behind the Practice

Purpose

To understand the way theory relates to the practice of action research

Content

Theory in action research has a different position and purpose than theory in quantitative studies.

Theory and Practice

The outcomes of action research are increased clarity and understanding that provide the basis for resolving the problem on which the study focused.

The Legitimacy of Action Research

The legitimacy of action research comes not from the criteria associated with quantitative research but from its ability to be successfully applied to problems and issues in people's everyday lives.

Power and Control

Postmodern perspectives show how attempts to control people's lives are confounded by the creative, complex, and dynamic construction of social life and behavior. This points to the need for more flexible, democratic, and creative ways of conceiving and organizing human activity.

The Next Generation

Action research suggests the need to liberate and empower people through collaborative and caring processes of investigation and action.

Representing People's Experience

Action research seeks to produce empathetic, evocative accounts that embody the significant experiences embedded in people's everyday lives and lead to greater understanding of the social realities within which people enact their social lives.

(Continued)

(Continued)

Scripts for Professional and Social Practices

The outcomes of action research provide "scripts" to guide new ways for enacting events and activities.

What We Learn From the Literature

A large body of literature provides diverse perspectives on the nature of action research, processes for enacting processes of inquiry, and its application to professional, organizational, and community settings.

In the Company of Friends

The end product of action research is a harmonious and productive sense of social life. It seeks to move people to cooperative, consensual ways of living that provide peace of mind and contribute to the pursuit of happiness.

3

SETTING THE STAGE

Planning a Research Process

DESIGNING EFFECTIVE RESEARCH

One of the major purposes of planning activities is to establish a positive climate that engages the energy and enthusiasm of all stakeholders. Programs, projects, and services that fail to capture the interest or commitment of the people they serve are often ineffective, inefficient, or both. Practitioners often assume that they can implement a program once they have gained official permission, only to discover that client groups refuse to participate. I have spoken with practitioners in many fields who have been frustrated by their inability to engage people in activities that appear, from their own perspective, to be highly desirable. Their comments and questions are indicative of their dissatisfaction:

- How can we get parents to participate in classroom activities? We can't even get them to come to the school.
- These young people must help us if we're to develop this facility for them.
- The mothers should bring their babies to the clinic more regularly, but they won't.
- We just can't seem to stop these kids from drinking or taking drugs or engaging in sex.

The language these practitioners use provides clues to the social dynamics involved. When we try to get people to do something, insist that they must or should do something, or try to stop them from engaging in some activity, we are working from an authoritative position likely to generate resistance. Such situations often are characterized by processes in which people in positions of authority already have defined the problem and formulated a solution. They fail to grasp that others may interpret the situation and significance of the problem in ways different from their own or may have different agendas in their lives, with other matters having much higher priority. My experience suggests that programs and projects begun on the basis of the decisions and definitions of authority figures have a high probability of failure.

I have seen many housing projects that failed miserably because of inadequate consultation with community members. In one community I visited regularly, the building coordinator was consistently frustrated in his attempts to hire local labor and failed to understand that the housing project had been imposed in that locality with little attempt to include members of the community in the planning phase. The building authority had met with two community leaders and had made determinations on that basis. Other sections of the community were, quite understandably, somewhat affronted by particular aspects of the plan and failed to invest their energies. Problems multiplied in the community from that time on.

This type of process, however, is common in many arenas. In classrooms I have personally discovered the joy and seen others delighted by the increase in effectiveness of their teaching when they engage their students in processes of planning their own learning. In business and industry it is now broadly accepted that operations and outcomes will be far more effective when workers and clients, at all levels, are included in the processes of investigation and planning. I now recognize the limitations of my own perspective and the power of processes that enable me to take advantage of the resources of the people with whom I work.

In Chapter 1, I introduced the three fundamental phases of a basic action research routine. In the first phase—*look*—participants define and describe the problem to be investigated and the general context within which it is set. In the second phase—*think*—they analyze and interpret the situation to extend their understanding of the nature and context of the problem. In the third phase of the process—*act*—they formulate solutions to the problem. This simple routine, however, masks a complex array of influences and activities. Multiple viewpoints and agendas constantly come into play, resulting in a continuous need to modify and adapt emerging plans. The research task becomes a social process in which people extend and reconstruct information emerging from their inquiry (data and analysis) through continuing cycles of exchange, negotiation, realignment, and repair.

SEEKING CONSENSUS: DESIGNING MEANINGFUL RESEARCH

The art and craft of action research include the careful management of research activities so that stakeholders can jointly construct definitions meaningful to them and provide the basis for formulating effective solutions to the research problem. Egon Guba and Yvonna Lincoln (1989) suggest that "the major task of the constructivist investigator is to tease out the constructions that various actors in a setting hold and, so far as possible, to bring them into conjunction—a joining with one another—and with whatever other information can be brought to bear on the issues involved" (p. 142). Constructions are created realities that exist as integrated, systematic, sense-making representations and are the stuff of which people's social lives are built. The aim of inquiry is *not* to establish the truth or to describe what really is happening but to reveal the different truths and realities—construction—held by different individuals and groups. Even people who have the same facts or information will interpret them differently according to their experiences, worldviews, and cultural backgrounds.

The task of the action researcher, therefore, is to develop a context in which individuals and groups with divergent perceptions and interpretations can formulate a construction of their situation that makes sense to them all—a joint construction. Guba and Lincoln (1989) designate this a hermeneutic dialectic process, because new meanings emerge as divergent views are compared and contrasted. The major purpose of the process is to achieve a higher-level synthesis, to reach a consensus where possible, to otherwise expose and clarify the different perspectives and to use these consensual or divergent views to build an agenda for negotiating action. The hermeneutic dialectic process is fundamental to action research, requiring people to work together with purpose and integrity to ensure the effective resolution of their issues and problems.

Because this activity brings people's work lives, and sometimes private lives, into the public arena, it requires a great deal of tact and sensitivity. Construction, consensus, and negotiation need to take place in conditions that recognize the impact of these activities on participants' pride and dignity and enhance their feelings of unity, control, and responsibility. The routines described in the following section, therefore, reflect a commitment to the working principles discussed in Chapter 1—relationships, communication, participation, and inclusion. At every stage of their work, research facilitators should ensure that procedures are in harmony with these guidelines, constantly checking that their actions promote and support people's ability to be active agents in the processes of inquiry. The underlying principle here is that human purposes are at least as important as the technical considerations of research.

ENTERING THE FIELD: BUILDING A PICTURE

The processes described in the following paragraphs are designed to furnish a context to stimulate stakeholders' interest and inspire them to invest their time and energy. Careful planning enables research participants, including the facilitator, to discover the makeup of the setting and establish a presence in that context.

Establishing Contact

In the early stages of a research project, facilitators should establish contact with all stakeholder groups as quickly as possible. Each group needs to be informed of events and needs to feel that all members can contribute to the research processes. A stranger who is heard speaking to some groups about issues of concern to other groups may arouse suspicion, antagonism, and fear. With that in mind, research facilitators should place a high priority on identifying stakeholders and informing them of the purpose of their activities.

Initial contact should be informative and neutral. A statement such as the following is appropriate:

> I'm Ernie Stringer. I've been employed by the Watertown Council to work with unemployed single parents. Some people seem to think there is a problem. I'm not sure if anything needs to be done, but I thought that I might talk with people to find out what they think.

This type of introduction provides a general context for a community-wide conversation. After contact has been established, a process of communication should be formulated; for example, "Thanks for talking with me. You've been most informative. I'd really like to talk with you again. Would that be possible?"

Facilitators should establish convenient times and places to meet with people and should, after initial visits, contact people regularly. This way people are more likely to feel that they are included in the process, that their input is significant, and that the project is theirs in some fundamental sense. This condition of *ownership* is an important element of action research.

When research facilitators talk with people, they should also ask about others who should be included in discussions. This will extend the facilitator's knowledge about the stakeholder groups and their membership. Networking, in this context, is not merely a political tool to be used to gain advantage but a social tool that ensures that all stakeholders are included in the process.

Sampling: Identifying Stakeholding Groups

In most research studies, one of the first tasks is to decide which people to include. In quantitative studies, random selection of participants is the most common method for determining who will take part, but qualitative and action research studies require a different process, often called purposeful sampling, that consciously selects people on the basis of a particular set of attributes. In action research, the major attribute is the extent to which a group or individual is affected by or has an effect on the problem or issue of interest.

Any problem or issue is likely to be affected by a wide range of people. A teacher's work, for instance, is likely to be influenced directly by students, colleagues, administrators, support staff, and parents, but teachers can also be affected by others who come into occasional contact with their classrooms—government officials, police, social workers, community leaders, and church leaders. Health professionals may likewise find their patients influenced by nurses, paraprofessionals, doctors, support staff, patients, and administrators. Social workers and agency staff also find their work with clients affected by others who work in the agency or provide support services.

Researchers, therefore, need to ensure that all stakeholders—people whose lives are affected—participate in defining and exploring the problem or service under investigation. Although it is not possible for all people to be thus engaged, it is imperative that all stakeholder groups feel that someone is speaking for their interests and is in a position to inform them of what is going on.

Research facilitators should conduct a social analysis of the setting to ensure that all relevant groups are included in the research process. Such a social analysis should identify the groups that have a stake in the problem under consideration, so that men and women from all age, social class, ethnic, racial, and religious groups, in all agencies, institutions, and organizations, feel they have a voice in the proceedings. It is important to cut across these categories to ensure adequate representation—a middle-class migrant person cannot always speak for lower-class migrant people, an older person for youth, or men for women. Members of groups that do not have voices in the proceedings will likely fail to invest themselves in the research processes and may then undermine any resulting activity.

> In many settings, I see middle-class professional people making decisions about programs and services that serve the needs of people about whom they have little understanding. The failure of schools to provide for the learning needs of minority populations signals the failure of school systems to engage minority people in the processes of educational planning. In one Australian town that I know, issues related to Aboriginal students are usually referred to a local Aboriginal pastor, although he represents only one of the Aboriginal groups there. The pastor speaks from the perspective of a Christian Aboriginal person and sometimes neglects the interests of other groups who are more closely bound to their traditional spiritual heritage.
>
> This is not an unusual situation. I have observed many instances in which certain people from a minority group are chosen to speak for all others because their middle-class social skills make them acceptable to mainstream institutions, despite their alienation from the people they are asked to represent.
>
> Youth programs often are set up so that well-mannered, clean-living, decent young people are inducted into courses intended to provide them with leadership skills that will enable them to provide appropriate direction to their peers and thus prevent drug problems, teenage pregnancy, and so on. Participants rarely are chosen by their peers, and few are closely related to the groups of young people who are actively taking drugs or engaging in sex. The real leadership in these situations is ignored in favor of the types of youth preferred by adult community leaders.

I participated in a training workshop in which agency workers sought ways of working with the members of a community group to stop them from drinking so much alcohol. The question asked was, "What can *we* do to stop *them* from drinking?" The answer, I thought at the time, was, "Precious little!"

Social mapping processes can help researchers identify all groups and subgroups affected by the issue at hand so they can fashion a comprehensive picture of the stakeholders in the setting. Charting the social dimensions of a setting can be useful in enabling people to visualize the diversity of groups in any social setting. All groups may not be involved in the research process, but the charting of stakeholders will help research participants identify those people who are primarily concerned with the issues at hand—sometimes known as the *critical reference groups.* Table 3.1, constructed by researchers who wished to identify the different groups in a Texas school district, is similar to such a chart. Another version of the same table also identified groups by sex, so that each row was split into male and female. For other purposes, it may be necessary to define categories for age groups. The information may be recorded in tabular or descriptive form, although a map of the context that locates groups physically is sometimes illuminating.

Sampling: Identifying Key People

Researchers sometimes feel disconcerted when people fail to engage in projects that the researchers consider significant. They are often surprised when obstacles appear without warning, when people fail to attend meetings, when tasks are not performed, or when antagonism is directed toward them. In many such instances, they have not only transgressed the boundaries of people's symbolic territory but failed to obtain permission to enter that territory.

An important preliminary task for research facilitators is to determine the formal structure of relevant organizations. They need to identify and communicate with people in positions of influence and authority and gain their permission to work there, when this is organizationally appropriate. At the same time, they also need to locate informal patterns of influence to ensure that all significant people—sometimes called *opinion leaders* or *gatekeepers*—are included in the early stages of the research process.

Table 3.1 Stakeholder Groups

	Anglo			African American			Hispanic			Asian		
	Lower SES	*Middle SES*	*Upper SES*	*Lower SES*	*Middle SES*	*Upper SES*	*Lower SES*	*Middle SES*	*Upper SES*	*Lower SES*	*Middle SES*	*Upper SES*
Students												
Families												
Teachers												
Administrators												
Businesses												
Churches												
Service agencies												

NOTE: SES = Socioeconomic status

In one community project I observed, the agency worker took pains to identify all key people. After two months, he became aware that many of the activities he was promoting were failing to make headway, despite positive responses from many of the townspeople. He eventually discovered that one of the farmers in the district who came to town infrequently was a key person in a number of groups in town. He was highly respected and had a significant impact on community affairs. Once the worker contacted this farmer and talked through the issues with him, many of the obstacles simply disappeared.

One technique for establishing or extending the people to be included in the study is to ask participants, a process sometimes called "snowballing." Researchers may ask, "Who else should we talk with about this issue? Who else is affected by it or has an effect on it?" "Who might provide a different perspective on the issue?" This signals the need to ensure that the people included in the study are drawn from groups or individuals having different experiences and perspectives.

Establishing a Role

Traditionally, researchers have carried with them the aura and status of the expert or scientist, expecting and being accorded deference. In action research, however, the role and function of the researcher differ considerably from that model. No longer laden with the onerous task of discovering generalizable truths, the researcher takes on a role carrying with it a unique status that, in a very real sense, must be established in the context of each study.

The research facilitator, therefore, first must establish a stance that is perceived as legitimate and nonthreatening by all major stakeholding groups. Problems will soon emerge if the researcher is perceived as a stranger prying into people's affairs for little apparent reason or as an authority attempting to impose an agenda. Although the researcher usually will be there under the auspices of some authority, that fact alone is insufficient to engage the attention or the cooperation of all groups in the setting. In many situations, associations with authority may be a marked hindrance, especially if people perceive that the researcher is there to judge, control, or interfere in their affairs.

Researchers, therefore, need to negotiate their role not only with those in positions of authority but with all the relevant stakeholder groups in the setting. The development of the role of the research facilitator in these circumstances can be conceptualized as having three elements: agenda, stance, and position.

Agenda

Research facilitators must establish their presence in a setting by informing people of their purpose. Initial introductions should include nondefinitive information that invites questions and states the agenda in the broadest terms. Initial statements should provide the tacit understanding that the researcher is a resource person whose role is to assist stakeholders, rather than to prescribe their actions. Researcher roles and functions, therefore, become overtly articulated in the process of introduction. The people involved can begin to understand what the researcher is concerned with and the part he or she plays.

As inquiry proceeds, agendas will begin to emerge and become more clearly formulated. At this early stage, however, it is necessary only to establish the focus of activity in the most general terms.

Stance

A researcher's presentation of self should be as neutral and nonthreatening as possible. Body language, speech, dress, and behavior should be purposeful, inquiring, and unpretentious. The all-knowing stance of the expert, the authoritative demeanor of the boss, or the swagger of the achiever is likely to be detrimental to participatory investigation. Many people, especially those in subordinate positions, are likely to respond negatively to any such stance. Researchers should aim to present themselves in ways likely to be perceived as skilled, supportive, resourceful, and approachable. A friendly, purposeful stance is appropriate for most situations.

Position

Position can be thought of as three entities to which any group in a social setting may stake a claim: physical space, social status, and symbolic territory. A family clinic, although ostensibly available to the whole community, for instance, may be claimed by an informal group known as young mothers. A community center may be *owned* by a particular ethnic group. Part of a school ground may be recognized as belonging to a particular clique of girls. These examples show how informal groups, despite no formal legitimacy, have powerful impacts on social life. When researchers conduct their social analyses, it is imperative that they get to know the interacting networks of social groups and identities that cut across the boundaries of the formal organization of a community, institution, or agency. The physical and symbolic territory that such groups occupy will have significant impact on the processes of investigation.

Networks of social identities are established more formally in such organizations as schools, hospitals, government agencies, social clubs, businesses, and churches. These institutions carefully delineate activities and allocate the people responsible for each territory. A high school English department, for instance, operates under the leadership of a senior teacher accorded higher status than the other English teachers. The department has responsibility for teaching English and related subjects and is probably located in a particular part of the school building. A hospital trauma clinic engages in medical emergency work, with orderlies, nurses, and doctors having different tasks and statuses—levels of importance—in that context. Churches likewise allocate a variety of functions, statuses, and locations for worship, child and youth services, finances, and so on to different groups or individuals.

Difficulties often arise when newcomers or people aspiring to change the status quo attempt to invade or change territory that is already occupied. The following comments illustrate situations in which people perceive territorial boundaries to have been crossed inappropriately:

- But Mrs. Jones and Miss Smith always have done the flowers.
- I'm a history teacher. How on earth can I teach English literature?
- Don Jones is part of my caseload. You have no right to interfere with him.
- Staff have never had access to the overall budget.
- The research methods class has never included action research before.

As researchers commence preparatory work, they should artfully position themselves so that they do not threaten the social space of the people with whom they will be working. They should take a neutral position in their status, activities, and physical location, expressing interest but showing no signs of designs on any territory.

Research facilitators also cannot afford to be associated too closely with any one of the stakeholding groups in the setting. Members of all groups need to feel that they can talk freely with facilitators, without fear that their

I disagree - You must have boundaries

comments will be divulged to members of other groups whom, for one reason or another, they do not trust. They also need assurance that their perceptions and agendas will be considered consequential. Researchers, therefore, should endeavor to spend significant periods in places associated with each of the major stakeholder groups—the practitioner's workplace, the administrator's office, and the places where client services are provided. They should make themselves available constantly in these diverse settings so that all stakeholder groups feel they have equal access. Visibility is important.

Researchers also should meet with people informally—in coffee shops, lunchrooms, sports arenas, bars, community centers, and even private homes, if invited. As they become known and accepted, they may tentatively request permission to attend events, meetings, activities, and so forth (e.g., "Would it be okay if I came along?"). The more freely researchers are able to participate in the ordinary lives of the people with whom they work, the more likely they are to gain the acceptance crucial to the success of action research. By meeting with people in places where those people feel at home, researchers enable them to speak more freely and, in the process, acknowledge the significance of their cultural settings.

I have seen many mistakes made in all these areas—agenda, stance, and position—by otherwise well-intentioned researchers whose personal presentation of self effectively distanced or alienated them from those with whom they intend to work. I have seen social workers whose fashionable, high-quality clothing was in stark contrast to the cheap and worn clothing of their clients, serving as a constant reminder of the difference in their status. I have observed stylishly coiffed, manicured, and made-up teachers who were unaware of the subtle yet powerful messages their images presented to parents whose incomes and lifestyles were unable to sustain this type of presentation of self on a day-to-day basis. I have encountered researchers and agency workers who always visited the administrator first, disappearing into an office for extended conversations that raised the suspicions of workers and clients. In one instance, I spoke with a school psychologist who drove to her work in the poorest part of the city in an expensive Mercedes-Benz sports coupe. And in the case of the visiting politicians and bureaucrats mentioned in Chapter 1, their suits and ties were in embarrassing contrast to the stained and worn clothing of their audience.

The agenda, stance, and positioning of research facilitators thus has considerable impact on the success, or lack of success, of any action research process. These elements of researchers' presentation carry many implicit messages that affect the extent to which other participants feel at home in the research process and are able to develop feelings of ownership. In summary, facilitators should take care to do the following:

- Present themselves as resource persons
- Be aware of their dress and appearance
- Establish their purpose in nonthreatening terms
- Associate with all groups, formal and informal
- Be visible
- Be accessible
- Meet in places where each stakeholder group feels at home

MAPPING THE CONTEXT: CONSTRUCTING A PRELIMINARY PICTURE

Initially, research facilitators should develop an understanding of the setting's social dynamics. They need to identify stakeholding groups, key people, the nature of the community, the purposes and organizational structure of relevant institutions and agencies, and the quality of relationships between and among individuals and groups.

Part of this process involves learning the history of the situation with which the researchers are concerned. This will be done in more detail at a later stage of the process, but researchers will need to know what has gone on with key issues prior to their arrival. Past events sometimes leave legacies of deep hurts and antagonisms that severely limit prospects for successful projects unless they are handled judiciously.

A community agency in a country town contracted with the community services unit for which I worked for help with a problem that threatened to close down the agency's operations. The agency had been set up to provide developmental services to a number of community groups in the

(Continued)

(Continued)

town and surrounding region. The government had discontinued funding, however, because it was alleged that the agency was no longer providing the services for which the funds had been provided. This was potentially a serious blow to a small community with limited resources.

We asked the agency executive committee and staff to provide their perspectives on the nature of the problem that had led to the current state of affairs. They provided a general picture of events (which was clarified further as different people presented their own parts of the story) that included groups and individuals involved and the parts they had played. Participants in this process included the agency staff—development officer, bookkeeper, secretary, and field officer—and members of the executive committee—chair, secretary, and committee members. They also identified key people in the funding body—regional manager and field officers—as well as other individuals and groups who supported or were associated with the agency—members of a church group, the town clerk, and workers in a community agency in a nearby town.

We were given permission to contact each of these groups or individuals and proceeded to meet with them. I spoke first with the field officer of the funding body, and then the regional manager, taking care to maintain a friendly, nonthreatening, yet businesslike relationship and to have each of them describe the situation from his or her perspective. From their points of view, the agency had ceased to function effectively, and staff members had become increasingly hostile each time they were approached to account for funds they had expended. I soon established that relations between the staff of the agency and the funding body were extremely antagonistic, making any communication problematic.

Reestablishing a working relationship between agency staff and officers of the funding body was difficult because agency staff members' attitudes seemed to change constantly. Although we discussed the need to establish a working relationship with the funding body and were able to arrange meetings with relevant people, agency workers would then quickly take a negative stance, criticizing the funding agency and decrying the activities of its workers. We eventually discovered that agency workers were meeting regularly with the agency's former bookkeeper, who fired them up each time they met about the deficiencies and character of the funding-body officers.

We met with the former bookkeeper and talked through the issues with him, learning more about the history of the situation in the process and asking him to suggest what could be done. By incorporating his suggestions in our preliminary plan and asking his assistance in carrying them out, we were able to defuse an uncomfortable situation that was hindering the project's progress.

One community worker used questions in the following list to guide the building of his own preliminary picture of a particular situation (McCauley, 1985). It was a picture he kept for his own information only, and it differed from the pictures built by the community groups he worked with, but it served to orient him to the setting and to enable him to keep the "big picture" in mind. He was careful not to impose his picture on others or use it as a tool to define the reality of their situation.

- Relationships
  - Who is related?
  - How are they related?

- History
  - When was the community started?
  - Who were the founders?
  - Why was it started?
  - What has been the main economic base?
  - Are the original families still there?
  - What about the history of minority groups?

- People
  - Important people
  - Elected people
  - Church people
  - Government departments
  - Local government
  - Community leaders
  - Community workers
  - Who is involved?

- Groups
  - Geographic groups
  - Social groups
  - Family groups
  - Community groups
  - Racial groups
  - Ethnic groups
  - Who is involved in each?
  - Who are the key people?
  - Which are the influential groups?

- Problems
  - What problems do you see?
  - What problems do others see?
  - What problems do the power brokers see?
  - What problems do local, state, and federal government officers see?
  - What problems do small groups see?

- Resources
  - What social resources are available?
  - What economic resources are available?
  - Who owns them?
  - Are they owned by individuals, groups, or government?
  - What is missing?
  - Why is it missing?

Research facilitators need to formulate their own questions according to the nature and extent of the inquiry in which they will engage. A more limited context, such as a classroom or agency office, may require a less extensive list of questions. The purpose of such questions is to ensure that researchers gain an adequate understanding of the setting in which they will work.

ETHICS IN ACTION RESEARCH

Ethical procedures are an important part of all research, and formal research institutions such as universities, agencies, and organizations all have rules and regulations covering the conduct of research. This arises because researchers

in the past have engaged in forms of inquiry that have put subjects or participants at risk. This does not necessarily arise because unscrupulous researchers
take advantage of people over whom they have control, though this sometimes
happens, but because they unwittingly or carelessly reveal information that put
their subjects in situations that are harmful.

The conduct of the Milgram experiments (1963) is perhaps the most
famous example. There, subjects believing they were administering severe
electric shocks to other participants were so traumatized that some required
extensive therapy. In anthropological studies, researchers have revealed
secret or sacred information that created havoc in the communities concerned. There is a long list of instances where researchers have consciously
or unwittingly engaged in ethically untenable practices or procedures. As
researchers we have a "duty of care" in relation to all people we engage in
processes of investigation.

In planning a study, therefore, researchers usually need to take specific
steps to ensure that participants come to no harm as a result of their participation in the research project. One of the principal tools to ensure this is to
clearly inform them of the purpose, aims, use of results, and likely consequences of the study, a process known as *informed consent*. This requires those
responsible for the study to provide written information about the aims, purposes, and processes of the study and to gain written acknowledgment of
participants' willingness to participate. Such written consent documents usually include statements indicating that

- People have the right to refuse to participate.
- They may withdraw from the study at any time.
- Data related to their participation will be returned to them.
- Any information (data) will be stored safely so that it cannot be viewed
  by others.
- None of the information that identifies them will be made public or
  revealed to others without explicit and written consent.

Because of the participatory nature of action research, ethical considerations work in a special way. The same provisions for duty of care apply, and
all stakeholders have the same rights to safety and informed consent that apply
in other forms of research. In action research, however, there is a particular
imperative to ensure that all participants know what is going on, that the processes are inherently transparent to all. Because participants in an action

research process have much more control than is usually accorded participants in a study, they are in effect engaging in a mutual agreement about the conduct of a study. Nevertheless, the need for informed written consent is still required for situations where people are at risk because of the sensitive nature of issues involved in the study.

In some cases, where practitioners engage their students, clients, or patients in routines of inquiry as part of their everyday engagement, formal consent may not be required. This may be the case in situations where teachers involve students in small projects to find better ways of attaining learning objectives, where social workers engage clients in personal explorations of issues in their lives, or where health professionals assist patients in a systematic exploration of a particular health issue. In these cases, the systematic processes of inquiry are part of the legal framework of duty of professional care, and no formal procedures are required to legitimize them.

Agreement to Participate

Goldburn Community Youth Group

Study of Youth Recreational Needs

Research Facilitator: Lyn Evans—Goldburn Youth Services Coordinator
Phone: 259–0892

The Goldburn Community Youth Group wishes to study the recreational needs of young people in the Goldburn area. The information used in this project will be collected by interviewing individual group members. Participants will be asked to engage in two interviews of approximately 1-hour duration each. The researcher will also have follow-up sessions with each person to check the accuracy of the information. Names will be kept confidential. Tape recordings and field notes always will be stored in a secure place by the researcher and not used for purposes other than the current study. Information that identifies individuals will only be used with their written permission.

If you wish to withdraw from the study at any time you are free to do so, and if you wish, all information you have given will be shredded or returned.

You may contact the researcher at any time via the above phone number.

I, _____, have read the information above, and any questions I have asked have been answered to my satisfaction. I agree to participate in this activity on the understanding that I may withdraw at any time without prejudice. I agree that the research data generated may be published provided my name is not used and that I am not otherwise identified.

Signed: _____ (Participant)   Date: _____
Signed: _____ (Facilitator)   Date: _____

Formal Ethics Approval: Internal Review Boards (IRBs) and Agency Procedures

In recent years people working in universities or government agencies have experienced some problems in acquiring formal approval to engage in action research. The enforcement of procedures and regulations designed to protect people participating in biomedical research, where drug trials and experimental medical procedures have the possibility of harming participants, has created real problems. Unthinking enforcement of regulations has resulted in unneeded and overburdensome ethical requirements. Social scientists have appropriately criticized biomedical IRBs for failing to adequately understand research methods such as ethnography, oral histories, and anecdotal evidence that often do not constitute "human subject research" as defined in the regulations for clinical research. The U.S. National Science Foundation (2013) has indicated that the regulations have some flexibility and rely on the common sense of the IRB to focus on limiting harm, maximizing informed consent, and limiting bureaucratic interference in valid research.

CHECKING FOR RIGOR

Much research is confounded by the lack of interest of the participants, but the collaborative processes of action research are designed to promote high levels of enthusiasm and active participation. Enthusiasm and interest, however, should not be mistaken for sound research processes. In their enthusiasm, researchers may fail to engage the systematic and rigorous processes that are the hallmark of good research. The basis for rigor in experimental research is founded in commonly established routines for establishing the reliability and validity of the research, but action research, being essentially qualitative, uses a different set of criteria. Rigor in action research is based on checks to ensure that the outcomes of research are trustworthy—that they do not merely reflect the particular perspectives, biases, or worldview of the researcher and are not based solely on superficial or simplistic analyses of the issues investigated.

Checks for trustworthiness, therefore, are designed to ensure that researchers have rigorously established the veracity, truthfulness, or validity of the information and analyses that have emerged from the research process. Lincoln and Guba (1985) suggest that trustworthiness can be established through procedures that assess the following attributes of a study:

- Credibility—the plausibility and integrity of the study
- Transferability—the possibility of applying the outcomes of the study to other contexts
- Dependability—research procedures that are clearly defined and open to scrutiny
- Confirmability—evidence that the procedures described actually took place

Credibility

In action research the credibility of research processes is a fundamental issue. Unless participants are able to trust the integrity of the processes, they are unlikely to make the personal commitments essential to a well-founded inquiry. The following issues assist them in gaining this feeling of trust:

- *Prolonged engagement.* A brief interview or conversation does not provide sufficient information to enable people to develop the deep-seated understandings necessary to outcomes of the research process. Interviews and focus groups should provide all participants with extended opportunities to explore and express their experience of the acts, activities, events, and issues related to the problem investigated.
- *Persistent observation.* Merely being present in a situation does not count as observation. The credibility of research is enhanced when participants consciously observe events, activities, and the context over

a period of time. Consciously observing and taking note of events places a premium on noting what is actually happening, rather than describing it from memory or from an interpretation of what people "think" happened.

- *Triangulation.* The credibility of a study is enhanced when multiple sources of information are incorporated. As Stake (2005) suggests, the inclusion of perspectives from diverse sources enables the inquirer to clarify meaning by identifying ways the phenomena are being perceived. These perspectives may be complemented and challenged by information derived from observations, reports, and a variety of other sources.

- *Member checking.* Participants are given opportunities to review the raw data, analyses, and reports derived from research procedures. This enables them to verify that the research adequately represents their perspectives and experiences. It also provides opportunities for them to clarify and extend information related to their experience.

- *Participant debriefing.* Member checking may also provide people with opportunities to deal with emotions and feelings that might cloud their vision, inhibit their memories, or color their interpretations of events. Debriefing focuses on the feelings and responses of the participant rather than the information participants have provided.

- *Diverse case analysis.* This criterion relates to the principle of inclusion. Researchers enhance the credibility of the study by ensuring that the perspectives of all stakeholding groups are incorporated into the study.

- *Referential adequacy.* Concepts and ideas within the study should clearly be drawn from and reflect the experiences and perspectives of participating stakeholders, rather than be interpreted according to schema emerging from a theoretical or professional body of knowledge. Reports and other communications therefore should be grounded in the terminology and language of the research participants to ensure that it reflects their perspective and can be clearly understood by them.

Transferability

Unlike traditional quantitative or experimental studies that enable the outcomes of research to be generalized to contexts and groups other than those involved in the research, action research outcomes apply only to the particular people and places that were part of the study. That does not mean, however, that nothing in the study is applicable to others. It indicates, however, the need for procedures that carefully explore the possibility that the outcomes of an action research study may be relevant elsewhere. The basis for that lies in the detailed description of the context(s), activities, and events reported as part of the outcomes of the study. It is possible for people not part of the study to make judgments about whether or not the situation is sufficiently similar to their own for the outcomes to be applied. These judgments indicate the degree of trust people have that the research outcomes may be transferred to their own situation.

Dependability

Dependability focuses on the extent to which people can trust that all measures required of a systematic research process have been followed. An inquiry audit provides a detailed description of the procedures that have been followed and provides the basis for judging the extent to which they are dependable.

Confirmability

Researchers must be able to confirm that the procedures described actually took place. An audit trail enables an observer to view the data collected, instruments, field notes, tapes, journals, or other artifacts related to the study. These confirm the veracity of the study, providing another means for ensuring that the research is trustworthy.

SOCIABLE RESEARCH PROCESSES

When we engage in research, we are not merely employing impersonal, technical routines that do not touch people's lives. The nature of any process of inquiry means that we enter cultural settings that are interactional, emotional, historical, and social. People interact at different times and places for different purposes, bringing histories of experience and understanding that orient them to the setting in particular ways. They suffer stress, enjoy a joke, argue, play, work, and socialize in myriad ways that contribute to the life of the community.

The processes of action research, therefore, are enriched by researchers who contribute to the lives of the groups with whom they work. Researchers increase their effectiveness when they immerse themselves in the richness of group life, talking with people about general events and activities, sharing a birthday cake, participating in informal or leisure activities, telling jokes, and so on. Scientific objectivity is not the purpose here. Although it is important to maintain a neutral stance in relation to interpersonal issues, participation entails the need to develop empathic understanding that comes about only through close involvement with people. In these circumstances, action research easily becomes an enjoyable human experience.

I've heard such comments as "All he does is sit around drinking coffee or tea with people"—remarks that, especially in the early stages of a project, contain a grain of truth. I am constantly aware of the symbolic significance of sharing food and drink, so I always take people up on the offer of a cup of tea or coffee, a beer at a bar after work, dinner, a party, or a sporting event. I've been invited to church and into people's homes; I've sat in gardens drinking wine, watched basketball games, and attended school functions.

It's not only that I enjoy socializing—the activity is all part of my work, but it allows me to enter people's lives in a "real" way. These social activities break down barriers to communication, help me develop good working relations with others, and give me greater exposure to the setting in a relatively short time. It's surprising how much work can be done in these contexts. People in the course of social talk will often discuss issues related to the project. They become less guarded in such nonthreatening contexts and reveal much that in more formal contexts they might have thought unimportant.

When this happens, I always make a formal visit to the people concerned soon afterward to ensure that they are comfortable with the conversation. I will say, "I had a great time with your friends yesterday. I enjoyed their company." Then, in the course of conversation, I also mention, "I was interested in what you had to say about. . . . I didn't know that." This enables the other person to check that the confidentiality and safety of our conversations still hold in these contexts. The information is confirmed and often extended, and working relationships are strengthened in the process.

COLLABORATIVE DESIGN: A FOUNDATION
FOR EFFECTIVE RESEARCH

The principles outlined in this chapter apply particularly in the planning stages of action research. More interactive processes that engage the research facilitator and other participants in carefully articulated processes of inquiry replace the detached, impersonal procedures associated with traditional research. The sociable nature of the research processes should not, however, mask the necessity for ensuring that rigorous and ethical procedures provide the basis for illuminating and effective investigations. As we do so, however, we need to take account of the ways in which the research study affects people's lives and the ways they respond to it.

When we enact action research processes, we are likely to engage approaches to work and community life at odds with the general conventions of the institutions and agencies that form the settings for much of our activity. The open dialogue that constitutes a core ingredient of our research processes runs the risk of disturbing a carefully controlled and regulated social environment. We may unconsciously disturb micropolitical alignments and threaten people who have established positions of power or influence. In these circumstances, therefore, it is essential to ensure that our initial entry to the setting is as "soft" as possible. We need to understand the complex interactions among people, events, and activities and to comprehend the ways in which they interpret their situations so that any activity we initiate sits easily in the minds of the people with whom we work.

Our ultimate goal is to provide a context that enables diverse stakeholders to work collaboratively toward solutions to the significant problems that confront them. The preliminary processes described in this chapter set the stage for this activity. They enable research facilitators to gain an overall picture of the situation, to develop positive relationships with people, and to help them think more deeply about their issues and concerns. The relationships and forms of communication that evolve set the stage for the inclusive and participatory processes that are the basis for common unity and productive action.

REFLECTION AND ACTION

Find a "cultural scene" to study—a place you might know a little but in which you are a "stranger." It might be a store, school, classroom, club or association, church, or any other public place. (If you have access to Spradley and McCurdy's *The Cultural Experience* [1972] you will get clues about the variety of places people can study.) Your task is to visit that "scene" and make contact with people there. Later you will engage in a ministudy of that place.

1. Visit the place. Stay there an extended period (around a half hour or more).

2. Look at what is happening. Introduce yourself to some of the "stakeholders" there.

3. Talk with some of them to find out what happens there.

4. Who are the "key people" in this place?

5. Who are the other stakeholders?

6. Why are they there? What do they do?

7. Reflect on this experience.

8. How did it feel to be in a place where you were a "stranger"?

9. How did people respond?

10. How much did you learn? Did you gain a deep or superficial understanding of the place?

11. What would you need to do to gain an in-depth understanding of this place?

12. Discuss this experience with colleagues or classmates.

Box 3.1   Setting the Stage: Planning a Research Process

Purpose

Research facilitators familiarize themselves with the context and design research plans in conjunction with stakeholders.

Process

Engage in Preliminary Activity

Establish contact with people in the setting
Identify stakeholding groups—those affected by the issue to be investigated

(Continued)

(Continued)

Identify key people—those in leadership positions or opinion leaders
Negotiate the researcher's role
Establish the position and role of the researcher: within which groups, in which places, doing what activities, with whom
Negotiate research agendas: which issues will be the focus of inquiry

Construct a Preliminary Picture of the Context

Stakeholders—groups and key people
Relationships
History of the situation
Problems
Resources

Ethics

Procedures to ensure well-being of participants
Privacy
Confidentiality
Informed consent

Rigor

Check the trustworthiness of procedures
Credibility
Transferability
Dependability
Confirmability

4

LOOK

Gathering Data

FOCUSING: FRAMING THE RESEARCH QUESTION

The basis of any investigation is a specific, usually problematic issue. Why are students in my class disengaged? How can we get young mothers in this area to have their babies vaccinated? Why is our customer base being eroded? What can we do about domestic violence? And so on. The underlying problem in action research is to establish the nature of the issue or problem and how it might be stated. Statement of the problem is a key issue that requires significant attention from the outset, since often problems are designated by people in positions of authority and defined in terms that either valorize their own perspective or demonize those central to the problem. As Denzin suggests (1989), policy makers, program managers, and others develop interventions and programs on the basis of their own experience rather than the experience of the people whom their policies are meant to benefit.

This is clearly the case in situations where marginalized groups are subject to research by authorities. Research proposals in Aboriginal contexts often start with a litany of grief that points to high levels of incarceration, high levels of domestic violence, low levels of employment, low levels of educational achievement, poor health . . . and so on. From the very start of a research project Aboriginal people are presented in negative terms, the focus being on the worst segment of their community lives. Such projects fail to recognize the significant majority who live well-ordered lives, within the bounds of their own social and cultural circumstances, and the deep well of experience available in almost any location.

Problems, in any case, are difficult to state clearly since any issue is usually enmeshed in a web of relationships, interactions, actions, events, and activities that make up the dynamic operation of any social setting. Statement of the problem is sometimes simple, but framing that problem as a question to be investigated often requires careful thought and some initial analysis. Research facilitators and participants need to think carefully through issues to identify key concerns related to the problem to be investigated. This type of reflection often reveals subsidiary questions that provide the basis for a more systematic and comprehensive investigation. Some of the questions we need to ask when identifying a problem are the following:

- What is the actual problem here?
- For whom is it problematic?
- How do stakeholders perceive the problem?
- Are problems and issues within or behind the initial problem?

An effective action research process therefore requires participants to work through the first cycle of investigation by exploring and examining the ways stakeholding groups describe or interpret the problem as initially framed. Only then can a research project frame questions that provide sufficient direction to an investigation that enables it to accomplish an effective outcome.

I was once asked to assist a school system to develop ways of engaging parents and communities in development of school resources.

Question: How can parents assist in the development of school resources?

Initial attempts by principals to engage parents proved ineffectual, and discussions with a number of parents indicated that they were suspicious that this was another strategy to have them "donate" more money to the school or to increase school fees. Preliminary workshops with parents in a sample of schools clarified this issue and asked parents to identify things they would be willing to do to develop school resources. The framework for action research workshops in schools in the system started with clarifying comments indicating why the school needed extra resources and that it was not intended to ask parents for donations of money. Subsidiary questions extended the original question to focus on actions.

Subsidiary questions:

What resources are needed?

How can parents assist in acquiring these resources?

What can they do?

How can they do it?

Framing the issue as a question rather than a request enabled parents to discuss many creative possibilities, and workshops in pilot schools were notable for their success in mobilizing parent energies in a wide range of activities and projects that, in the end, significantly enhanced their school's resources.

GATHERING DATA: ACQUIRING INFORMATION

The primary objective of the Look phase of the process is to gather information that enables researchers to extend their understanding of the experience and perspective of stakeholders—those mainly affected by or having an influence on the issue investigated. The first cycle of an action research process is therefore qualitative, requiring researchers to gather information about participants' experiences and perspectives and to define the problem or issue in terms that "make sense" in their own terms. We seek to understand participant experiences in order to work toward a viable solution in which people will invest their time and energies. Participants, especially primary stakeholders, are therefore consciously engaged in the process of describing the nature of the problem and gathering information.

This differs from traditional hypothesis-testing research in two significant ways. First, participants are knowingly engaged in seeking to develop understandings and solutions, objectivity not being the primary aim of the process, as solutions need to make sense to the subjective experience of the participants.[1] Second, researchers do not hypothesize an answer to the research question but seek to understand the nature of related events—how and why things happen the way they do. Gathering data, therefore, has quite a different purpose.

There is a real sense, however, that we seek a sense of objectivity as we gather data, as we need to ensure that information is gained directly from the participants and is not tainted by the perspectives, biases, or experiences of research facilitators. When we frame research questions for interviews or questionnaires, for instance, we need to be very careful that we don't inadvertently incorporate our own views or ideas. Leading questions that implicitly suggest an answer to the problem taint the research process with the perspective of the researcher.

In the Think phase of the research, analysis of information emerging from responses to questions provides insights from which "interventions"— actions to remedy the situation—are formulated. Continuing research cycles enable evaluation, reformulation, and redevelopment of actions, leading to increasingly effective solutions to the problem at the heart of the research project.

I've seen many examples of action research processes that have provided effective outcomes for the key stakeholders. Lisa, a special education teacher, worked with her students to understand why they were so disinterested in reading. By increasing her understanding of their experience of reading she was able to formulate effective strategies that greatly improved her students' interest and engagement.

In another school in the same city, a group of Hispanic parents expressed concern about the quality of their children's schooling. With the support of the principal they engaged in an action research project that focused on improving communication between the school and the students' families. Volunteers from a Hispanic neighborhood group interviewed parents and teachers to understand their experiences of parent–teacher conferences. They were able to identify a range of ways that both parents and teachers could improve the conferences and in the process also discovered other ways to improve communication between the school and the students' families.

Initial phases of exploration are designed not to gather concrete evidence or objective data but to reveal the reality that makes up people's day-to-day experience, bringing their assumptions, views, and beliefs out in the open and making them available for discussion. The process of talking about their experience provides people with rich insights that enable them to achieve greater clarity about events and activities in their lives. As they share experiences they gain greater understanding of the realities of the situation and the potentials of constructing solutions to the problem that take these realities into consideration. By working collaboratively, participants develop collective visions of their situation that provide the basis for effective action. At its best, this type of activity is liberating, enabling people to master their world as they see it in a different way—a tangible process of enlightenment.

At a community health workshop focused on problems related to alcohol, participants were asked to describe the types of drinking behavior displayed by groups in their community. At the end of the workshop, one of the health workers exclaimed excitedly, "I used to see alcohol as a blanket covering my community. Now I see it in a different way. I can see the different ways that people use alcohol and the different outcomes of that use. Now I can see areas where things can be done." An explanatory framework that focused on descriptions of alcohol use, rather than alcoholism as a whole, resulted in a new vision that provided novel possibilities for action.

This anecdote contains an important message: Problems do not exist in isolation but are part of a complex network of events, activities, perceptions, beliefs, values, routines, and rules—a cultural system maintained through the life of the group, organization, or community. As people reveal relevant details of their situation, they see more clearly the ways in which the research problem or focus is linked to features of their organizational, professional, and/or community lives. This type of exploration leads people past their taken-for-granted perspectives and promotes more satisfying, sophisticated, and complete descriptions of their situation.

SOURCES OF INFORMATION

Information to be gathered in any investigation will be determined to a large extent by the nature of the issue or problem investigated. The remainder of this chapter identifies the types of data that might be collected and the processes for gathering that information. As participants explore the issue at hand, they may discover the need for other types of information, and data gathering becomes an ongoing process that emerges as the investigation proceeds. This contrasts with procedures of experimental research in which the data to be gathered are precisely defined in the research design.

A social worker I know set out to investigate why young teenagers in her town engaged in so much vandalism. By talking with some of them she discovered that the underlying reason was boredom, and the sources of boredom included schooling that was boring, the lack of sports facilities, and the closure of parks and gardens. Her investigation broadened to include discussions with the local principal and some teachers, local sports people, the local government office responsible for parks and gardens, and the town police. She discovered that sports clubs lacked facilities to accommodate teenagers, that parks and gardens had been closed for economic reasons, and that the schools were locked into a mandated curriculum that was marginally relevant to the needs and interests of the young people in that region. The information she was able to acquire and share with the stakeholders enabled them to take action to increase leisure activity opportunities for teenagers, with a consequent dramatic drop in acts of vandalism.

I have elsewhere (Stringer, 2004) mentioned Lisa, a special education teacher who was concerned about her students' lack of interest in reading. Initially she tried different teaching strategies to try to increase their engagement—but without success. As she talked with her students, however, she discovered a number of issues that affected their reading activities and was able to take appropriate and successful action to remedy the situation by taking these matters into account. She discovered that students responded to different types of reading activity, the physical arrangement of seating, the social arrangements related to learning activities (some liked solitary reading activities; others liked to work in groups), and the types of reading material she used. She had not been able to "guess" these in her first attempts, but the appropriate data emerged through collaborative work with her students.

The primary data in action research are derived from interviews with primary and key stakeholders. As the focus of investigation and the issues to be incorporated in the emerging investigation become clearer, other sources of data may become relevant. Research participants may also become involved in events and activities that are themselves informative, or they may systematically observe a site or context. As they do so, a variety of other sources may provide information that further clarifies or extends understanding of the issue being investigated. These may include information derived from

- Interviews
- Focus groups
- Participant observation
- Questionnaires
- Documents
- Records and reports
- Surveys
- The research literature

Researchers need to be parsimonious in selecting information specifically pertinent to the issue, as a mass of peripherally relevant information may create less rather than greater clarity.

INTERVIEWS: GUIDED REFLECTION

Interviews provide opportunities for participants to describe the situation in their own terms. It is a reflective process that enables the interviewee to explore his or her experience in detail and to reveal the many features of that experience that have an effect on the issue investigated. The interview process not only provides a record of participants' views and perspectives but also symbolically recognizes the legitimacy of their experience. To initiate an interview, research facilitators should

- Identify themselves, their role, and their purposes
- Ask permission to talk with people and to record information
- Check that the time is convenient for an extended discussion
- Negotiate alternative times and places for interviews, if necessary

Interviews should be characterized as informal conversations. For example, the research facilitator might say, "I'd like to talk with you about how things are going for you, Jenny. Could we have a talk sometime? When could we do that?" Allowing participants to designate the time and place maximizes the possibility that they will suggest contexts in which they feel comfortable. One of the key features of successful interviews is the need for participants to feel as if they can say what they are really thinking or to express what they are really feeling.

As interviews progress, research facilitators may be presented with viewpoints that appear limited, biased, or wrong. Interviewers should, however, avoid discussion or debate with interviewees, since this detracts from the ability of participants to express views of their own experiences and perspectives. Challenges to participant views will occur naturally as differing perspectives are presented in more public arenas. The task at this stage, to adapt the words of a well-known anthropologist, is "to grasp the natives' point of view, to realize their vision of their world" (Malinowski, 1922/1961, p. 25). Questioning procedures described shortly therefore are drawn from ethnographic procedures that seek to elicit information from an insider's perspective, technically known as emic knowledge or understanding, in contrast to etic constructs and terminologies derived from people who do not naturally "inhabit" a particular social domain.

Semistructured Questioning Procedures

A major problem with the interview process is that questions are easily tainted by the researcher's perceptions, perspectives, interests, and agendas. Professional practitioners are confronted with practical problems and issues that they usually resolve by applying skills and procedures drawn from their professional stock of knowledge. They are confronted with difficult clients who seem unable or unwilling to follow designated procedures, students who seem unable to perform or behave appropriately, or dysfunctional family or community groups. In these instances research always starts with a general question: "Why are the clients unable to follow their care plans?" "Why can't these students learn this material?" "Why do they engage in these inappropriate or disruptive behaviors?" or "Why are people in this organization or family always arguing?"

Common professional procedures require practitioners to hypothesize an answer to these questions, formulate a potential solution, and then test it out by having clients, students, or groups follow procedures implied by that solution. In action research, the practitioner "brackets"—holds in abeyance—his or her professional stock of knowledge and starts by having the client, student, or group explore the issue *in their own terms*. Practitioner perspectives are included at a later stage, when primary stakeholders have described both the situation and the issue in their own terms.

Questioning procedures are very delicate because participants are likely to react negatively if there is an implied judgment or criticism embedded in the question. In the beginning, research facilitators will ask very general questions that enable them to understand the way participants experience the context—"How are things going for you, Jenny?" "Tell me about this school (or your class)"—and following questions enable participants to extend their exploration of their own experience and their own perspectives on issues that emerge in the course of the interview. Questions, in fact, are merely triggers that enable participants to explore and describe what is happening in their lives or to reflect on events associated with issues of concern. Sensitive questioning processes enable them, in effect, to tell stories of their own experience. These not only allow them to recount the everyday context in which events emerge but sometimes also to explore epiphanic events—those defining moments of experience that occur in problematic interactional situations and reveal underlying tensions and problems in a situation (Denzin, 1989). The procedures described momentarily and summarized in Box 4.1 follow Spradley (1979) and provide a useful framework of relatively neutral and nonleading questions that minimize the extent to which participants' perceptions will be governed by language and concepts inadvertently imposed by researchers.

Grand tour questions enable participants to describe the situation in their own terms (e.g., "Tell me about [your work]") and provide focus without giving direction or suggesting responses. An initial grand tour question may be followed by questions that assist respondents to extend their descriptions.

- *General* grand tour questions enable participants to describe the setting or issue in their own terms (e.g., "I've recently come to [town, this office, the school] and don't know much about it. Could you tell me about this place?").
- *Typical* questions encourage respondents to describe how events usually occur (e.g., "How does your group usually work?" "Describe a typical day in your office").
- *Specific* questions focus on specific events or phenomena (e.g., "Can you tell me about yesterday's meeting?" "Describe what happened the last time." "What happens in the recreation room?").

Researchers can further extend accounts by using activities that enable participants to visualize their situation more clearly:

- A *guided tour* question is a request for an actual tour that allows participants to show researchers (and, where possible, other stakeholders) around their offices, schools, classrooms, clinics, centers, or agencies (e.g., "Could you show me around your center [office, classroom, clinic]?"). Throughout the tour, participants may explain details about the people and activities involved in each part of the setting. Researchers may ask questions as they go (e.g., "Tell me more about this part of the clinic [room, office, class]." "Can you tell me more about the social workers [clients, patients, young people] you've mentioned?").
- A *task* question aids in description (e.g., "Could you draw me a map of the place you've described?"). Maps are often instructive and provide opportunities for extensive questioning and description. Participants can also demonstrate particular features of their work or community lives (e.g., "Can you show or tell me how you put a case study together?").

Further information may be acquired through the skillful use of prompts that enable participants to reveal more details of the phenomena they are discussing.

- *Extension* questions (e.g., "Tell me more about . . ." "Is there anything else you can tell me about . . .?" "What else?")
- *Encouragement* comments or questions (e.g., "Go on." "Yes?" "Uh huh?")
- *Example* questions (e.g., "Can you give me an example of that?")

Researchers may gain more detailed information by pursuing a *minitour* that focuses on issues and events emerging from grand tour questioning. Minitour questions focus on each issue and explore it using the types of questions described earlier (e.g., "You previously mentioned [blank]. . . . Tell me more about that." "Can you describe a typical . . .?"). Combinations of typical, specific, tour, task, extension, encouragement, and example questions provide opportunities for extensive exploration of the setting, events, and activities.

Box 4.1   Grand Tour and Minitour Questions

Grand Tour Questions

> *General:* Allow participants to describe the context in their own terms
>
> *Typical:* Enable participants to describe how events or activities usually occur
>
> *Specific:* Focus on specific events, activities, or other phenomena

Activity Questions

> *Guided tour:* Participants show researchers places and describe what happens there
>
> *Tasks:* Participants are asked to perform tasks that enable them to describe the setting, events, activities, or issues with greater clarity—maps, drawings, demonstrations, and so on

Prompt Questions

> *Extension:* Assist participants to talk further about something they have mentioned
>
> *Encouragement:* Prompt participants to continue talking
>
> *Example:* Encourage participants to describe specific events, activities, and people

---

Source: Adapted from Spradley, 1979.

Research facilitators should take a neutral stance throughout these activities and neither affirm nor dispute, verbally or nonverbally, the information that emerges. At the same time, they should remain keenly attentive, recording responses as accurately as possible. It is essential that they capture participants' own terms and concepts for later use in formulating accounts.

Questions should be carefully formulated to ensure participants are given the maximum opportunity to present events and phenomena in their own terms and to follow agendas of their own choosing. Researchers should be particularly wary of leading questions that derive from their own interpretive schemata and are not directly related to participant agendas. These types of questioning are distinctively different from those formulated for use in surveys that often require researchers to hypothesize variables influencing the issue investigated and frame questions around those.

Field Notes: Applying the Verbatim Principle

Participant researchers should carefully record details of interviews, using field notes or tape recordings for this purpose. Taking field notes is a skill that requires some practice, as it is important to apply the *verbatim principle,* recording precisely what is said, using the respondent's language, terms, and concepts. Researchers should resist the impulse to summarize what is said or record it in terms with which they are familiar or comfortable. This requires researchers to write at speed, so that notes may be rather untidy. If possible, use forms of short-hand in note taking (e.g., *t* for *the, takg* for *taking, w* for *with,* and so on).

As an interview commences, or when rapport has been established, the interviewer should ask, "Do you mind if I take a few notes as you speak? I'd like to remember what you've said." As the interview progresses, you might also ask, "Could you just hold on for a moment? I'm a bit behind."

Following the interview, the interviewer should "member check," reading back the notes and asking whether they are an accurate record of what was said. Alternatively, he or she may choose to type up the notes later and have the respondent read them, preferably with the interviewer present, to check for accuracy.

My own experience suggests that most people enjoy being interviewed using these techniques. They appear to like the fact that someone is listening carefully to what they are saying and consider it of sufficient worth to record it. The "member checking" process is also informative, providing respondents with opportunities to reflect on ideas or events they have presented and to extend or modify their comments. "Yeah, well, I know I said that, but what I really meant was..." "Yes, and now I remember what was going on then. We had been..."

Tape Recorders

The use of a tape recorder has the advantage of allowing the researcher to record accounts that are both detailed and accurate. The use of tape recorders can have a number of disadvantages, however, and researchers should carefully weigh the merits of this technology. Technical difficulties with equipment may damage rapport with respondents, and people sometimes find it difficult to talk freely in the presence of a recording device, especially when sensitive issues are discussed. A researcher may need to wait until a reasonable degree of rapport has been established before introducing the possibility of using a tape recorder. When using a recorder, the researcher should be prepared to stop the tape to allow respondents to speak "off the record" if they show signs of discomfort.

Follow these steps for using a tape recorder:

- Prior to the interview, check that the tape recorder is in working order and batteries are charged. Have sufficient tape or recording space for the length of the interview(s).
- Ask the interviewee's permission to record the interview.
- Transcribe the tape as soon after the interview as possible.
- Provide the interviewee with a copy of the transcription to check for accuracy.
- Store tapes and transcriptions in a safe place to ensure confidentiality.

FOCUS GROUPS

Focus groups provide another means of acquiring information and might be characterized as a group interview. Participants in a focus group should each have opportunities to describe their experience and present their perspective on the issues discussed. As with interviews, carefully devised questions provide the means to focus the group on the issue at hand and enable them to express their experience and perspective in their own terms, without the constraints of interpretive frameworks derived from researcher perspectives, professional or technical language, or theoretical constructs. Focus questions should follow the same rules and formats as those used for interviews, employing neutral language and maximizing opportunities for participants to express themselves in their own terms.

The following steps provide a basic framework for facilitating focus groups: Set ground rules. For example,

- Each person should have opportunities to express his or her opinions and perspectives.
- Participants should be respectful and nonjudgmental of each other.

Explain procedures clearly.

- Designate a leader and recorder for each group (or have the group elect a leader).
- Provide and display focus questions.
- Explain recording and reporting procedures.
- Designate time frames for each activity.

Facilitators should

- Ensure each person has an equal chance to talk.
- Ensure discussions relate to the focus question(s).
- Keep track of time for each activity.
- Assist the group in summarizing the perspectives emerging from their discussions and identify key features of their experience and perspective.

Recorders should

- Keep note of what people say, using their own words.
- Record the outcomes of the summarizing process, preferably on a chart.

Plenary sessions offer feedback and clarification.

- Gather groups for plenary sessions, ensuring adequate time for the process.
- Each group should present the outcomes of its discussion, using the charted summary.
- Where one person presents, provide opportunities for individuals within the group to extend or clarify points presented.
- The facilitator should ask questions that clarify or extend the information presented, extending understanding of the group's perspective.
- Ensure that new information emerging in this process is recorded on charts.

Combined analysis. Have participants

- Identify common features across the charts.
- Identify divergent issues or perspectives.
- Rank issues in order of priority, using some form of voting procedure.

Planning: What happens next?

- Make an action plan, starting with an issue of highest priority.
- Designate tasks, persons, time lines, and resources.
- Designate a person to monitor these tasks.
- Designate a time and place to meet to review progress on the action plan.

PARTICIPANT OBSERVATION

Participant observation is distinctively different from observational routines common in experimental research or clinical practice, where the things to be observed are specifically defined. Observation in action research is more ethnographic, enabling an observer to build a picture of the lifeworld of those being observed and to develop an understanding of the way they ordinarily go about their everyday activities. It enables teachers to see how students go about the tasks that have been assigned them, social workers to observe how mothers interact with their children, marketers to study how customers interact with a business or commercial environment, or consultants to see how people go about the work of an organization.

Observation enables researchers to record important details that become the basis for formulating descriptions from which stakeholding groups produce their accounts. Although field notes are commonly used for observations, videotapes and photographs may also provide a powerful record of events and activities. As researchers observe stakeholding groups, they have opportunities to gain a clearer picture of the research context by observing the everyday settings in which participants undertake activities relevant to the research focus. By recording their observations as field notes, they acquire a record of important elements of the context of the participants. Researchers should record these notes during or soon after events have occurred, incorporating information that will later provide the means to describe a context or event. The schema depicted in Box 4.2 assists observers to include all relevant details in their description.

Box 4.2   Elements of Observation

- *Places:* offices, homes, and community contexts; locations of activities and events; physical layouts
- *People:* individuals, types of people, formal positions, and roles
- *Objects:* buildings, furniture, equipment, and materials
- *Acts:* single actions that people take (e.g., reading a report on a client)
- *Activities:* a set of related acts (e.g., formulating a case study)
- *Events:* a set of related activities (e.g., case conference)
- *Purposes:* what people are trying to accomplish
- *Time:* times, frequency, duration, and sequencing of events and activities
- *Feelings:* emotional orientations and responses to people, events, activities, and so on

As I talked with people in a community resource agency about their work, I also observed the conditions under which they worked, the resources available to them, the interactions among the types of workers, and the tasks in which they were engaged. Through time, I gained a much clearer understanding of the operation of the agency than I had initially. I interviewed people and made similar observations during my visits to the funding agency with which the resource agency was in conflict and during visits to other relevant agencies and organizations in town. I recorded information about all these settings, noting those features that seemed relevant to the investigation. I returned to some of the settings to record more details as the need for additional information arose. When agency workers complained of lack of equipment, materials, and stationery, for instance, I was able to assist them in performing a rough inventory and, in the process, was able to build a detailed picture of available resources.

I also visited key people in client groups and other agencies to acquire descriptive information about the general context of the town, the conditions in which its client groups lived, and other details of the community context. This information provided the materials from which I produced a general account of the context, which I presented as a preliminary report at the next meeting of the agency committee. I was careful to present an account that represented the different perceptions and interpretations of the situation given to me by participants in the setting. I asked the committee to discuss each section of the report and then made modifications and additions on the basis of their comments.

Participation in research contexts also provides research facilitators with opportunities to engage in interviews and conversations that extend the pool of information available. Appropriate questions enable researchers to describe the situation in the participants' own terms. For instance,

- What are all the (places, acts, events, and the like)?
- Can you describe in detail the (objects, times, goals, and the like)?
- Can you tell me about all the (people, activities, and the like)? (Spradley, 1979, p. 79)

This process also provides opportunities for researchers to check the veracity of their own observations. Phenomena such as purpose and feeling can be inferred only superficially by an observer and need to be checked for accuracy. I might record, for instance, "The principal met with faculty to present a written statement of the new school policy. The faculty appeared rather disgruntled with the new policy but made no comment about it." Here I have noted information related to the purpose of the meeting and the feelings of the faculty. This is potentially relevant information, but I would need to check with the principal and faculty to verify the authenticity of my interpretation. The principal may have other unstated purposes, the presentation of policy merely providing the context for meeting with faculty, and the faculty themselves may have been disgruntled about those other (hidden) agendas.

DOCUMENTS, RECORDS, AND REPORTS

Researchers can obtain a great deal of significant information by reviewing documents and records. Documents and records may include memos, minutes, reports, policy statements, procedure statements, plans, evaluation reports, press accounts, public relations materials, information statements, and newsletters. Organizational literature from schools, hospitals, clinics, centers, churches, businesses, and so on may include client records, policies, plans, strategies, evaluations, reports, procedural manuals, curricula, public relations literature, informational literature, and so forth. These types of documents are often prolific, and researchers need to be selective, briefly scanning their contents to ascertain their relevance to the issue under investigation.

Researchers should inspect official directories, where available, and keep records of the documents reviewed. They should record any significant information found in documents and note its source. In some cases, research-ers may be able to obtain photocopies of relevant documents.

Researchers should prepare summary statements of information they have acquired and check them for accuracy with relevant stakeholders. In the pro-cess, they should ascertain which information may be made public and which must be kept confidential. The intent of the summaries is to provide stakehold-ers with information that enables each group to review and reflect on its own activities and to share relevant information with other stakeholding groups. This information provides the key elements from which a jointly constructed account will be formulated.

VISUAL MEDIA

The electronic age has provided the means to greatly enhance people's ability to represent their lives in visual form, greatly extending our ability to present representations of people's experience in ways that capture the reality of any context. A wide range of media, produced relatively easily through the use of still and video cameras, enables production of photographs, films, charts, post-ers, books, magazines, newsletters, and so on that greatly enhance an action research process. Not only do they more clearly depict the realities of people and contexts, but they provide ways in which participants in an action research process can provide a more empathetic understanding of their situation and the issues within it. Lists of some of the available resources to help develop these types of material are listed in the Participatory Visual Methods section of Chapter 5 and the Social Media and Online Collaborative Tools section of Chapter 9.

Photographs and Videos

"A picture is worth a thousand words." Written text is often an inade-quate means of developing understanding, and simple photographs often provide a powerful means of presenting images of events and other phenomena—resources, offices, housing, and so on—relevant to the issue under investigation. Although the images themselves can provide a useful ongoing record, they also enhance reports and presentations produced as part of an investigation.

A particularly powerful use of photographs is provided by participatory visual methods such as Photovoice, Picturevoice, Paintvoice and Comicvoice (see Chapter 9: Social Media and Online Collaborative Tools). These include techniques of photo elicitation, wherein participants describe and comment on photographs of events or contexts in which they have participated and are assisted to create visuals that capture their individual or group experiences and perspectives. Participants can take control of the camera, taking images that seem most relevant from their perspective, and learn how to develop visual materials—books, charts, posters, menus, cards, and so on. Simple visual materials produced with common word-processing programs can be enhanced by more sophisticated productions as people develop their skills. Applications such as iBook and similar programs provide the means for people, with a little assistance, to produce materials that greatly enhance an action research process.

The development of videos is likewise within the grasp of many people through computerized programs that enable them to develop simple but powerful films that capture their experience and provide the means for more empathetic understanding of their situation or the issues they investigate. Researchers can loan cameras or video recorders to participants and work with them to think through—as part of the Look, Think, Act process—what images, events, activities, or situations they will record. This provides them with the means to control their worlds, framing and focusing according to their own terms of what is significant and how it should be presented.

Where photographs are used, it is usually necessary to first ask those being photographed permission to do so. If the photographs or video footage is to be shown publically, then written permission is needed, in accordance with the ethical guidelines suggested in Chapter 3.

In Warburton, an Aboriginal community in a remote region of Western Australia, a group of women started a school breakfast program that eventually evolved into a community catering service. In order to be able to tell others of the way these activities had emerged and the significance of them they initially developed a simple script that described the operation of the breakfast program. They first used the script for presentation in a webinar (a web-based seminar) that spoke to audiences in many parts

(Continued)

(Continued)

of the nation. This script was then used as the basis for developing a book that included photographs of key elements of the breakfast program and was published as an iBook. Further development of their script resulted in a poster that formed the backdrop for conference presentations to a variety of community and agency audiences. Video footage shot by the women and a facilitator provided the means for an agency worker, who had the required skills, to work with them to develop short but highly effective videos of aspects of their work together. At all stages the women, who necessarily spoke to their audiences in English—a second or third language to the women—continued to extend their capacity to speak publicly in situations where formerly they would have been embarrassed. The visual materials, however, provided the means that enabled them to keep their presentations relatively brief, simple, and highly effective.

SURVEYS

Surveys are of limited utility in the first phases of an action research process because they provide very limited information and are likely to reflect the perspective, interests, and agenda of the researcher. In later stages of action research, however, a survey may provide a very useful tool for extending the data collection process to a broader range of participants. It provides the means to check whether information acquired from participants in the first cycles of a process is relevant to other individuals and groups.

To conduct a survey, researchers should

Establish the purpose and focus of the survey. Carefully define

- The issues to be included
- Information to be obtained
- The respondents to be included in the survey sample

Formulate the questions for the questionnaire:

- Construct *one* question for *each* issue or piece of information.
- State the question in clear and unambiguous terms.
- State the question in positive rather than negative terms.

- Do not include jargon or technical terms that may be unfamiliar to respondents. Keep questions short and to the point.

Construct response formats:

- Open response: for example, "What factors have the most impact on your ability to do your work?"
- Fixed response: "How long should employees have for midmorning break: 5 minutes, 10 minutes, 15 minutes, 20 minutes?"
- Dual response: yes/no; either/or; agree/disagree
- Rating response: There are two major forms of rating: the Likert scale, where respondents rate their response to a statement by circling or checking that which is most appropriate (1. Strongly agree___ 2. Agree___ 3. Neutral___ 4. Disagree___ 5. Strongly disagree), and the semantic differential, where respondents rate the degree of their response to polar opposites ("The service provided was . . . fast___ ___ ___ ___ ___ ___ ___ slow."
  $$3 \quad 2 \quad 1 \quad 0 \quad \text{-}1 \quad \text{-}2 \quad \text{-}3$$

Provide introductory information for respondents:

- Purpose and nature of the survey
- Likely duration of time to complete responses
- Examples of types of response required

Test the questionnaire:

- Select a small pilot sample of respondents.
- Have them complete the questionnaire or respond to interview questions.
- Analyze responses to identify problematic or inadequate questions.
- Modify those questions.

Conduct the survey:

- Administer questionnaire or interview respondents.
- Collect responses.
- Thank people for their participation.

Analyze the data:

- Collate information for each question.
- Compute appropriate statistical measures—sum, mean, standard deviation, and so on.
- Identify significant results.

Report on the outcomes of the survey.

REVIEWING THE LITERATURE: EVIDENCE FROM RESEARCH STUDIES

In the first stage of action research the purpose of investigations is to extend and clarify participant understanding of the issue. Research participants seek to understand how and why events happen as they do. Often, however, people's "common sense"—the taken-for-granted knowledge accumulated through their personal experience—comes into conflict with other people in the setting. We need to find ways of checking the validity of these differences in perception, and we also need to check whether commonsense interpretations of the situation can be otherwise verified. Sometimes people assume the truth of a statement at odds with other credible sources of information. This is particularly true of distortions arising from media sensationalist reports or the grandstanding of political figures.

In these situations we have available a stable and powerful body of knowledge, established through a long history of systematic investigations, that enables us to check the validity of statements often presented as "facts." While the research literature does not provide definitive answers to all issues, it does provide information that sometimes has been thoroughly established through rigorous and systematic studies that provide much higher degrees of certainty than gained from other sources—press reports, political statements, and so on. When matters of fact are at issue, research can often help resolve disputes or provide information that has a more solid grounding than "What I think is . . ." or "It's just common sense!" Research can assist us in finding the extent to which the following types of assertions have any basis in fact:

- Crime is increasing.
- Students are performing poorly in schools.
- Taking "soft" drugs leads to "hard" drug usage.

- Youth engage in sexual activity (or become pregnant) much younger than they did previously.
- This treatment definitely is successful in creating weight loss (or stopping smoking, improving health).

The outcomes of research, presented as statistical information, can often provide clear evidence to either support or reject the veracity of such assertions. It is important, however, to check the history of any given set of information to ensure that though a situation may look bad, it may represent an improvement in the situation. It is also important to check a variety of studies because single studies often provide inadequate evidence upon which to make judgments. Review reports provide a useful source for information.

Many parents at a school at which I worked were incensed when the principal informed them that she would need to introduce some mixed-grade classes. At a meeting with parents she was able to present strong research evidence that students' academic performance did not suffer when they were placed in mixed-grade classes and that there were a number of psychological and social benefits. Most parents present at the meeting were gratified to have this level of information presented to them and were satisfied that their children's education would not suffer. The strength of the information was adequate to calm fears they had expressed early in the meeting.

A recent politically inspired "law and order" campaign in my city, aimed at greatly increasing legal penalties, was based on statements from political and community figures that indicated an increase in crime. Research recently completed by a local university, however, showed clearly that crime, in almost all areas, had decreased markedly in that period.

Access to the research literature is usually found in university libraries, largely in academic or professional journal reports. Though this is still the greatest repository of research reports, the Internet now provides a number of avenues to enable community-based researchers to acquire this type of information through web searches. A number of powerful search engines—Google, AltaVista, Yahoo, and so on—and websites now provide the means to access information derived from a large body of research. Google Academic provides a general resource, while derivatives of the old ERIC system still provide access to reports and reviews of educational research. Where matters of fact are involved, research participants now have the ability to acquire solid information from the huge array of research currently available (see Chapter 9).

To conduct a web search, researchers should

- Identify and describe the issue or topic.
- Identify key terms that characterize the topic.
- Log on to an appropriate search function. (Click on the "search" function incorporated into most computer programs.)
- Enter key terms.
- Review relevant websites.

GATHERING STATISTICAL INFORMATION—HOW MANY . . .?

An action research project may make use of statistical information for a variety of purposes. Records of numbers of events, participants, and so on can contribute to a clearer picture of the status of a research project. An action research project might include the following numerical information:

- Occurrences: the number of people, events, behaviors, participants, and so on
  - A record of the number of people engaged in a project, using a service, participating in activities, and so on provides the means of keeping track of events and estimating the degree to which the project is reaching intended audiences.

- Comparisons: differences in occurrence between groups
  - Interesting information can be obtained by comparing people from different groups—men and women, people from different age groups, people of different race or ethnicity, and so on.

- Trends or histories: changes in occurrence over time
- A single "snapshot" provides information that, by itself, may be misleading. Sometimes significant accomplishment or success is masked by a low "score" that fails to reveal considerable improvement over time.

- Central tendencies: the average number of people, occurrences of events, and so on

    o Mean scores help us keep track of occurrences of phenomena, especially where large numbers are involved. We can be better informed of the number of people participating in events, the scores on tests, and so on.

- Distributions: the extent to which scores or occurrences are clustered or widely spread

    o Attention to the distribution of occurrences assists us in understanding whether or not there is a wide dispersal of scores in a sample. The distribution may signify the need to treat groups differently or to pay further attention to individuals or groups who appear to be different in some way, either through the lack of participation indicated by the data or through the outcomes of the activities in which they have been engaged.

EXTENDED UNDERSTANDING: DESCRIPTIVE ANALYSIS

The first phases of an action research process are designed to provide well-grounded understandings of the experience and perspective of participants. Further information from observations and so on provides additional data that can complement, clarify, and extend understanding of the events and other phenomena associated with the issue at hand. Preliminary observations and interviews may lead to more extensive processes that enable participants to construct more sophisticated and detailed accounts of their situation, enabling them to see the complex web of interactions and activities within which problematic events are played out.

The following section therefore provides three alternative procedures researchers may use to assist people in extending their understanding of their situations and the issues investigated. These are similar to ethnographic processes used in qualitative research and have been applied successfully in many community, organizational, and group contexts. Although each process is intended to provide a separate alternative approach to the development of a descriptive account, researchers may find in practice that they include any combination of these procedures. Chapter 5 provides a set of procedures for identifying the features and elements to develop descriptive accounts.

Alternative 1: Working Ethnographically—Collaborative Descriptive Accounts

The processes outlined in the interviewing section in this chapter may be applied to group contexts. Grand tour and other questions may be directed to a single group or to varied groups attending a meeting rather than to individuals. The research facilitator should elicit multiple responses to these questions verbally, using group processes where appropriate, and should record them in summary form on charts. This material can then be used in the formulation of descriptive accounts (see the Formal Reports section in Chapter 8).

Alternative 2: Six Questions—Why, What, How, Who, Where, When

The first question—why—provides a general orientation to the focus of the investigation, whereas succeeding questions—what, how, who, where, and when—enable participants to identify associated influences. The intent is not to define causes but to understand how the problem is encompassed in the context or setting. *How* and *what* questions are more productive than *why* questions. The former provide opportunities for revealing direct experience, whereas the latter often lead to explanations remote from people's experience. Examples of appropriate initiating questions include the following:

- *Why* are we meeting today? What is the purpose?
- *What* is/are the problem(s)? What is happening?
- *How* does it affect our work or lives?
- *Who* is being affected?
- *Where* are things happening?
- *When* are things happening?

Answers should focus on acts, activities, and events related to the problem; participants should not attempt to evaluate or judge individual or group behavior. An initial pass through these questions will lead to further questions that can provide increasingly detailed information. This will include the history of the situation (how it came to be as it is), the people involved in or affected by the problem, interactions and relationships among these people, resources (people, space, time, funds, current use, access, availability), dreams, and aspirations.

Alternative 3: Community Profile

A community profile provides a descriptive snapshot of the context in which the investigation is placed. It enables stakeholders to formulate an over-view that describes significant features of their context. Smaller projects in restricted sites, such as classrooms, schools, community centers, and govern-ment agencies, may require information that focuses only on dimensions of the setting itself—that is, the classroom, school, agency office, and so on. In many cases, however, persistent problems require investigations that extend into the neighborhood, town, city, or region.

There is often a profusion of information about community contexts, and it is essential that the work of preparing a profile remain focused. Following preliminary activity that briefly describes the setting (see Chapter 3), research-ers should ask major stakeholders for their views about the types of information pertinent to the investigation. This will help researchers choose judiciously from a potentially vast array of information and minimize the time spent amassing inconsequential information. Research facilitators should assist stakeholders in developing a community profile framework that appears most appropriate to the task at hand. A community profile might include any of the following:

- *Geography:* location, landforms, climate
- *History:* history of the setting, major events, developments, history of the problem(s) under investigation, major laws affecting the site or the problem(s)
- *Government:* impacts and places of local, regional, state, and federal government policies and agencies; boundaries
- *Politics:* parties, organizations, representatives
- *Demographics:* population size; gender, race, ethnic, and age distributions; births and deaths
- *Economics:* sectors (e.g., business and industry), employment, wages and salary levels, general status (prospering, declining)
- *Health:* services, agencies, facilities, special populations (e.g., older persons, children, persons with disabilities)
- *Education:* schools, institutions, services, sectors (e.g., primary, secondary, college), resources, community education
- *Welfare:* services; institutions, agencies, and organizations (govern-ment and nongovernment); personnel (e.g., social workers, counselors)
- *Housing:* number, type, and condition of dwellings; forms of accom-modation (e.g., low rent, transient, hotel)

- *Transportation:* public and private transportation, accessibility and availability, areas serviced, road conditions, types (road, rail, air)
- *Recreation:* type, number, condition, and accessibility of facilities and services; clubs and organizations; age groups targeted
- *Religion:* type and number of churches, levels of attendance, activities and services
- *Intergroup relations:* social groups (race, ethnic, religious, or kinship affiliations), coalitions, antagonisms
- *Planning:* regional, city, town, or local plans

Community profiles usually provide demographic information, much of which can be gained from official or documentary sources, but information may also be acquired during preliminary observations and interviews. John Van Willigen (1993, after Vlachos, 1975) suggests a format that embodies cultural information in addition to the types of demographic data just described. The type of information collected necessarily requires extended ethnographic work with people within the setting. Van Willigen's framework incorporates cultural tracts that include the following:

- *Lifestyle:* economic status, communication (including language, proxemics, and expressive media), religious sites and practices, housing (styles and clustering of dwellings, place of kin networks), geographic location, institutional characteristics, health definitions and practices, education, leisure and recreational activities, politics
- *Historical features:* contemporary and historical artifacts and physical representations
- *Worldviews, beliefs, perceptions, and definitions of reality:* cognitive systems (how people think about and organize everyday reality), religious systems (spiritual reality), values systems, belief systems, perceptions of one's own group and others, intercultural perceptions

Once the researcher has acquired the information for the community profile, he or she can organize and present it in a form that people from all stakeholding groups can readily understand. The profile can be made available for their scrutiny as part of the process of formulating accounts (see Chapter 5). A community profile provides a structured way for participants to determine clearly the range of influences likely to have an impact on the problem under investigation. The information ensures that a broad range of relevant features of the situation are taken into account and paves the way for effective and sustainable projects and programs.

MEETINGS: GROUP PROCESSES FOR
COLLABORATIVE INQUIRY

The most successful and productive action research occurs where participants have the opportunity to talk extensively about their experiences and perceptions. Interview processes enable people not only to reveal the issues and agendas but also to reflect on the nature of events that concern them. Where individual interviews are not possible, research facilitators may organize meetings that bring people together to explore the issue under investigation. In these circumstances they should use carefully articulated group processes to ensure that each participant has extended opportunities to describe his or her situation and to express his or her issues and concerns.

Preliminary Meetings

When diverse stakeholder groups are brought together, it is often fruitful, particularly where there has been a history of conflict between parties, for researchers to do some preliminary work to ensure harmonious and productive meetings. Holding prior meetings with each of the conflicting parties can enable them to define their own agendas and to clarify the purposes of the larger meeting. In these contexts, researchers should work to formulate statements that are nonjudgmental and nonblaming yet clearly articulate participants' perceptions and concerns.

> When I worked on community projects, I always indicated the need for joint action between stakeholding groups. After I had established contact with individuals and groups and provided them with opportunities to express their viewpoints, I would signal the possibility of linking with others. I would comment that there are a number of other people (or groups) who are concerned with this issue, and it might be useful to meet with them to discuss it.

A common mistake of researchers intent on community-based action is to call a "public meeting" to discuss issues and formulate plans. Often, such meetings are held in places—schools, universities, agency offices—alien to many stakeholders. In consequence, many groups are poorly represented, and the organizers become disconcerted by the apparent apathy of the people they wish to engage. School principals, social workers, and health workers, for instance, cannot understand why certain parent groups will not come to meetings called specifically to deal with their children's problems. They frequently comment in these circumstances on the parents' "lack of interest" and fail to perceive how threatening formal or official environments can be for some people.

I have been involved in many situations in which parents, especially those from lower socioeconomic environments, perceive schools and government offices as threatening and judgmental bastions of authority. Meetings held in institutional arenas often reinforce these perceptions, as articulate and self-confident people hold the floor and determine the course of events and the texts—resolutions, statements, records, and so on—that finally emerge. Persons who are less articulate are effectively silenced, their concerns unheard and their agendas unmet.

In some instances, public meetings provide contexts in which individuals or groups in conflict meet for the first time. Without preliminary work, these types of meetings may degenerate into conflict-laden situations that serve only to reinforce antagonisms and exacerbate existing problems. Public meetings, therefore, should be used only after stakeholder groups have had the opportunity to meet in safe and comfortable contexts to explore their issues and to clarify their thoughts and perceptions. Where there is no other alternative, researchers should carefully facilitate group processes, as suggested in the following section, to enable all participants to express their views in safety and have their issues recognized.

Organizing Meetings

Meetings don't "just happen"; careful planning and preparation must take place to ensure that participants can work through their issues and attain their objectives without the distractions of poorly articulated activities, inadequate materials and equipment, or uncomfortable or irritating conditions. The following are critical issues research facilitators need to take into account when organizing meetings.

Participants

Meetings should reflect the participatory intent of action research; it is important, therefore, to ensure that people who can legitimately speak for the interests of each stakeholding group attend. Having one or two persons represent a diverse ethnic group, for instance, may ignore the deep divisions that lie among families, cliques, and social class groupings within that population. Researchers should review their initial social analysis to confirm that all groups are appropriately represented by individuals who can legitimately take on the role of spokesperson. Meeting conditions—time, place, and transportation—should maximize the opportunities these people have to attend.

Leadership: Facilitating a Productive Meeting

A meeting is best led by a neutral chair or facilitator—a person perceived as having no overriding loyalty to any particular stakeholding group. Researchers can act as facilitators, but it may be appropriate in some circumstances for a respected community member to act in this role. It is important that participants accept the chair or facilitator as a legitimate or appropriate person to direct proceedings. Only in exceptional circumstances, for example, would a meeting investigating women's issues have a male chair.

The task of negotiating diverse perspectives in a research process can become difficult if strong and determined people try to impose their own agendas and perspectives. The chair or facilitator should employ judicious, diplomatic, yet firm processes to ensure that such people do not stifle the diverse agendas and perspectives that are essential components of the process. For that reason, researchers should ensure that the chair or facilitator has the formal authority and the procedural skills to maintain the integrity of the meeting process. A formal statement, written or verbal, that acknowledges the chair or facilitator's authority should be obtained from key stakeholders prior to the commencement of the meeting. This may take the form of a letter or memorandum to participants or may be included in a welcoming speech at the meeting.

Significant differentials of power between the research facilitator and other participants are not conducive to productive meetings. Researchers should ensure that people of appropriate status are engaged to facilitate or lead meetings.

I learned of a situation in which an inexperienced junior professor and a graduate assistant were asked to facilitate a workshop at a conference of senior educational administrators. Within a short time, the administrators had marginalized the professor and graduate assistant and had taken control of proceedings.

Ground Rules and Agenda

Researchers may ask groups in advance to suggest meeting ground rules in order to minimize the possibility of conflict and to provide conditions conducive to productive work. Meeting procedures should be planned carefully to minimize the possibility that they degenerate into heated debate, accusation, and blaming. Each meeting should begin with the presentation of a broad agenda that includes statements about the purpose of the meeting, the manner in which the meeting will proceed, and the activities in which participants will engage. Time may be allocated for people to comment on the agenda and to suggest alternative procedures. These preliminary activities, however, should not take so much time that they detract from the main activities of the meeting.

> I once attended a one-day workshop in which two of the six available hours were expended on establishing ground rules and formulating an agenda. This use of the available time created a great deal of frustration among many of the participants because the time remaining was insufficient to deal with the intended workshop agenda.

Procedures

Meeting procedures can ensure that each group has an equal opportunity to express perceptions and concerns and to have them included in the meeting's generated statements and accounts. By making frequent use of small-group processes, facilitators can provide opportunities for people to articulate their thoughts and ideas in safety. This ensures that multiple perspectives are elicited and that forceful people do not dominate proceedings. In one useful type of small-group process, the facilitator or meeting leader follows these steps:

- Divide the meeting into groups of, usually, no more than six members.
- Describe the activities to be performed or the questions to be discussed (these may be selected from any of the frameworks for developing descriptive accounts presented in this chapter).
- Provide adequate time for these purposes to be achieved.
- Have each group write a summary of activity outcomes on a chart.
- Have all participants reassemble and display their charts.

- Have each group present its summary verbally. As each group presents, questions from the facilitator or audience may allow group members to clarify meanings and in some cases extend their descriptions. This additional information may then be added to the chart.

Decision Making

Meetings should operate on the basis of consensus, rather than on majority vote. The latter encourages competitive, divisive politicking, which usually ensures that the least powerful groups will not have their interests met. Although consensus is sometimes difficult to attain, it is a powerful instrument for change when it is achieved. When agendas are pushed through to accommodate time pressures, bureaucratic pressures, or the interests of powerful groups, the outcomes are likely, in the long run, to be unproductive. Time is an essential element in any collaborative activity; it cannot be compressed without damaging the essential participatory nature of a action research process.

Venues

Initial meetings may be held in people's homes, cafes, offices, community centers, or any other venue where the stakeholder group itself is comfortable. When people talk in the comfort of their own territory, they are more likely to be honest and forthcoming. Public venues are appropriate when all stakeholder groups meet to work through issues and agendas. Even then, however, researchers should take care to select meeting sites where the least powerful groups will feel comfortable. If a meeting is held in their territory, they are more likely both to attend and be willing to contribute to the proceedings. A local community hall, church halls, hostels, community health clinics, lodge halls, and even parks may provide appropriate contexts.

Communicating and Reporting

Action research requires all stakeholders to be informed of activities and events as they occur. Where groups engage in activity—sometimes with great enthusiasm—but fail to inform other participants of what they are doing, the process is likely to be disrupted in a number of ways. People may have their feelings hurt, feel excluded, become suspicious, or feel unwanted. In these and many other ways, failure to maintain communication can lead to a loss of commitment and loss of ownership. Continued communication can be achieved informally by regular meetings in which people report on their activities, e-mail, phone calls, or use of social media. Reports may also be made in the form of meeting minutes, newsletters, or verbal presentations. Formal reports, as described in Chapter 8, may require more extended and complete reporting procedures, though the primary purpose is to ensure that all stakeholders are fully informed of the progress and outcomes of the project.

REFLECTION AND ACTION

1. If possible, return to the cultural scene you previously visited. Using the techniques presented in this chapter, interview someone who is part of the scene. If you have chosen your own workplace, interview at least one of the stakeholders there. Your purpose is to learn how the person interviewed describes the scene, including significant important events that are part of ongoing operations of the setting.[2]

2. Before you start you will need to prepare the following:
   - How you will introduce yourself and the purpose of the interview
   - The type of questions you will ask (using formats suggested in this chapter)
   - The method of recording information—notebook or tape

3. After the interview read back the notes you have taken to the person interviewed. Ask whether your notes accurately reflect what he or she said.

4. Reflect on the process and discuss with another person. How did that feel? What did you note about the interview process? How might you have improved? (Keep the notes [data] for later analysis.)

5. Observe the setting for an extended period of time (at least a half hour), using techniques suggested in this chapter. Record what you observe. (Keep these observations for later analysis.)

6. Reflect on the process of observation. How did that feel? What did you learn about the process of observation?

7. From the interview and observation, list what else you would like to learn about that setting. Formulate a short questionnaire around those issues.

8. Return to the setting and interview a number of persons using that questionnaire.

9. Alternatively, prepare a number of copies of the questionnaire and ask people to complete it.

10. Reflect on the differences between the use of a questionnaire and the interview process for gathering information. How do they differ? What are their strengths? What are their weaknesses?

11. Identify an issue, question, or problem arising in your interviews or observations. Do a search of the research literature on that topic. Identify studies that have been done and summarize what they reveal.

NOTES

1. Very few action research contexts provide the means to incorporate the necessary research design that would enable a practitioner to rigorously test a hypothesis or to generalize the results outside of the research contexts. Transferability to other contexts (Lincoln & Guba, 1985; Stringer, 2004) may be possible if appropriate "thick" descriptions result from the study. The use of faux experiments in action research is likely to lead to spurious results (results that cannot be attributed to the dependent variable or the intervention) because of the inability to control variables in an action research setting.

2. This can be a useful exercise right at the beginning of a workshop or class. Participants should initially work in pairs, interviewing one another to identify key features of their life—who they are, where they're from, and so on, as well as interesting events or experiences. Interviewers should take notes to assist their memory. When interviews have been completed, pairs should join to form into groups of four to six people. Interviewers should then introduce their subject to the group, in terms derived from the interview. Interviewees should then be given the opportunity to evaluate, clarify, and extend information given.

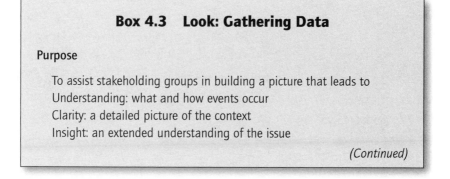

Box 4.3   Look: Gathering Data

Purpose

To assist stakeholding groups in building a picture that leads to
Understanding: what and how events occur
Clarity: a detailed picture of the context
Insight: an extended understanding of the issue

(Continued)

(Continued)

Process

Gather Information

Sources of information
Interviews: key people from each stakeholding group
Observation: significant settings, events, or activities
Other sources: documents, records, reports, surveys, research literature

Record Information

Record information as
Notes: a written record of what people said or did, or key points from documents, records, or the research literature
Audiotapes: audio record of interviews
Videotapes: video record of events, people, places, and so on
Photographs: photographs of events, people, places, and so on

Extend Understanding

Construct frameworks for descriptive accounts
Collaborative descriptive accounts
Six questions—why, what, how, who, where, when
Community profiles

Organizing Meetings

Participants
Leadership and facilitation
Ground rules and agenda
Procedures
Decision making

Communicating

Inform people of research activities by distributing reports to participants and stakeholders as
Meeting minutes
Bulletins
Interim reports

5

THINK

Reflection and Analysis

In their day-to-day lives in work and community settings people act and behave according to well-established routines and recipes that have emerged from their socialization or professional development. In organizational and agency settings these taken-for-granted procedures and processes are usually incorporated into common practices based on particular ways of thinking about activities in that setting—care plans, lesson plans, interview procedures, meeting procedures, administrative arrangements, and the many other ways that people structure and organize their professional or community activities. These are often so deeply ingrained in people's experience that they are not conscious that the very forms of organizing and implementing activity may themselves be part of the problem they wish to investigate.

Action research processes are designed not to take these procedures for granted but to include them as necessarily part of the investigation. They need to "re-search," look again, at things they have never seen as problematic, making them subject to investigation and analysis and ultimately as potentially in need of change. Rather than being assumed to be an immutable part of the context, the taken-for-granted becomes available for inspection and analysis. People need to be able to think about all aspects of the situation, to critically examine all features of the setting so they are able to fashion effective solutions to the problems they confront. The following processes therefore provide the means by which people can "re-theorize" the situation, to look past the taken-for-granted theories and explanations for events that are embedded in their everyday work, professional, and community lives.

The purpose of the Think phase is to sift through the accumulating body of information that emerges from the Look phase—identifying significant features and elements that seem to have a significant influence on events. These are then organized into a framework of ideas or concepts that enables participants to better understand problematic features of the situation. These systematic processes of analysis provide the means for a deeper or more extended understanding of the situation that lead to a more effective and sustainable resolution of the problem or issue investigated.

I sometimes work with people who indicate that "I'd like to be able to do that, but it's too time consuming. I'm just too busy to do that." In these circumstances they continue to implement practices that are a part of their professional "stock of knowledge," experiencing frustration and irritation when, despite their best attempts to devise better ways of doing the job, they fail to accomplish their objectives. I've seen teachers who continue to be frustrated when children in their class continue to achieve poorly and remain "turned off" and fractious; social workers angry at clients who fail to achieve "targets" to which they have agreed; health professionals whose patients' health continues to decline because they fail to make changes to a lifestyle that is the nominal cause of their problems; and so on. Often they are held in place by mandated requirements of their organization or agency to apply particular procedures to client, student, or patient problems. These cases emphasize the need to include all stakeholders at all levels of a system and all relevant aspects of the situation if effective resolution to problematic events is to be achieved.

INTERPRETATION: DEVELOPING UNDERSTANDING

Denzin (1989) has written of the need to make the problematic, lived experience of ordinary people directly available to policy makers, welfare workers, and other service professionals, so that programs and services can be made more relevant to people's lives. He suggests that an interpretive perspective identifies different definitions of the situation, the assumptions held by interested parties, and appropriate points of intervention:

> Research of this order can produce meaningful descriptions and interpretations of social process. It can offer explanations of how certain conditions came into existence and persist. Interpretive research can also furnish the

basis for realistic proposals concerning the improvement or removal of certain events, or problems. (p. 23)

The task of the research facilitator in this phase of the research process is to interpret and render understandable the problematic experiences being considered. Interpretation builds on description through conceptual frameworks—definitions and meaning—that enable participants to make better sense of their experiences. It uses experience-near concepts—terms people use to describe events in their day-to-day lives (rather than, e.g., theoretical concepts from the behavioral sciences)—to clarify and untangle meanings and to help people illuminate and organize their experiences. The researcher must provide the opportunity, in other words, for participants to understand their own experiences in terms that make sense to them.

Interpretive activity exposes the conceptual structures and pragmatic working theories that people use to explain their conduct. The researcher's task is to assist participants in revealing those taken-for-granted meanings and reformulating them into "constructions [that are] improved, matured, expanded, and elaborated" and that enhance their conscious experiencing of the world (Guba & Lincoln, 1989). These new ways of interpreting the situation are not intended as merely intellectualized, rational explanations; rather, they are real-life constructs-in-use that assist people in reshaping actions and behaviors that affect their lives.

"Interpretation is a clarification of meaning. Understanding is the process of interpreting, knowing, and comprehending the meaning that is felt, intended, and expressed by another" (Denzin, 1989, p. 120). The purpose of interpretive work, therefore, is to help participants to "take the attitude of the other" (Mead, 1934), not in a superficial, mechanistic sense but in a way that enables them to understand empathetically the complex and deeply rooted forces that move their lives.

In some instances, initial interpretive work provides the basis for immediate action. Some problems, however, are more intransigent and require extended processes of exploration, analysis, and theorizing. The form of analysis should be appropriate to the problem at hand. Complex or highly abstract theories, when applied to small, localized issues, are likely to drain people's energy and inhibit action. Explanations and interpretations produced in action research processes should be framed in terms that participants use in their everyday lives, rather than those derived from the academic disciplines or professional practices.

When I began working at the community level, I would often present explanations for problems as derived from my background in the social sciences. I would include concepts such as social class, racism, power, authority, and so on. In few instances did these forms of analysis strike a chord with the people with whom I was working.

On one occasion, I presented an analysis to a group of Aboriginal people that implied that their responses to racism were inappropriate. My explanation outlined a theory of minority responses to racism that high-lighted apathy, avoidance, and aggression as typical behaviors that derived from a history of oppression. The anger directed at me by the Aboriginal people present was a humbling experience.

In retrospect, I understand their anger and wonder at my naiveté. Not only was I interpreting their situation from my perspective; I was also judging their behavior in stereotypical ways, implicitly criticizing their responses to situations they faced. Today, I ensure that any analysis I make is drawn from terms known to the people with whom I am working, is expressed in their language, and is derived from their experience-near concepts. My own role in this process is to assist them in articulating their ideas and to ensure that they express their ideas clearly and accurately. I also ask probing questions that challenge the rigor of their interpretations to ensure that their interpretations will hold up in the court of public scrutiny and future action.

The use of experience-near concepts does not eliminate the need for rigorous inquiry. Restricted or cursory analyses that produce superficial solutions to deep-seated and complex problems are unlikely to be effective. Researchers and facilitators can ensure that explanatory frameworks are sufficiently rigorous to move people past stereotypical or simplistic interpretations of their situations, but these frameworks must be grounded in the reality of their everyday lives. They must acknowledge the experiences and perspectives of those to whom programs and services are directed, rather than of those who deliver those services.

In the early phases of a recent project in East Timor, principals and superintendents often commented that parents were not interested in their children's schooling—that it would be difficult to get them to participate in school life. Through a series of parent workshops I was able to demonstrate that parents had high levels of interest in their children's schooling. Using participatory processes of inquiry based on small-group techniques, these workshops gave parents opportunities to express their concerns about the school and to suggest ways that they might be able to engage in activities that would assist the staff of the school in dealing with the issues that emerged. In most schools parents identified a number of ways that they would be willing to participate in improving the school, and many successful projects emerged—fund-raising; school repair and maintenance; garden maintenance; teaching materials manufacture; local crafts, art, songs, and dances; and assisting with school security arrangements. Parents found many ways that they, with their limited education and resources, could make a difference in their children's schooling.

ANALYSIS AND INTERPRETATION PHASE I: DISTILLING THE DATA

Two major processes provide the means to distill the data that emerge from the ongoing processes of investigation. The first is a *categorizing and coding* procedure that identifies units of meaning (experience, perception) within the data and organizes them into a set of categories that typify or summarize the experiences and perspectives of participants. The second data analysis process selects *key experiences* or transformational moments and "unpacks" them to identify the elements that compose them, thus illuminating the nature of those experiences. Researchers may use either or both of these techniques of data analysis as they seek to acquire clarity and understanding by distilling and organizing the information they have gathered.

Categorizing and Coding

The major task of this procedure is to identify the significant features and elements that make up the experience and perception of the people involved in the study (stakeholders). *All* analysis is an act of interpretation, but the major aim in analysis is to identify information that clearly represents the perspective and experience of the stakeholding participants. Those involved in data analysis must "bracket" their own understandings, intuitions, or interpretations as much as possible and focus on the meanings inherent in the world of participants.

This difficult task requires some practice and feedback to identify the ways in which we tend to view events through our own perspectives, and it points to the need to ground our analysis in participant terms, concepts, and meanings. This is tricky ground, especially when we come to coding procedures, where we must use a term or heading to represent the data within a category:

> Maria Hines, a member of a city neighborhood collective, is most explicit about her experience of analyzing data in a project in which she participated. With a slight frown she describes how "I never knew how difficult it was *not* to put my own words and meanings in. We had to really concentrate to make sure we used what people had actually said and not put it in our own words. It was *hard*." (Stringer, 2004)

To minimize the propensity to conceptualize events through their own interpretive lenses, researchers should, wherever possible, apply the *verbatim principle,* using terms and concepts drawn from the words of the participants themselves. By doing so they are more likely to capture the meanings inherent in people's experience.

Because stakeholders are likely to have different experiences and perspectives on any issue, analysis of each stakeholding group should initially be kept separate and more general categories developed at later stages of a project. Thus initial analysis will keep, for example, teacher, student, and parent perspectives separate to identify ways that these stakeholders see the situation. Even within these groups, however, there will be groups and individuals who describe and interpret events in different ways. Analysis should identify these diverse perspectives in ways that enable research participants to understand the elements their perspectives have in common and the ways in which they diverge. Likewise, city planners, businesspeople, and residents may have differing perceptions of a neighborhood development project that all need to be acknowledged and incorporated into planning procedures. Managers, professional staff, administrative staff, and customers or clients may differ in the way they describe their experience, affecting the way a business or agency operates.

Procedures for this form of analysis involve

- Reviewing the data
- Unitizing the data
- Categorizing and coding
- Identifying themes

- Organizing a category system
- Developing a report framework

Reviewing the Data

Commence this phase by first reviewing the issue on which the study is focused and any associated research questions. The purpose of analysis is to identify data (information) pertinent to these issues and questions. As data analysis continues, there may be considerable amounts of data that are either irrelevant or peripherally relevant, so that choices need to be made about which data to incorporate into processes of analysis.

Researchers should first review transcripts or records of interviews, reading them to familiarize themselves with the contents and to get a feel for the views and ideas expressed. Other types of information will be incorporated in further cycles of analysis.

Unitizing the Data

As people talk about their experience and perspective, their narrative is composed of a wide range of related and interconnected ideas, activities, and events. They will often change direction or focus on the many parts of the story that compose the interrelated aspects of everyday experience. The next phase is to identify the discrete ideas, concepts, events, and experiences incorporated into their description to isolate the elements of which their experience is composed.

Using a photocopy of the original data, block out each separate item of information using a pencil to identify units of meaning. A unit of meaning may be a word, phrase, sentence, or sequence of sentences. You can then literally cut out each of these pieces and paste it onto a card, labeling the card to indicate the origin of that unit—the interview from which it was drawn.

Teachers and parents came to the next meeting / and talked of starting a PTA (Parent Teacher Association). / Some parents refused to consider this / due to their experience of past associations. / The parents then identified other parents who had good ideas, / who had the interest and enthusiasm, / and who would work with teachers / to improve the school. / They decided they needed to inform other parents / of the possibilities for starting a Parent Teacher Association.

When pasting units onto a card, extra information may need to be added to make the meaning clear. For example, to the unit "Some parents refused to consider this," researchers would need to add in brackets "starting a Parent Teacher Association." The intent is to identify *units of meaning*—statements that have discrete meaning when isolated from other information.

Categorizing and Coding

Once the data has been unitized, the units of meaning must be sorted into related groups or categories. The previous boxed example provides information about parent activities, experiences, and perspectives about a PTA. It provides the basis for a category that may be identified (coded) as "Parents' perspectives on a PTA." Information from other interviews could be added and the category resorted to identify different dimensions of their perspective. Each pile of cards, or category, could then be labeled to identify the particular dimension; for example, an initial set of categories based on the previously discussed data might be "Starting a PTA," "Parents with good ideas," or "Parents with interest and enthusiasm." As data from other interviews are included, however, these categories might be seen as inappropriate and the code revised.

As the data are analyzed, categories might emerge that enable a large number of activities to be included under a relatively small number of headings. For instance, analysis of interviews that focus on PTAs might reveal the following categories: "Organizing a PTA," "The structure of a PTA," "Parent activities," "Improving the school," and so on. This is a natural way of organizing information. Many people would include oranges, apples, pears, and peaches within a category called "fruit." Likewise, shirts, shorts, slacks, and sweaters might be categorized as "clothing."

Identifying Themes

When the categories associated with each stakeholding group have been placed in a system of categories it may be possible to identify themes held in common across stakeholder groups. Within a school we may see that teachers, students, and parents are concerned about "results," even though their concerns are expressed differently. Neighborhood stakeholders, similarly, may be concerned about the effect of a new roadway, though they may see that effect in either positive or negative ways. All perspectives would need to be incorporated under the overarching theme "Effect of a new roadway."

Research participants therefore need to identify themes—issues, experiences, or perspectives that people have in common—by comparing categories and subcategories across stakeholding groups.

Organizing a Category System

The category system must then be recorded in some rational form, providing a clear picture of the categories and subcategories of information related to the topic investigated.

A manager of a service agency engaged in a project to investigate the operations of one of the agency's services. The analysis identified the key features emerging from analysis of interviews with agency staff, clients, and client parents and the elements comprising each of those features:

Relationships

    Between staff
    Between staff and
        families
    Between staff and clients

Information Sharing

    Written
    Verbal
    Meetings
    Recruitment
    Social events

Skills

    Assess and record
    Reviews
    Participation

Family Input

    Plans
    General
    Outcomes
    Significant events

Confidentiality

    Consent

Environment

    Maintenance
    Personalization
    Safety issues

Health

    Food preparation
    Diet

Developing a Report Framework

This type of category system provides a framework for reports or presentations that communicates the outcomes of this phase of the research to relevant stakeholders. Themes, categories, and subcategories provide the headings and subheadings for this purpose but may be preceded by an introduction that provides contextual information and the purpose of the report and followed by a conclusion that presents the outcomes of the investigation.

Analyzing Key Experiences, Epiphanic Events, or Critical Incidents

The purpose of this approach to analysis is to focus on events that seem to have a marked impact on the experience of major stakeholders. Denzin (1989) talks of moments of crisis, or turning-point experiences that have a significant impact on people. Such events may appear as moments of crisis, triumph, anger, confrontation, love, warmth, or despair that have a lasting impact on people. They may result in a "lightbulb" or "a-ha" experience that provides people with greater clarity about puzzling events or phenomena or leaves them with deep-seated feelings of alienation, distrust, anger, or hopelessness. Key experiences or epiphanic events, however, can be moments of joy and triumph, wonderful experiences that affect people's lives in positive ways. Analysis of events where people overcome great obstacles to achieve something momentous, or when they work exceedingly hard to accomplish something important, can provide great insight into the underlying dynamics of people's lives.

The analysis of critical incidents has an extended history in the human service professions, for as Tripp (1993) indicates, this enables teachers to acquire the means to self-monitor their techniques and routines in order to increase the power of their professional judgment. Analysis of critical incidents now extends to a wide range of areas, including education, counseling (Juhnke & Kelly, 2005; Tyson, Perusse, & Whitledge, 2004), and management (Hinkin, 2005).

As we interview people systematically over an extended period they are likely to focus on events that have special significance for them. By unpacking these events we can learn the features that make them so meaningful, and in the process we extend our understanding of the way the issues affect their lives. This may require ongoing cycles of investigation with participants to explore the significance of the identified events or incidents. This type of analysis requires researchers to

Review the Data

Review the data as suggested in the Categorizing and Coding section.

Identify Key Experiences

For each participant, identify events or experiences that appear to be particularly significant or to have an especially meaningful impact on them.

Identify Main Features of Each Experience

For each significant event or experience, identify the features that seem to be a major part of that experience.

Identify the Elements That Compose the Experience

For each feature, identify the elements that compose the detailed aspects of that experience.

Identify Themes

List experiences, features, and elements for each participant. Compare lists to identify experiences and features of experience common to groups of participants. List these as themes.

Case Example: Facilitating Workshops

This example demonstrates how a piece of data can be analyzed and the category system used as the basis for a report on workshop facilitation. The analysis commences with a piece of raw data and identifies a key experience and its associated features and elements.

This is an excerpt taken from field notes written while observing a project team facilitating a planning workshop.

"I remember the anxiety that used to sit in the pit of my stomach as I watched my colleagues commence a workshop, my mind racing with details of what needed to happen and the 'what-ifs' that haunted me. My organizational mind was constantly working on plans to institute if things failed to eventuate as they were intended. It was something that nagged me and caused me many sleepless nights.

"I eventually learned that the start of a workshop was always likely to be a bit 'lumpy' and that, provided facilitators were well prepared and flexible enough to accommodate the needs and capabilities of participants, we would almost always accomplish our goals.

(Continued)

(Continued)

"So now I can watch team members facilitating the workshop, appreciate the careful planning that has occurred, and sit proudly as they work competently with the participants, engaging their attention and enthusiasm. I watch the energy of the participants as they focus on the real issues emerging from their work. I feel that I have become blessedly redundant and that my colleagues have the capacity, evolved from their previous work with me, to carry on the business at hand. They're clear, competent, and well-spoken, able to achieve excellent results and to enable participants to achieve the solutions they have sought through their participation."

Key Experience
Experiencing an effective workshop

Features and Elements

- *Anxiety*
  - Feelings
  - Sleeplessness
  - "Lumpy" start to workshop
- *Careful Planning*
  - Identify outcomes
- *Identify Learning Tasks*
  - Sequence tasks
  - Report
  - Evaluate
- *Flexible Processes*
  - Explain each task
  - Demonstrate or model the activity
  - Participants enact the activity
  - Debrief or feedback (evaluation)
  - Repeat if necessary
  - Timing according to participant needs, skills, or understanding
- *Accomplishing Purposes*
  - Engaging attention and enthusiasm
  - Focusing on real issues
  - Working competently
  - Having the capacity
  - Achieving solutions
  - Feeling proud, redundant

This example provides the key features of Anxiety, Careful Planning, Identifying Learning Tasks, Flexible Processes, and Accomplishing Purposes.

The elements composing details of the first and last features are drawn from the previous data. A following interview revealed the elements composing Careful Planning and Flexible Processes. These features and elements provide the basis for a report that enables agency administration to understand how the team had presented an effective workshop.

ANALYSIS AND INTERPRETATION PHASE II: ENRICHING THE ANALYSIS

The first cycles of an action research process enable researchers to refine their focus of investigation and to understand the ways in which primary stakeholders experience and interpret emerging issues. In following cycles other information is incorporated that further clarifies or extends participants' understanding by adding information from other stakeholders and data sources. In a school research process, the perspectives of parents might be added to those of students and teachers, and school or student records or the research literature might provide relevant information. In a health program, patient and health professional perspectives might be complemented by evidence-based information from the professional literature.

The purpose for this activity is to provide the means for achieving a holistic analysis that incorporates all factors likely to have an impact on achieving an effective solution to the problem investigated. Thus the part that each major stakeholder plays will be taken into account, as well as the substantial information from policy and program documents and the research literature.

Figure 5.1   Incorporating Diverse Data Into an Emerging Analysis

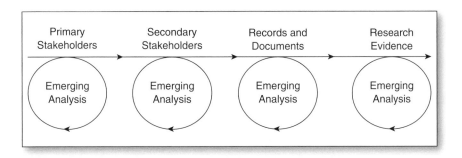

The example previously presented of parent concerns for mixed-grade classrooms provides an example of this process. Parents were able to clearly articulate their desire to ensure that their children's education would not suffer from these arrangements, and information from the research literature provided them with reassurance. The diagram in Figure 5.1 presents ways that different types of information may be incorporated into cycles of an action research process.

FRAMEWORKS FOR ENRICHING THE ANALYSIS

When people engage the significant issues embedded in long-standing or highly contentious problems, they sometimes need to engage in extensive research to identify the underlying issues involved in the situation. Frameworks of analysis that enable them to delve beneath the surface of events can provide rich understandings that enable them to make sense of the situation and deal effectively with the complex problems that often are part of their experience. Four alternative approaches or frameworks that assist stakeholders in this process of sense making and clarification are presented in the following sections: interpretive questions, organizational review, concept mapping, and problem analysis. Larger or complex projects may require more extended and detailed frameworks, such as those found in the literature on management, planning, community development, or applied anthropology (e.g., Black, 1991; Van Willigen, 1993; Whyte, 1984).

Alternative 1: Interpretive Questions—Why, What, How, Who, Where, When

For relatively simple projects, participants might work through a series of questions that enable them to extend their understanding of the problems and contexts they have previously described. Interpretive statements that result from this process should help them develop accounts that reveal the nature of the problem at hand and important features of the context that sustain it. Interpretive questions might include the following:

- Why are we meeting? (purpose, focus, problem)
- What are the key elements and features of the problem?
- How is the problem affecting us? What is happening?

- Who is being affected?
- Where are they being affected?
- When are they being affected?

It may be useful for the facilitator to repeat each of these questions a number of times to enable participants to build more information into their interpretations.

More complex projects may require more detailed and extended questioning strategies to reveal such elements as the following:

- The history of the situation—how it came about
- The individuals, groups, and types of actors involved
- Interactions and relationships among the people involved
- The purposes and intents of the people involved
- The sequence and duration of related events and activities
- The attitudes and values of the people involved
- The availability of and access to resources and their use

The following types of questions may be relevant:

- Why?
  - Why are we studying this issue?
  - Why is it significant?
  - To whom is it significant?
  - What do we hope to achieve?

- What?
  - What major activities, events, or issues are relevant to the problem?
  - What is each person or group doing or not doing?
  - What are their interests and concerns?
  - What are their purposes? What do they want to achieve? What do they want to happen?
  - What do they value?
  - What resources are available? (people, material, equipment, space, time, funds)
  - What resources are being used? By whom?

- How?
  - How do acts, activities, and events happen?
  - How are decisions made?

– How are resources used?

– How are individuals or groups related to each other?

– How do individuals and groups affect the situation?

– How much influence do they have?

- Who?

  – Who is centrally involved? (individuals, groups)

  – Who else is significant?

  – Who are the influential people? What is the nature of their influence?

  – Who is linked to whom? In what ways?

  – Who is friendly or cooperative? With whom?

  – Who is antagonistic or uncooperative? With whom?

  – Who has resources? Which ones?

- Where?

  – Where do people live, meet, work, and interact?

  – Where are resources located?

  – Where do activities and events happen?

- When?

  – When do things happen?

  – When are resources available?

  – When do people meet, work, and engage in activities?

  – When does the problem occur?

  – What is the duration of occurrences of the problem?

Not all these questions will be relevant to any one situation. The questions the facilitator selects will depend on the context of the problem and the setting. The researcher should record in detail answers to the questions and should write a summary on a chart that can be seen by all members of the group. Such charts help participants visualize the situation they are interpreting and provide records that can be employed in subsequent activities.

Alternative 2: Organizational Review

In some circumstances—where, for instance, different sections of the same institution or agency experience similar problems—it may be appropriate for the researcher to conduct a review of the whole organization. This activity is intended to reveal different interpretations of problematic features of the organization and sources of the problems. It is intended not as an evaluation of competence or assessment of performance but as a method for discovering points where action can be taken. Participants in the review process should focus on the following features of the organization:

Vision and Mission

- *Vision.* What is the overarching or general purpose of the organization? Education? Health improvement? Assistance for the needy?
- *Mission.* In which ways does the organization seek to enact its vision? Providing educational services, courses, and classes? Engaging in health promotion programs? Providing welfare services?

Goals and Objectives

- *Goals.* How does the organization seek to achieve its purposes? In what activities does it engage?
- *Objectives.* What are the desired outcomes of these activities? For whom?

Structure of the Organization

- *Roles.* Are roles clearly delineated? Who works with whom? Who has authority over whom? Who supervises and gives directions? To whom?
- *Responsibilities.* What types of people are responsible for which activities? Who performs which types of tasks?
- *Rules and procedures.* Is it clear what needs to be done and how it is to be done?
- *Resources.* Are the resources required for tasks adequate and available (e.g., time, materials, skills)?

Operation

- Is each person clear about his or her roles and responsibilities?
- How effectively is each person enacting his or her roles and responsibilities?

- What factors hinder the enactment of those responsibilities (e.g., lack of materials, time, skills, or support)?
- Are there tasks and responsibilities to which no one is clearly assigned?
- What is not happening that should be? What is happening that should not be? Where are the gaps? Where are the barriers?

Problems, Issues, and Concerns

- What problems, issues, and concerns are expressed by stakeholders?
- Who is associated with each?
- How do stakeholders explain or interpret problems, issues, and concerns?

As participants work through these issues, they will extend their understanding of the organization and aspects of its operation relevant to their problems, issues, and concerns. The outcomes of their inquiries should be recorded in detail and summarized on charts for use in later stages of the research process.

I once worked as a consultant with a community child care agency whose mandate was to find appropriate foster homes for children and to ensure that the foster families were adequately supported. The agency was experiencing a number of difficulties in performing these functions. Staff members were stressed and overworked, and funding sources questioned the effectiveness of the agency's services. When we charted the purposes for which the agency had been formed and matched those against its actual activities, we discovered that staff were engaged in work of peripheral relevance to the agency's stated main function. They were attempting to provide a wide range of support services to foster families—furniture, clothing, food, and counseling—that could be provided by other agencies funded for those purposes. When they saw what was happening, staff and committee members decided to terminate many of those activities and to link clients to other relevant agencies when such needs arose.

Alternative 3: Concept Mapping

Long-term, entrenched problems frequently defy the remedial efforts of professional practitioners. Occurrences of drug abuse, eating disorders, lack of interest in schoolwork, youth crime, and other problems are so pervasive that they often appear beyond the reach of ordinary programs and services. They exist as part of a complex system of interwoven events and circumstances deeply embedded in the social fabric of the community.

Attempts to remediate these problems are unlikely to be successful if they focus merely on one aspect of the interrelated factors that make up the situation. Quick-fix, "spray-on" solutions rarely work. Participants need to reconceptualize such issues in ways that clearly identify the interrelationships among all the significant elements that affect the situation. The intent of this type of activity is to help participants find a way to pursue multiple holistic and inclusive strategies that assist people in dealing with the problems that affect their lives.

In the first phase of the research process, delineated in Chapter 4, participants describe the problem and define key elements or characteristics of the situation. In concept mapping, those elements are plotted diagrammatically, so that participants can visualize the ways in which components of the situation relate to the problems they are investigating. To guide participants in formulating a concept map, the facilitator should take the following steps:

- Begin by printing on a large piece of paper or a board visible to all participants a word or phrase that characterizes the central problem, and then enclose the word or phrase inside a geometric figure (e.g., a square or circle).
- Add to the chart other geometric figures labeled to represent elements associated with the problem.
- Link the figures containing the elements that seem to be related to each other.
- Extend the mapping process to include additional figures until each participant is satisfied that all significant elements have been included.

An example of a concept map is provided in Figure 5.2. This interpretation of poor school behavior of youth in a rural town is ascribed by stakeholders to a number of interlinked factors—poor attendance, low academic attainment, general family issues, parent issues, financial problems, and poor health. All issues are seen to contribute to the identified behavior problem and need to be addressed as part of the process of defining a solution to the problem of poor school behavior. Further analysis may have extended this map to delineate factors associated with health problems, financial problems, and so on. Financial problems, for instance, may be associated with high unemployment in the town, which in turn may relate to closure of businesses or other economic conditions.

Figure 5.2   Concept Map of Poor School Behavior

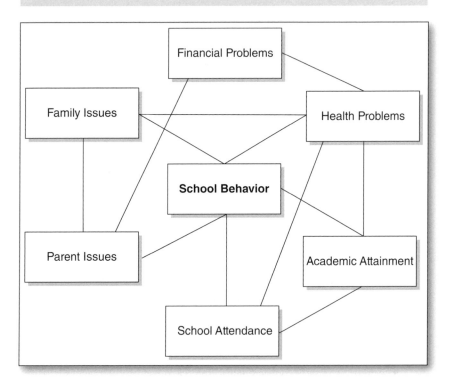

Concept maps help participants visualize the major influences that need to be taken into account and assist them in evaluating whether all relevant stakeholders have been included in the investigation. In Figure 5.2, the appearance of family issues signals the need to involve relevant family members in the inquiry process. The young people who are themselves the focus of the problem should be central to the concept-mapping process. Incorporating additional stakeholders in turn may extend the factors incorporated into the map and thus the elements that need to be considered when action is planned. Activities from other interpretive frameworks (e.g., interpretive questions) can be used to further expand this form of analysis.[1]

The explanatory frameworks produced in this process are not meant to be scientifically or professionally defensible. We are looking not for the best or the correct explanation but for one that makes sense to or can be accommodated by all the stakeholders. In all the processes described earlier, it is essential that each stakeholding group provide input about its own situation. Analyses based on other people's interpretations do not provide an appropriate basis for action. In Figure 5.2, for instance, teacher or administrator perspectives on the family are less relevant than the perspectives of the family members themselves. Outsider interpretations often are incomplete or inaccurate and are sometimes judgmental; they may tend to create divisiveness and hostility, which are antithetical to the participatory principles of action research.

Alternative 4: Problem Analysis—Antecedents and Consequences

An approach similar to concept mapping enables participants to identify the antecedents of existing problems (i.e., elements of the situation that led up to the problems) and the consequences that derive from those problems. In this process, the facilitator should have each stakeholder group identify the following elements and describe them on a chart:

- The core problem
- Major antecedents to the problem
- Other significant factors related to those antecedents
- Major negative consequences
- Other significant consequences

A committee of agency workers and community representatives investigated the high incidence of juvenile crime in a small country town. A process of exploration revealed that criminal activity appeared to be related to the lack of leisure activities for teenagers and to poor school attendance. No one in town accepted responsibility for organizing activities, there were few facilities available for that purpose, and the school provided little in the way of afterschool programs or activities. Poor school attendance was directly related to poor school performance, uninteresting or irrelevant curricula, and family poverty.

As a result of increases in juvenile crime, burglary, petty theft, and vandalism, there was a general increase in alienation of some groups of young people from other sectors of the community. There were increasing incidents of conflict between youth and members of the community, businesspeople, law enforcement personnel, teachers, and so on and deterioration in employment opportunities for young people.

(Continued)

(Continued)

The long-term prospects of some youth also seemed likely to be affected by the negative outcomes of incarceration in prisons and other institutions and growing criminal records. This situation is drawn as a concept map in Figure 5.3.

Figure 5.3 Antecedents and Consequences of Juvenile Crime

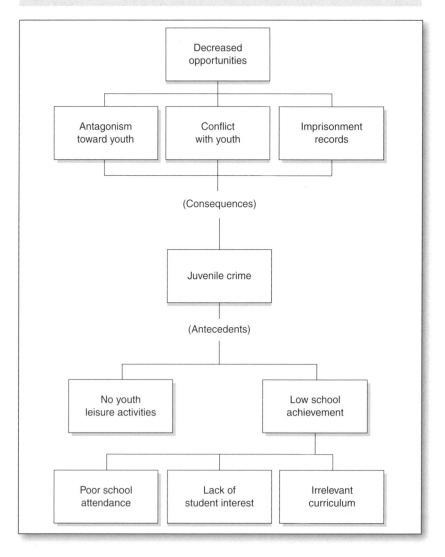

WRITING REPORTS COLLABORATIVELY

Researchers commonly work independently to analyze data and formulate reports on the basis of their own interpretive lenses. In the process they tend to lose the interpretive perspective of other participants and to fashion a report that often fails to adequately represent the perspective of those with whom they work. The following procedures provide the means to engage stakeholding groups in the processes of analysis, thus ensuring that the end result integrates their perspectives and priorities. Research facilitators help participants engage in meaning-making discussion and dialogue—hermeneutic dialectic processes—with the intent of developing mutually acceptable accounts of the issues and problems they are investigating. To facilitate these processes, researchers assist selected participants with organizing meetings, setting an agenda, reviewing descriptive accounts, and analyzing information and developing accounts and reports.

Organizing Meetings

Research facilitators work with key stakeholders to organize meetings (see Chapter 4). Members of the principal stakeholding group, for whom the problem or issue is most central, should have a key role in the organization of meetings. These members should ensure that representatives who can speak for each of the stakeholding groups are able to attend.

Procedures for Analysis

Setting the Agenda

In this phase of the process, participants learn something about the people involved, the purpose of meeting, and the activities in which they will be engaged. The facilitator's role includes the following duties:

- Inform people of the purpose of the meeting.
- Provide an opportunity for participants to introduce themselves and identify the groups to which they belong.
- Present a broad agenda for the session.
- Allow time for participants to discuss, clarify, and modify the agenda. Do not discuss the issues at this time but focus on the processes of the meeting.

Reviewing Descriptive Information

The purpose of this activity is to give participants a chance to review the descriptive information produced in previous meetings. This is especially important when stakeholding groups have done some initial work separately. Facilitators should provide opportunities for each stakeholding group to do the following:

- Send written versions of the descriptive accounts or give them to participants prior to the meeting.
- Present a verbal report that summarizes descriptive information produced by their previous activities.
- Present the key elements of these reports on a chart.
- Allow time for meeting participants to discuss and clarify the accounts, avoiding extended or detailed discussion unless there are contentious issues that need to be resolved.

Distilling the Information: Analysis

Using one of the processes for data analysis presented earlier, participants should work collectively to organize the information in the charted summaries into sets of categories. They should identify converging perspectives (i.e., those ideas, concepts, or elements common to all or a number of groups) and diverging perspectives (i.e., those ideas, concepts, or elements found in the accounts of only one or a few groups). Because this activity is time consuming, it may sometimes be appropriate to formulate a working party to carry it out.

- Participants should select elements from the charts that are perceived to be significant features or characteristics of the issue investigated.
- Participants should sort elements into categories, so that those associated in some significant way are clustered together. The idea is to rationalize the large number of individual ideas, accounts, or issues to create a smaller number of categories. In doing so, facilitators should ensure that the process of categorizing does not erase important information. A category labeled *youth issues,* for instance, might erase important distinctions between early and late teens or between males and females. Decisions about ideas that can be incorporated into

particular categories and those that must remain separate should be made through discussion and negotiation.

- Participants may organize categories in a variety of ways. A color-coding system may be used, for example, wherein similar items are identified on charts with colored markers. Alternatively, each idea, issue, or concept may be copied onto a card, and the cards can then be sorted into piles according to their similarities or common characteristics. Groups may also use large-sized self-adhesive labels, placing all elements on a large wall and allowing participants to move them around into groups associated together. Participants should know that there is no right way or correct answer for this process. The way they organize the information is the way that makes the best sense to them collectively.
- When participants have reached agreement on the categories and the information contained in each, they should classify each group of concepts according to a label or term that both identifies and describes the category. This process is represented symbolically in Figure 5.4.

Constructing Reports

The previously described process provides material that forms the basis for reports and identifies actions to be taken by participants. Research facilitators should continue to meet with participating stakeholders—a working group to formulate a report. The working group should

- Review materials
- Use the category system developed during analysis as a framework for writing a report
- Use the outline to write a detailed written report (Detailed records from meetings should provide the content of the report; see sections on reporting in previous chapters and in Chapter 8.)
- Provide the time and opportunity for all members of the working group to read the report and give feedback
- Modify the report on the basis of their comments
- Meet again with the working party if any members suggest significant revisions
- Distribute the report to all stakeholders

Figure 5.4   Example: Issues Derived From Categorized Information

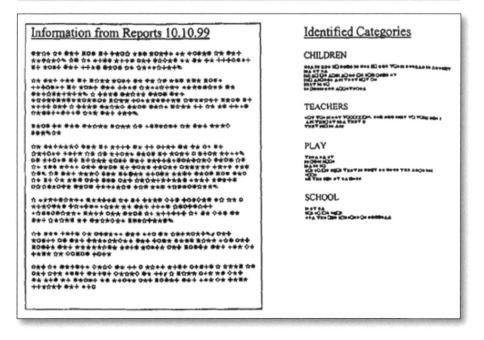

Participatory Visual Methods: Presentations and Performances

In his book *Interpretive Ethnography,* Denzin (1997) signals the need for forms of reporting that more clearly represent people's lived experience. Current formats tend to render people's lives in forms that are stiff, formalistic, and often encompassed in technical language. They silence the voices of the people to whom they refer and mask the realities of their day-to-day lives. Denzin suggests the need for reports that are more evocative, enabling readers to more readily understand people's experiences. Such reports would be open-ended, multifaceted, and multivoiced and would not indulge in abstract terminology or privilege the perspective of persons in positions of authority. Thus he suggests the need for reports that experiment with genre, voice, and narrative style, so that official reports may take on the appearance of writing more usually associated with fiction or poetry.

He extends this argument to suggest that such writing may be envisaged as *texts waiting to be staged.* That is, people may be better able to represent their ideas and experiences through performances than through written reports. Thus it may be possible to present the outcomes of a research process through the following types of performance:

- Drama
- Role plays
- Simulation
- Dance
- Song
- Poetry
- Works of art
- A combination of the above

This move to performance is especially important in action research because participants often include people whose feelings of well-being are diminished by the intrusion of formalistic texts. Researchers need to find ways of communicating that do not disempower groups of participants.

A researcher once showed me a report she had written for a government agency that presented an Aboriginal community's account of a research process in which they had engaged. I asked her how many people in the community had read the report, and she admitted that few would wish or be able to read what was a rather thick and formal report. "How," I asked her, "will people get to know about the information in the report?" Her first impulse was to write another version of the report, but I suggested she think of a concert. This would enable different groups to present their perspectives in ways that were more in keeping with the life of the community. Thus people could choose to use song, dance, drama, poetry, humor, role plays, or other forms of presentation to get their message across.

Creative approaches to presentation likewise provide the means for participants to present the outcome of their inquiries to a variety of audiences. Presentations can take a variety of forms, including discussion and workshop formats that enable research participants to engage their audience in dialogue that enables them to more clearly understand that which is presented. Presentations may be enhanced by use of the following types of visual materials:

- Charts
- Posters
- Photographs
- Booklets
- Summary reports

Modern technology opens up possibilities for communication that were not available in the past. Groups may choose, for instance, to use carefully scripted video presentations to present information in their own voice and in their own way (Schouten & Watling, 1997). This form of presentation provides many dramatic and effective possibilities for communicating the outcomes of a research process.

I recently participated in a departmental review process whereby each of the units of the department reported on their activities for the year. The administration section staff, largely younger women, were somewhat shy and loath to present personally, so they produced a video. Taped in their offices, in a swimming pool, and in the garden, all members of the administrative staff reported on their activities. Their presentations were often touched with humor, as was the case of one woman who would speak to the camera only through a hole in a paper bag over her head. The video presentation was engaging and informative and provided other staff with a clear understanding of the work in which administrative staff were engaged and the issues that confronted them.

There are contexts and purposes, therefore, that may be better served by more creative thinking about the best ways for communicating information to audiences of stakeholders. Although formal written reports may be useful in some contexts, it is possible that more innovative uses of narrative texts, staged performances, or electronic productions may enhance the work in which we are engaged. Researchers need to keep the audience and the purpose clearly in mind as we formulate ways to communicate effectively the outcomes of our research processes.

CONCLUSION

The processes of analysis in this chapter provide the means by which people can rethink an issue and formulate clear, sophisticated, useful explanations and interpretations of situations. The specific ideas and concepts contained within these interpretive frameworks provide the basis for planning concrete actions to remedy the problems on which the research has focused.

For complex problems involving multiple stakeholder groups, the activities described in this chapter may be enacted as separate parts of an action research process. For simpler problems within discrete settings, such as classrooms, offices, and small organizations, they may be incorporated into processes that move more rapidly from description, through interpretation, to problem solving. It is well to keep the distinction between these activities in mind, however, to ensure that people are clear about the nature and purpose of the processes in which they are engaged.

As presented here, the procedures may seem long-winded and complex, but experience will show researchers when and how to consolidate or abbreviate them to ensure a brisk, purposeful flow of activity. Researchers should be wary, however, of simplifying the research process by confining it to a small inner circle or by omitting "troublesome" stakeholders. Participation boosts personal investment in the process, extends people's understanding of the contexts and social processes in which they are involved, and minimizes the possibility that the research will bog down in conflict. Action research is not just a tool for solving problems but a valuable resource for building a sense of community.

REFLECTION AND ACTION

Using the field notes gathered in interviews for previous activities,

1. Analyze the information using a coding and categorizing process. (If you have extensive notes, you may focus on one issue that emerged within the interview.)

2. Present the resulting framework of key features and elements to a friend, colleague, or working group.

3. Explain how that framework enables you to provide an account of the person you interviewed.

4. Reflect on and discuss the process of analysis. What did it feel like? What are some of your concerns or questions about the process? How was it informative or helpful?

5. Repeat that process using the technique for analyzing key experiences.

6. Reflect on and discuss that process. How were the outcomes of the two processes different?

7. Using features and elements from one of the frameworks, draw a concept map. Use one issue as the central element of the map.

8. Using features and elements from each framework, present short reports to your friend, colleague, or classmate.

9. Reflect on your presentations. Are there more effective ways you might have presented that information using some of the techniques suggested in the Presentations and Performances section?

10. Analyze the notes from your observations, using a coding and categorizing process. Write a short report about that setting.

NOTE

1. Deshler (1990) provides a more extensive treatment of concept mapping.

Box 5.1   Think: Reflecting and Analyzing

Purpose

To use interpretive processes to distill the information gathered, identify key features and elements of people's experience, and enable participants to understand more clearly the way the issue affects their lives and activities.

Process

Frameworks for Analysis and Interpretation

Categorizing and Coding

    Review and unitize the data.
    Formulate categories and code them.

Identify themes across the categories.
Organize a category system.
Develop a report framework using the category system.

Analyzing Key Experiences

Review the data and identify key experiences.
Identify main features and elements of each experience.
Identify major themes across experiences.
Organize a report framework using features and elements.

Enriching Analysis Using Frameworks for Interpretation

Interpretive questions: why, what, how, who, where, when
Organizational review: vision, mission, structure, operation, problems
Concept mapping: issue, concepts/influences, links
Problem analysis: problem, antecedents, consequences

Writing Reports Collaboratively

Organizing meetings
Procedures for analysis
Setting the agenda
Reviewing information
Distilling information—analysis
Constructing reports

Presentations and Performances

Use drama, song, dance, art, or poetry for effective presentations.
Use visuals to enhance presentations: photographs, charts, videos, slides.

6

ACT

Action Plans—Implementing Sustainable Solutions

CONSTRUCTING ACTION PLANS

Chapter 5 described how analysis enables participants to identify the problematic features and elements of the issue on which research is focused. In the next phase of action research, participants work creatively to formulate actions that lead to a resolution of the problem(s). What can we do, they should ask, that will enable us to achieve better results or a more positive outcome? What steps can we take to ensure that we accomplish the outcomes we desire? Elements and categories that have emerged from the interpretive processes described in the previous chapter suggest key areas or aspects of the situation that need to be dealt with in any plan for taking action. Participants then identify *what* they will do to gain a more positive outcome and *how* they will go about the tasks required.

Action plans often can be incorporated into the regular operations of organizational life, so that practitioners may work with students, clients, customers, or colleagues to devise lesson plans, care plans, case management plans, marketing plans, urban renewal plans, and so on. This chapter therefore presents systematic ways of planning and implementing the action plans that distinguish action research from other approaches to inquiry.

I've seen superb results achieved through action research processes. In classrooms I've seen students, previously unengaged and uninspired, excitedly and animatedly focusing on their work. I've seen teachers, exasperated with the apparently inflexible nature of their context, find concrete and productive ways of reframing their classroom activities. In one school a single interview was sufficient to provide a teacher with the time to run quickly through a Look, Think, Act routine, a quite unintended but palpably productive process. She described the situation, subjected it to analysis, and formulated solutions almost instantaneously.

"Dr. Stringer, I don't know what I can do about parent-teacher conferences. We only have 10 minutes with the parents for each child, and that's only time to go through the report, and time's almost up. We can't really engage in any decent conversation about the child's progress or any problems we're experiencing." [Look] As she extrapolated on these comments she started to explore the issue further. "It's very frustrating, because parents can really be a great help when they work with us. What I really need to do is to spend time explaining how I set up lessons, what I'm trying to achieve with their child, and the problems they are having. They'd then understand what's happening and might be able to help their child do what needs to be done to improve their work." [Think] She then started to think of ways that she could achieve these purposes. "You know it's impossible to do all that in the time available. What I could do is to meet with groups of parents and explain my teaching processes and problems that their children experience. We could then talk about how parents could do some things to assist with this or provide their children with specific ways of helping them. We wouldn't need to . . . " She then explored a number of ideas related to this and left, bubbling with excitement and enthusiasm. [Act] Although I left that city shortly after, I heard later that she and other teachers had instituted a number of ways to improve parent-teacher conferences and that the process had proved so productive that the school had allocated more time to these activities.

Although all problems are not as easily resolved, it now never surprises me when people are able to see how to modify and adapt their activities and come up with effective solutions to the problems they are experiencing. The process of action research has, for me, high levels of success.

People often assume that a professional analysis provides the best way of envisioning a problem and that all that is then needed is to provide a "recipe" or prescription that people can follow. The problem with generalized recipe-like solutions is that they fail to take account of the underlying issues that have made the experience problematic for participants in the first place. Recipe-based solutions often are based on the professional expertise of the practitioner and fail to take account of the deep understandings that people have of their own experience and the underlying issues that are a central part of the problem. Professional knowledge can only ever be a partial and incomplete analysis of the situation and needs to complement and be complemented by the knowledge inherent in participant perspectives. This is especially true in situations where practitioners interact with people whose personal history, culture, or social background are markedly different from their own.

Participants, especially the primary stakeholders whose issues are the central focus of the research, participate in planning to systematically devise the tasks and activities that will enable them to achieve a resolution to the issues at the heart of the action research process. The following procedures are based on a framework of action that involves three phases:

- Planning, which involves setting priorities and defining tasks
- Implementing activities that help participants accomplish their tasks
- Reviewing, in which participants evaluate their progress

PLANNING

In the planning phase, research facilitators meet with major stakeholders to devise actions to be taken. As stakeholders devise a course of action that "makes sense" to them and engage in activities that they see as purposeful and productive, they are likely to invest considerable time and energy in research activities, developing a sense of ownership that maximizes the likelihood of success.

Identifying Priorities for Action

Sometimes the results of analysis identify a single issue needing attention, and research participants may formulate a plan immediately. Often, however, there are multiple related issues requiring action, so participants will need to make decisions about the issue on which they will first focus and some order of priority for other issues.

To accomplish this, participants should

- Identify the major issue(s) on which their investigation focused
- Review other concerns and issues that emerged from their analysis
- Organize the issues in order of importance

- Rate the issues according to degree of difficulty (it is often best to commence with activities that are likely to be successful)
- Choose the issue(s) they will work on first
- Rank the rest in order of priority for action

Constructing Action Plans

Participants then plan a series of steps or tasks that will enable them to achieve a resolution of the issue(s) investigated. Each issue is first restated as a goal. For example, the issue of increasing juvenile crime might be restated as a goal: "to decrease juvenile crime." The features and elements related to this issue, revealed through the processes of analysis, are restated as objectives. The analysis of juvenile crime depicted in Figure 5.3 (in Chapter 5), for instance, suggests that features related to increased juvenile crime include "lack of youth leisure activities," "poor school attendance," and "lack of after-school programs." These could be stated as a set of objectives: "to develop youth leisure activities," "to improve youth school attendance," and "to organize afterschool programs." Teams of relevant stakeholders should develop a plan for each issue and bring them to plenary sessions for discussion, modification (if necessary), and endorsement.

A related set of outcome statements provides the means for evaluating the success of the planned activities. Such outcome statements describe the outcomes more clearly—using the previously mentioned objectives, for example, results in outcome statements that answer how many leisure activities have been organized, how well attended they were, and within what time line they occurred; the specific extent to which school attendance is to be improved; and what type of afterschool programs were there, with what attendance, within what time line.

It is essential that each planning group include a member from each of the major stakeholding groups. The issue of poor school attendance, for instance, should have a team that includes teachers, youth, school administrators, and parents. A simple six-question framework—why, what, how, who, where, and when—provides the basis for planning:

- *Goal (Why)*

   State the purpose of the project—for example, to combat juvenile crime. (This can be defined as a goal statement that describes the broad issue to be addressed.)

- *Objective (What)*

  State what actions are to be taken as a set of objectives—for example, to organize an afterschool program for teenagers and to develop a youth center.

- *Tasks (How)*

  Define a sequence of tasks and activities for each objective. List them step by step.

- *Persons (Who)*

  List those responsible for each task and activity.

- *Place (Where)*

  State where the tasks will be done.

- *Time line (When)*

  State when work on each task should commence and when it should be completed.

- *Resources*

  List resources required to accomplish the tasks. Include funds needed to pay for materials or services or list these separately.

Action plans should be recorded on a chart or whiteboard so that people can get a clear picture of how they will achieve their goal(s) (see Figure 6.1). They provide a concrete vision of the active community of which they are a part and enable participants to check on their progress as they work through the stages of the project together. Once planning is completed, participants can check that each issue has an action plan and that each person is clear about his or her responsibilities. They can also check the availability of material and human resources required for the tasks they must complete.

Outcome Statements

Outcome statements describe what will be achieved—the end result of the activities delineated in the plan. Where objective statements present a list of intentions, outcome statements describe what is actually going to be done. The following examples map out the outcomes for the youth center and afterschool program plans that emerged as actions to be taken to decrease youth crime (see Figure 6.1).

Figure 6.1 An Action Plan

| | Goal (Why): What are we trying to achieve? | | | | | | |
| | To decrease youth crime by providing an afterschool program of activities | | | | | | |
Objective What	Tasks How	Person(s) Who	Start When	Finish When	Location Where	Resources	Funds
1. Establish a youth center.	a. Obtain permission to use old school building. b. Repair and renovate. c. Plan organization of sports center.	Mrs. Farole Parent volunteers Students volunteers	3/4/08	6/2/08	Disused school building	Paint Timber Tools	$15,000 School district Village council Government grant
2. Establish an afterschool program.	a. Establish an art program. b. Establish a sports program. c. Establish a tutoring program.	Mr. Baldwin Jose Marina Venus	4/1/08	7/3/08	Sports center	Art materials Sports equipment	$3,500 School district Fees

Youth Center Outcomes

By June 2, 2008, the Youth Center team will have

- Obtained permission from the principal and the school board to use the disused independent classroom for a youth center
- Completed repairs to flooring and repainted the classroom
- Formulated a plan for the operation of the youth center as a venue for afterschool activities

Afterschool Program Outcomes

By July 3, 2008, the afterschool program team will have

- Established an art program
- Identified and engaged a volunteer to run the program
- Planned the program
- Obtained relevant supplies and materials
- Prepared and delivered promotional materials to the school, local youth clubs, sports clubs, and churches
- Ensured an adequate supply of furnishings

A similar set of outcome statements would apply to the other elements of the afterschool program.

Action planning can be an energizing process for those involved. In my recent work in East Timor I was heartened by the sense of excitement and anticipation that resulted from the development of action plans. In a Parent Teacher Association (PTA) workshop in one school, I watched the interest building as parents worked in small groups to identify activities in which they could engage to assist in improving the work of the local school. Their interest grew to excitement at the planning session, their faces glowing with anticipation as the plans emerged, so that they could clearly see the step-by-step processes through which they could accomplish their goals.

A group of tough-looking farmers, having decided they would build a small "fish pond (farm)" to raise money for the school, grew quite animated as they formulated their action plan with the assistance of a facilitator:

"What do you want to do?"

"We want to build a fish farm."

"How will you do this?"

"We need to find some land to build the fish farm."

"How can you get land?"

"I know someone who will donate the land."

"What will you do next?"

"We must build the dikes to hold the water."

"Who will do that?"

"We can do that ourselves."

"What else will you need to do?"

"We need a net to cover the pond so the birds won't get the fish."

... and so on.

After the facilitators had recorded all the information, they drew an action planning framework on a chart taped to the chalkboard and inserted details. Missing elements led to more questions that resulted in a complete plan for the development of the fish pond. The sense of pride and accomplishment among men in the group was evident, for here they could see clearly how to put their ideas into practice—a great sense of empowerment.

I have a photograph that shows the men standing by their pond some months later, proudly showing visitors the completed project. They are clearly invested in the school, and I've heard that they have been able to sell fish in the local market to provide funds for materials needed to assist in the reconstruction of the classrooms that had so cruelly been burned by the previous occupying military.

Quality Check

The heart of action research is not the techniques and procedures that guide action but the sense of unity that holds people to a collective vision of their world and inspires them to work together for the common good. The planning processes detailed earlier provide a clear set of tasks and activities, but they are not complete until these activities are checked against a set of principles. The essence of this part of the planning process is not only to check that the tasks have been described adequately but to ensure that each of the participants is aware of the need to perform them in ways consonant with community-based processes.

Each participant should have the opportunity to discuss his or her tasks and activities, so that all describe what they will do and the way in which they will go about doing it. Facilitators should assist this process by having participants check their activities against the criteria for the well-being of the people (see Chapter 1). Each person should be sure that his or her tasks and activities are enacted in ways that will enhance other people's feelings of

- *Pride.* Feelings of self-worth (Will these activities enhance people's images of themselves?)
- *Dignity.* Feelings of autonomy, independence, and competence (Are we doing something for people instead of enabling them to do it, either by themselves or with our assistance?)
- *Identity.* Affirmation of individuals' social identities (Are the right people performing the tasks? Are women, for instance, performing tasks related to women's issues?)
- *Control.* Feelings of control over resources, decisions, actions, events, and activities (Can people perform the tasks in their own way?)
- *Responsibility.* People's accounting for their own actions (Are we trusting them to perform the tasks in ways that make sense to them?)
- *Unity.* The solidarity of groups of which people are members (Do they have to alienate themselves from their group to perform the tasks?)
- *Place.* Places where people feel at ease (Can they do the tasks in their own places?)
- *Location.* Locales to which people have historical, cultural, or social ties (Do we need to relocate some of our activities?)

Facilitators also need to have people check whether their activities are consonant with the set of principles outlined in Chapter 1, which focuses on

- *Relationships.* Are processes encouraging productive working relationships between people?
- *Communication.* Are regular times for sharing information included in plans?
- *Participation.* Do major stakeholders engage in tasks set in the plans?
- *Inclusion.* Are all major stakeholders included in the plan?

The time and energy spent on this quality check constitutes a sound investment of personal resources, as it is likely to minimize delays and blockages by ensuring that all stakeholders are acknowledged and respected. The participatory and inclusive relationships enacted in action research provide the benefit of a harmonious, supportive, and energizing environment that is not only personally rewarding but also practically productive.

IMPLEMENTING

Collaborative processes often start with a flourish. Much enthusiasm and energy are generated as plans are articulated and people set off to perform their designated tasks. The best of intentions, however, often run up against the cold, hard realities of daily life. Participants in the research process reenter family, work, and community contexts, where responsibilities and crises crowd out new activities. As participants attempt to implement the tasks that have been set, research facilitators should provide the emotional and organizational support they need to keep them on track and to maintain their energy, model sound community-based processes, and link the participants to a supportive network.

Supporting

In the early stages of activity, people often find themselves, to some extent, out on a limb. If the preliminary work has included all people affected by the research process—the stakeholders—then the performance of new tasks or different approaches to routine tasks will usually proceed with few impediments. Even so, people usually take risks when they change their usual routines and processes, and sometimes they experience criticism and disapproval. In addition, the best of plans cannot take all contingencies into account, and performing new tasks may turn out to be much more difficult than people had anticipated. To a greater or lesser extent, they will experience feelings of doubt, threat, or anxiety that impede their ability to continue with research activities.

In these circumstances, the press of continual work and life demands can easily lead to delayed or neglected research tasks. The main job of the research facilitator is to provide the practical support that will enable people to continue their research activities. Support can be provided in many ways, some of which are described briefly in the following paragraphs.

Communication

Facilitators should communicate with each participant regularly and organize simple ways in which participants with similar or related tasks can communicate. Such interactions may take the form of prearranged regular visits, telephone calls, arrangements for emergency contact, and informal social contacts—meeting for lunch, a beer after work, and so on. It is important that each person be linked with others so that participants can discuss their problems, celebrate accomplishments, maintain focus, and sustain their sense of identity with the research project.

I once assisted a group of community development workers in forming a support network for themselves after they had attended a planning conference. Because they were located in communities many hundreds of miles apart, opportunities for interaction were limited. I arranged a regular telephone conference call in which they could discuss issues, share ideas, and generally "unload." Later, each of them commented on how important that contact was. It lessened their feelings of isolation and enabled them to stay on track when other agendas and problems threatened to divert their energies.

I have also encouraged other groups to develop small support networks that can meet easily on a regular basis. Meeting for coffee, during lunch breaks, or for dinners, these groups can provide a relaxing and safe environment in which the members can talk through their problems and gain emotional support as they do so.

Personal Nurturing

As people work through their assigned tasks, their worlds are often changed in some fundamental way. They sometimes gain a deeper understanding of themselves, their need to trust both their own judgment and that of those around them, and the extent of the risks they are taking. In such circumstances, people often need personal reassurance and affirmations of their competence and worth. Facilitators should be constantly sensitive to the need to provide affirming comments to people engaged in research activities, not in a patronizing or mechanical way but authentically and specifically.

I recently asked a young teacher to speak to a university class about the work she was doing in her classroom. At first she hesitated, recommending that instead I ask another person who is an "expert" in the field. "Amy," I said, "I've heard you talk about your work and really like the ideas you have and the way you link them to the practical, daily realities of teaching. I think you would be much better for the job than an 'expert' who may have many good ideas but can't make the direct links you can. In addition, the young women in the class will be able to identify directly with you, because you are like them in many ways." Not only did she agree to speak to the class, but she also provided an excellent presentation that was applauded by the class.

Reflection and Analysis

Visits and conversations provide researchers with opportunities to ask questions that can help participants performing tasks describe and reflect on their activities. Such questions may touch on some of the following areas:

- *Relationships.* How have people responded to this (new) activity? Are they supportive? Has anyone caused any problems for you?
- *Patterns of work and organization.* Can you combine your activities with your work? Does this cause any problems? Do your tasks conflict with other people's ways of working?
- *Communication.* Who have you talked with about your tasks or activities? Have you talked with your supervisor, manager, or administrator? Your fellow workers, teachers, or clients? What have their responses been? Who would be useful to talk with from time to time? Who can support you?
- *Difficulties and solutions.* Are you having any problems? Have you overcome them?
- *Progress.* How are things working out for you? Have you made much progress? What have people been saying about your activities?

Facilitators should not judge the performance of the participants, even if asked to do so. There is a great difference between saying, "Things don't appear to be going very well" and asking, "How are things going for you?" Facilitators should encourage participants to review each aspect of their tasks, talking through the processes in which they are engaged and touching base on the principles. For example, "Who have you talked with about this? Will you be able to continue with this task? How are people responding to your activities?"

Assistance

When participants experience difficulties, research facilitators may need to provide assistance. They can assist directly with some activities, providing or seeking out information, doing small tasks, or acquiring needed materials. Research facilitators should not take over tasks but merely provide sufficient help to enable the participant to initiate or complete them successfully. Researchers need to develop the facility to do things *with* people and not *for* them; they need to be especially wary of the temptations that arise when working with others in areas in which the researchers have expertise. It is usually more important that the people involved develop the skills to maintain the process rather than just get the job done. When facilitators take over a job, they implicitly highlight the incompetence of other participants and disempower them in the process.

Conflict Resolution

Conflicts, whether minor disagreements or major arguments, are not uncommon in action research. The researcher who has maintained a relatively neutral stance in the research process can take the position of a disinterested party in a dispute. In these situations, the researcher's mediating role is to assist the parties in conflict in coming to a resolution that is satisfactory to everyone. The task is to manage the conflict so that all parties can describe their situations clearly, analyze the sources of conflict, and work toward a resolution that enables them to maintain positive working relationships.

Modeling

The ways in which research facilitators enact their supportive role provide direct cues to other participants regarding their own ways of working. Researchers' availability and the manner in which they provide assistance and support should implicitly demonstrate community-based processes. Their openness and authenticity should illustrate the difference between a community-based approach and a patriarchal, bureaucratic, controlling style of operation.

Mahatma Gandhi said, "Be the change you wish to see in others!"

As they work with other participants, research facilitators should ensure that their procedures and working styles enact the processes and principles of community-based research. Their conversations can describe their own and other people's activities, and they should find opportunities to give "gifts"—news, information, snacks, a telephone number, or a flower. As they describe their own activities, research facilitators provide information analytically that demonstrates ways in which people may reflect on their own work. For example,

> I've managed to help Mary find someone who can assist her with her project. They've already been able to. . . . She says that she's really starting to feel good about that and intends to. . . . She feels more comfortable now that she's able to talk with the other people in her office. Next time I see her, I'll . . .

Extended discussions provide opportunities for facilitators to pass on information but also to encourage people to reflect on their own activities. Modeling is one of the most powerful means of instituting the social processes inherent in community-based research. The doing is worth much more than the saying.

> I recently taught a successful graduate course called Community-Based Ethnography. Of all the student feedback I received, the most consistent comments related to the way in which I taught the course. One student noted, "The instructor not only teaches about community-based research; he does it."
>
> A member of a community in which I worked once criticized a consultant who had failed to live up to his expectations. "He can talk the talk," he said, "but he can't walk the walk."

Linking

A support network is a key ingredient in the success of a project. This is true not only for the research process itself but for each of the participants involved. As people plan their tasks and activities, they can nominate the people who are likely to support them and take steps to establish relationships with them. Participants will do much of this work themselves, but the facilitator's knowledge of the broader context will often enable him or her to link workers with other people sympathetic to their activities or who can provide important information or other resources. Linking participants to a supportive network provides them not only with emotional support but often with organizational and community support.

Linking participants in networks of support sometimes enables them to engage new people in research activities and extends the breadth and power of the research process itself. When people display interest, it may be appropriate to ask them if they would like to participate in activities or to help research workers perform their tasks. In this way, linking not only extends the support network for individual participants but generates the energy that sustains a community-building process.

As research facilitators assist other participants in developing supportive links, they should be wary of inserting themselves as permanent intermediaries in the linking process. When they continue to act as "middlemen," research facilitators inhibit the development of positive working relationships between participants and others with whom they work. They maintain control and increase their own power in the situation at the expense of those they are assisting. Figure 6.2 depicts a situation in which information transfer, discussion, or interaction cannot take place except through the research facilitator. A linking, supportive network, conversely, provides multiple opportunities for exchange, conversation, and consultation (see Figure 6.3).

REVIEWING

Participants should meet on a regular basis to review their progress. The plan should be displayed at these meetings, and stakeholders and each of the participants performing tasks should be given the opportunity to do the following:

- *Review* the plan (Focus question: Have you had any thoughts on our plan?)
- *Report* on progress (How are you doing with your tasks?)
- *Modify* sections of the plan, if necessary (Are you having any difficulties? Do we need to change our approach? Do we need to change the tasks you've been assigned?)
- *Celebrate* successes (What have we achieved?)

Figure 6.2   A Controlled Network

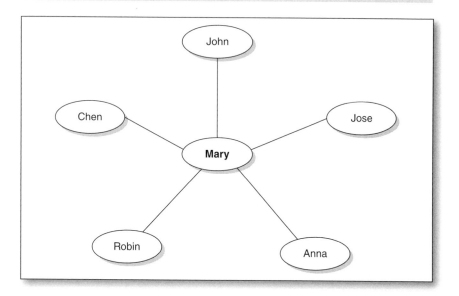

Figure 6.3   A Linking Network

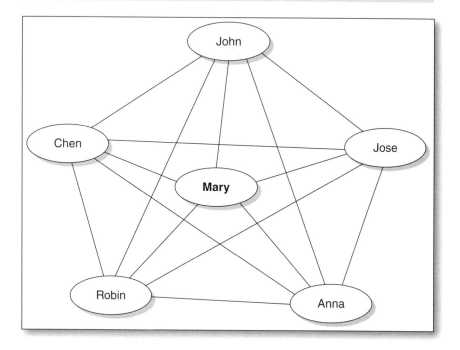

These activities motivate people by highlighting accomplishments or reassuring them if they have failed to make significant progress; in addition, they provide a context that reinforces their sense of community. As people strive to perform their tasks and report on their successes and struggles, they share their worlds in a real, direct way and, in the process, extend their understanding of the contexts in which they are working.

These processes also present opportunities for rethinking aspects of the description, interpretation, and planning processes and provide extra support for people experiencing difficulty. Participants may find, for instance, that they require more information, that the tasks they have been assigned turn out to be inappropriate in some way, or that their activities are being blocked. In these cases, the plan will need to be modified to take these exigencies into account.

The reiterative nature of action research soon becomes apparent. Where people struggle to implement activities derived from a fixed vision or version of their world, they will soon be confronted by the dynamic realities of the context. To the extent that they can construct and reconstruct their vision, taking into account the increased understanding that comes from each reiteration of the process, they will successfully negotiate the complex web of meanings, interactions, and discourses that compose social life.

EVALUATING

At some stage, the need for a formal evaluation of the project may become evident. People who contributed funds and personal or political support will probably appreciate some statement or report that provides information about the extent to which progress has been made or desired ends have been achieved.

Evaluation requires processes similar to those used to formulate joint stakeholder descriptions and interpretations. A full treatment of the process is provided in Guba and Lincoln's *Fourth Generation Evaluation* (1989). Evaluation is carried out as a joint construction of stakeholder groups who

- Place their claims, concerns, and issues on the table for consideration
- Review information obtained from interviews, observation, documents, and group constructions

- Resolve claims, issues, and concerns
- Prioritize unresolved items

Tasks and activities that have resulted in a satisfactory resolution are delineated, and those that are unresolved become subject to continued action. As Guba and Lincoln (1989) point out, different values held by stakeholders will lead to disagreement about priorities for further action. The research facilitator's task is to negotiate these points of disagreement and seek ways to reformulate the issues so that participants can agree on the next steps to be taken.

This method of evaluation is consonant with the constructivist philosophy inherent in action research. It defines outcomes in ends that are acceptable to stakeholders, rather than those whose degree of success may be measured against some set of fixed criteria.

Sometimes there is considerable pressure to provide a "definitive" evaluation, especially from people who wish to use numbers to justify expenditure or their personal involvement. Numbers, however, are illusory and usually reflect a distorted vision of the research process. Nevertheless, there are occasions when some quantitative information is useful and may be properly included in an evaluation process. We may provide numbers of students enrolled in a course, youth attending a program, mothers attending a child care clinic, and so on. Numbers by themselves are misleading, however, and often oversimplify the state of affairs. They also risk reifying—creating an illusory preeminence about—certain aspects of a project or program. People may focus on tables that quantify relatively trivial features or disregard significant features of the project. Research participants should be wary, therefore, of engaging in forms of evaluation contrary to the principles of action research. (A number of appropriate evaluation strategies are summarized by Yolanda Wadsworth in her book *Everyday Evaluation on the Run* [2011].)

CONCLUSION

This chapter describes the phase of a research project where "the rubber hits the road." It is the point at which we start moving and where action occurs; where we set out to do something about the problems that have been the driving force behind all the activity. I have described routines that suggest ways to work with stakeholders to plan tasks and activities, implement them, sustain them, and evaluate them. The end point of the process should be the resolution of the problems with which we started.

Social life is rarely as simple as that, however. We usually find that myriad issues emerge when we start to poke at a problem, which can transform the problem itself and our orientation toward it. Steps taken to solve one problem sometimes take the lid off a whole range of related issues and problems. Further, the broader the context in which a problem is held, and the greater the number of stakeholders, the greater the complexity of the task confronting researchers. Chapter 7 focuses on these more complex situations and provides guidance to researchers who wish to engage deep-seated problems within diverse social, organizational, and community settings.

Generally, however, clearly articulated plans based on systematic and inclusive processes of inquiry have a high probability of achieving successful results. The investment of the time required to enact action research is amply rewarded by the significant outcomes that usually result. Where people say, "Oh, I'd like to be able to do that, but it would take too much time," they usually reinscribe the problem by using standard routines or procedures that have a long history of failure. Quick-fix solutions may give the impression that "we're doing something about this," but such approaches almost always fail to deal with the underlying issues that create the problems in the first place. By systematically identifying the significant elements that make up people's experience of problematic events, and planning concerted action that deals with the real issues affecting people's lives, we can achieve effective solutions that improve the quality of those lives.

REFLECTION AND ACTION

Identify an issue or problem that emerged from one of your interviews or that was apparent in the setting you observed. Alternatively, you may focus on an issue or problem from within your own work setting. Reflect on the following questions and discuss them with friends, colleagues, or classmates.

1. How would you go about formulating a solution to the issue or problem?

2. Who needs to be involved?

3. Working with a group (if possible, the people you interviewed or observed), formulate a solution.

4. Using the framework presented in this chapter, map out an action plan to enact that solution. Make sure you identify the people involved and the steps, actions, or activities in which they will be engaged.

5. Review the action plan with your group. Identify strengths and weaknesses of the plan. Modify the plan to strengthen it.

6. Identify a process for monitoring, supporting, and reviewing the implementation of the plan. Identify who should do these activities and when.

7. With your group, map out an action plan for evaluating the planned activities.

Box 6.1   Act: Action Plans—Implementing Sustainable Solutions

Purpose

To plan and implement practical solutions to problems that have been the focus of research

Process

Planning

Identify priorities for action.
Develop action plans that incorporate
Goals: the actions required to resolve issues
Objectives: specific activities required to accomplish goal(s)
Tasks: the sequence of tasks required to accomplish each activity
Persons: those who will carry out the tasks
Time: the time frame within which each task will be completed
Resources: materials, equipment, and funds required to complete tasks

(Continued)

(Continued)

Implementing

Implement the tasks described in the action plan.
Support people systematically by
Communicating: inform people of each other's activities
Nurturing: praise people's efforts
Reflecting: assist participants in reflecting on problems and progress
Assisting: actively assist people when difficulties hinder progress
Resolving conflicts
Modeling appropriate behavior
Linking people in mutually supportive networks

Reviewing

Review progress.

Evaluating

Review the plan.
Assess the effect of activities.
Revise the plan if needed.
Prioritize unresolved issues.
Celebrate achievements.

7

STRATEGIC PLANNING

MANAGING SUSTAINABLE CHANGE

Chapter 6 provided routines for moving a simple research process from the interpretive or analytic stage to practical action within limited contexts such as classrooms, offices, and small organizations. This chapter focuses on more complicated contexts, in which practitioners, managers, workers, and community groups engage the complex issues and deep-seated problems often contained within large and diverse organizations, such as school systems, health services, government agencies, and business corporations, or that cover multiple community or organizational contexts in cities, regions, and states.

The intent is to ensure that changes evolving from action research are systematically integrated into the life of the agency, organization, department, or institution in which the research took place. Unless research participants take systematic steps to incorporate changed procedures into the ongoing life of the organization, changes are likely to be short-lived and have little impact. Systematic and principled action research has the potential to extend its influence to all sectors of activity that have an impact on the issue or problem originally investigated. It enables research participants to engage the significant changes that need to be incorporated into the organization and to do so in ways that ensure the continuing and improved effectiveness of its operation.

In the time following the establishment of independence in East Timor, I acted as a UNICEF consultant for the Ministry of Education, Culture, Youth, and Sports. My task was to find ways of involving parents and the community in the rebuilding and management of local schools devastated at the

(Continued)

(Continued)

time of Indonesian withdrawal (Stringer, 2007). Initially, I facilitated participatory workshops with parents and teachers to engage them in action research processes that identified ways parents could contribute to the reconstruction and development of their local schools. At the same time, I engaged in interviews, focus groups, meetings, and workshops with directors and superintendents of education, school principals, and community leaders. Input from these sources provided information that was incorporated into a well-received policy paper that became the basis for developing Parent Teacher Associations (PTAs) in East Timor (Stringer, 2002).

In the following year I assisted a team of East Timorese educators in planning and facilitating a "preliminary pilot" parent workshop in one school and then left them to implement similar workshops in six pilot schools across the nation. Evaluation workshops held some months later indicated that they had been highly successful in initiating parent participation in a broad range of activities—rebuilding classrooms and furniture, making teaching materials, raising funds through gardens and fish farms, providing the school with a water supply, organizing security, and many other activities.

Workshops were then initiated across the nation by a team of trained facilitators who planned the implementation strategies they would employ in each district. Careful and systematic processes of preparation and planning enabled district teams to systematically integrate these developments over an extended period. Thus the participatory processes of action research, initially focused on a relatively small number of people, grew into a national program that provided the basis for much-needed development of the East Timorese school system.

Much of the success of this project was due to the strategic planning and support processes that included stakeholders at all levels of the school system, from senior ministry officials to parents and community leaders in local schools. Not only were the participatory processes of investigation, planning, and implementation effective at a practical level; they were also consonant with the national imperatives of this new nation. As one team member exclaimed with great jubilation, following a highly successful workshop, "This is so democratic!"

Although the basic Look, Think, Act framework remains the same for more complex projects, practitioners need to modify and adapt their procedures and acquire additional skills to enable them to accomplish the multiple intents of action research. This chapter therefore focuses on planning and organizational arrangements to help participants maintain control and direction of their activities in these more demanding circumstances. The following sections describe appropriate orientations to management, planning, implementation, and evaluation and the value of celebration.

MANAGING PROCESSES OF CHANGE AND DEVELOPMENT

As an integral part of a complex social system, researchers always affect other people's lives in some way when they modify their work practices or initiate new activities. Researchers are likely to disrupt long institutionalized practices that affect people's egos, dignity, power, status, and career opportunities. In almost all situations, some people will resist changes of any sort unless the processes are carefully defined and their interests taken into account.

Significant change is also likely to connect with many agencies and organizations, so that participants may find themselves subject to pressures to develop controlling and bureaucratic styles of operation that lose their community focus and override the principles of action research. Facilitators must work with participants to ensure they are able to maintain the autonomy and integrity of their work but avoid the style, manner, and forms of operation that typify many bureaucratic settings. They need, above all, to maintain approaches to development that engage the participatory processes and foster a sense of community among all participants. This strategic approach to developmental work requires time and resources that must be factored into scheduling and budgeting plans.

The unit for which I once worked was asked to produce a program to provide management training for people in community agencies. We estimated that development processes would take a minimum of 6 months and resisted efforts to get us to contract to do the job in 6 weeks, a period that would have allowed no time for consultation with client groups. The contract was given to another organization, which developed a set of training programs within the 6 weeks allotted. After 6 months of ineffectual activity, however, the training programs folded. We eventually acquired

(Continued)

(Continued)

funding for a 12-month developmental process, which resulted in a program that is still operating successfully today across all regions of the state.

In another instance, we estimated that we would need 6 months to consult local groups and formulate a redevelopment strategy for a regional community organization. Although we were funded, after negotiation, for only 4 months, we found ways of completing the job satisfactorily in that time. Today, many years later, that regional organization continues to operate effectively.

To integrate their activities with existing organizations and agencies, participants should constantly refer to the working principles of action research. They need to inform themselves of approaches to management consonant with those principles so that they can enact their organizing activities in appropriate ways. A vast array of literature informs the fields of management, leadership, and organizational development, but sources consonant with the approach to action research presented in this book include *The Empowered Manager: Positive Political Skills at Work* (Block, 1990); *A World Waiting to Be Born: Civility Rediscovered* (Peck, 1993); *The Fifth Discipline* (Senge, 2006); *The Dance of Change: The Challenges of Sustaining Momentum in Learning Organizations* (Senge et al., 1999); *Leading Organizations: Perspectives for a New Era* (Hickman, 2009); and *Organization Change: Theory and Practice* (Warner Burke, 2010).

Block (1990) suggests a way of conceptualizing the difference between what he typifies as *bureaucratic* and *entrepreneurial* organizations. Bureaucratic organizations, he suggests, are characterized by patriarchal systems that emphasize a top-down, high-control orientation to organizational activity. These types of organizations breed power-oriented people who use manipulative tactics to further their myopic self-interests, which focus on advancement, approval by organizational superiors, money, safety, and increased control, rather than on service. Block further suggests that one outcome of this style of operation is the creation of cautious, dependent people who work in ways that maintain the status quo.

A sign in bold capital letters on the wall of an alternative school program proclaimed, "If you keep doing what you always do, you'll keep getting what you always get."

Entrepreneurial organizations, conversely, are characterized, according to Block (1990), by people who act out of "enlightened self-interest." Enlightened self-interest focuses on activities that have meaning, depth, and substance; that genuinely serve the interests of clients or users; that have integrity; and that have positive impacts on people's lives. Entrepreneurial organizations are based on trust and a belief in the responsibility of people. The business of such organizations is managed directly and authentically, so that people know where they stand, share information, share control, and are willing to take reasonable risks. Supervision, in these circumstances, becomes oriented toward support and consultation rather than control, and success is defined as contribution to service users, clients, or customers.

Although Block's conceptual frameworks have a business orientation, his entrepreneurial approach to management emphasizes a service-oriented definition of self-interest in harmony with the principles of action research. He proposes that management is not necessarily as highly controlling and exploitative as is sometimes perceived but can be enacted in consonance with more humanistic and democratic forms of organizational life.

As research projects increase in extent and complexity, the tools and resources of management become increasingly relevant. Research facilitators and other participants need organizational and management skills to supervise the wide range of activities, constraints, forces, and pressures that impinge on their activities. They also need, however, to be consciously aware of the model of management they are enacting so that they are not drawn into procedures based on traditional, hierarchical models of authority and control that damage, rather than enhance, research processes.

STRATEGIC PLANNING

Difficult problems and complex settings often require long-term and large-scale strategic planning. Strategic planning encompasses carefully defined and inclusive procedures that provide participants with a clear vision of their directions and intentions. It enables stakeholders to describe

- A *vision* of their long-term aspirations
- An *operational plan* that defines the particular projects or activities that will accomplish this vision
- *Action* plans that lay out the tasks and steps required to enact each of these projects or activities

A Unifying Vision

As people work toward a collective vision that clarifies the nature of the problems that have brought them together, they gain a greater understanding of the complexities of the situation in which they are enmeshed. They also gain a more holistic understanding of the multitude of factors within which problems are embedded and realize the need to formulate increasingly sophisticated plans to resolve them.

The use of drugs by youth, for instance, may encompass a whole range of factors, including education, family, lifestyle, work, leisure activities, and the media. A community seriously intent on dealing with the issue of drug abuse will need to take all these factors into account in planning. Although community members need to focus on activities that will have immediate impact on some aspects of the problem, they also need to do "upstream" work that goes to the problem's sources rather than dealing only superficially with its manifestations.

> The story goes that one day a man found himself rescuing a number of people that were drowning in a river that flowed past his house. Eventually, he tired of dragging one after the other from the river and walked upstream, where he observed a bully pushing people into the water. He struggled with the bully, who was eventually arrested and taken away. The problem of the drowning people was solved by his upstream work.
>
> When we engage in action research, we are often placed in situations where we need to be pulling people from the water and working upstream at the same time. It is important, however, that we go to the source of the problem rather than do nothing but cope constantly with its outcomes.

As their analysis reveals the factors with which they must contend, stakeholders may be able to rationalize their activities. By planning carefully, they may find they are able to incorporate a diversity of activities into a few broad schemes or to connect a multitude of activities in ways that increase their effectiveness. A vision of the future that encompasses many facets of their common life may start to emerge.

A vision statement should clearly define the long-term aspirations of stakeholders. It should attempt to articulate the ultimate ends of an action research project by encompassing statements about particular goals within a broader framework of ideas. Such a statement may take the following form:

> Students, administrators, and teachers at Downerton School will work with parents and other relevant community groups to provide a high quality of education for families in the district. They will develop a curriculum and a school organization that is relevant to the lives of students and enables them to
>
> - Achieve the highest levels of academic success of which they are capable
> - Gain and maintain high levels of self-fulfillment
> - Develop and enact moral and ethical standards appropriate to their family and community lives
> - Live in harmony with fellow students, staff, and the community at large
> - Gain the skills and knowledge that will enable them to be a viable part of the workforce

The development of a vision is an attempt to integrate the many agendas that emerge from analyses in the Think phase of action research.

The vision statement should provide the rubric under which the concerns of all participants are incorporated—academic standards, student behavior, boring teaching, irrelevant curriculum, teen pregnancy, and so on. Although participants—teachers, administrators, students, and parents—might have different agendas and priorities, they should all identify with and accept ownership of a vision statement within which they can recognize their own agendas and interests.

Vision statements should be publicly developed as part of the planning processes outlined in Chapter 6. The previous statement would result not solely from the activities of school administration, faculty, and the school board, for instance, but from an extended process including all stakeholders—students, parents, community groups, business interests, and so on.

Vision statements are not the beginning point of an action research process. They arise only after considerable work has been undertaken to define specific problems and result from efforts to rationalize issues and concerns that have emanated from initial research processes. The "big plan" is an emergent reality rather than a predefined and predefining one.

Operational Statements: Enacting the Vision

An operational statement delineates the specific projects that enable participants to realize their vision. The previous vision statement, for instance, may be operationalized as follows:

The Downerton School will enact its vision through

- A school curriculum development process
- Site-based management processes
- Parent participation projects, including classroom volunteers, fund-raising, afterschool programs, and short-term specific-needs projects
- A student governance organization
- A peer counseling program
- Community outreach and education programs
- Staff development programs

The intended actions stated here are based on what the primary participants view as necessary to help them deal with their issues and concerns. Students cannot demand that their teachers engage in staff development programs; teachers should not initiate peer counseling programs for students on their own initiative. Actions must derive from the people who are the targets of any suggested action. The teachers themselves are likely to be unresponsive to staff development programs that have been mandated without consultation, and students are likely to see a peer counseling program as yet another imposition of the adult world unless it results from their own analysis of their needs.

I once observed a group of practitioners planning a program to decrease teenage alcohol consumption in one community. Their basic premise was, "How can we stop them from drinking?" The only role they envisaged for teenagers involved using some "respectable" teens to act as models. There was no thought of involving teenagers who actually consumed alcohol. I do not know the actual outcome of the program, but I would be very surprised if the group's efforts resulted in a decrease in alcohol consumption.

There is sometimes a tendency to "gang up" on a problem by eliciting the support of many people and agencies. Plans to solve youth problems in a community sometimes start with meetings of concerned citizens or community leaders, who then seek the aid of social workers, teachers, other community leaders, service organizations, churches, government agencies, and politicians to develop appropriate plans. Although any or all of these may be appropriate at some stage, action research emphasizes the primacy of the principal stakeholders— those whose interests are centrally at stake. Action essentially must derive, in this case, from the youth themselves, who must ultimately formulate plans and decide what and who will be involved in the solutions they define.

Operational statements should be comprehensive and describe the activities required to enable the primary stakeholders to accomplish the aspects of the vision that are significant to them. Participants may not be able or willing to institute all the activities at once, but the operational statement should clearly articulate all the factors that need to be taken into account to resolve the problem effectively. Research facilitators should arrange meetings that enable participants to review their vision and operational statements from time to time so that they are aware of the extent to which they have made progress toward solution of their problems. An operational statement diminishes the possibility that people will look to one-shot jobs as instant solutions that focus on one related element.

Action Plans

A separate plan should be developed for each of the activities or projects delineated in the operational statement. As each plan becomes activated, participants should define the following:

- The *objectives* of the project
- The *tasks* to be done
- The *steps* to be taken for each task
- The *people* involved
- The *places* where activity will occur
- The *time lines* and durations of activities
- The *resources* required

Processes for developing action plans are described more fully in Chapter 6.

As different teams or committees formulate their action plans, they should come together to reveal their activities and directions to each other. This provides opportunities for the smaller groups to rationalize and coordinate activities, so that plans do not work at cross-purposes or waste resources by inadvertently engaging in activities in the same areas.

Reviewing the Plans

As participants prepare to implement activities, they should appraise the strength of each plan according to the internal and external forces that impinge on it. A simple framework involving an analysis of the internal strengths and weaknesses of the plan, and external opportunities and threats, guides this process.

Strengths and Weaknesses, Opportunities and Threats

- *Strengths*. What are the strengths of the group (e.g., people and purposes)? What are the strengths of the plan (e.g., processes, resources, funds, materials, places)?
- *Weaknesses*. What are the weaknesses of the group? Of the plan? Who is not included? What resources are unavailable? What skills or knowledge do we need to obtain? Are there any gaps in our planning?
- *Opportunities*. What can we do that we have not yet planned to do? Have we taken full advantage of the people and resources we have? Who might potentially assist us? What resources are available that we are not yet using?
- *Threats*. Who might resist our efforts? What might they do? Are we invading other people's territory? Who might perceive us as a threat?

As answers to these and other relevant questions emerge, they should be restated in the form of objectives or tasks and assigned to individuals or groups as part of their responsibilities. For instance, a weakness identified as "inadequate funds" should be restated as an objective: "to investigate possible sources of funding" or "to commence the following fund-raising activities." People can be assigned these tasks as part of the project.

Political Dimensions

In the 1960s, change processes were often driven by campaigns in which groups achieved their objectives by engaging in overtly power-oriented social and political action. The approach to action research presented here is not oriented toward this type of social action, being more aligned with change processes promoted historically by people like Mahatma Gandhi and Martin Luther King Jr. Its purposes and objectives are to formulate links with and among parties who might be seen to be in conflict and to negotiate settlements of interest that allow all stakeholders to enhance their work, community, and personal life. To the extent that research facilitators are able to do this, they will increase the potential for the common unity at the heart of this approach to research. When researchers engage in political processes based on polarities of interest, they are likely to engage in conflictual interactions that generate antagonism. Although the potential for short-term gains is enticing, long-term enmities, in my experience, have a habit of coming back to bite you. The first impulse in action research must be to build links and formulate complementary coalitions rather than to divide the social setting into friends and enemies.

Through my work with Aboriginal people, I have become increasingly sensitive to the tendency of some individuals to constantly cast Aboriginals as oppressed peoples who are victims of colonization. To define Aboriginal life in such terms is to build a vision that has the potential to demean and diminish a group whose cultural strengths and spiritual wisdom have significance that goes far beyond their small numbers. To portray them in such terms is, from my perspective, an act of envictimization.

This does not mean that I wish to deny the exceedingly violent history visited on Aboriginal people in Australia or to diminish the social, cultural, and political problems they face. There are times when we need to confront those issues directly and forcefully. When I consider the strength and integrity of my Aboriginal colleagues and friends and the vitality of their family lives, however, I see a broader reality that goes far beyond this vision of Aboriginal as victim. I don't want to diminish their human potential by constantly highlighting their oppression or portraying them as victims. The words that my Aboriginal colleagues use to speak of their experience provide a vision of familial, cultural, and spiritual strength that is a much more powerful basis for action. I would rather build from that strength than struggle through a perspective based on weakness.

There may be times when obdurate, inflexible, ambitious, or fearful people will try to block the progress of a project. Research facilitators need to be aware of the political dimensions of the settings in which they work to deal with these situations. They can compile a list of those individuals and groups likely to assist them or be in favor of their activities, as well as those likely to resist because they believe the researchers' activities to be against their interests. All these people should be included as stakeholders from the beginning of the research process.

Only when researchers have failed, despite their best attempts, to engage people in their projects, and when people have purposively set themselves against the researchers' aims, should researchers fall back on the strategies envisaged in such books as Coover, Deacon, Esser, and Moore's *Resource Manual for a Living Revolution* (1985) or engage in the "campaigning" mode suggested by *Rules for Radicals* (Alinsky, 1989); and Kelly and Sewell in *With Head, Heart, and Hand* (1988).

Budgeting and Financial Planning

Funding sometimes can be a contentious and awkward aspect of a project, and research facilitators need to handle finances carefully and openly to maintain the integrity of the research process. Facilitators should assist participants in formulating a clearly defined budget that links financial requirements to each of the tasks and activities defined in the original planning process. The budget must be set out clearly so that all stakeholders can understand it. They should be presented with a copy of the budget, prior to meetings if possible, and have the opportunity to discuss it during meetings.

The budget should estimate the costs involved in establishing a project as well as continuing (recurrent) costs. These may be set out as shown in Table 7.1, which is based on a budget used in a youth leisure project.

An extended project that involves complex processes may require the services of someone with budgeting expertise, but participants can learn to formulate budgets for less complex projects. It is important that all costs be itemized and that decisions be made about expenditures—whether, for instance, people are to be hired for some tasks, what equipment is required, and what travel is necessary.

Finances are often the most contentious part of a process because of most people's experiences with bureaucratic organizational settings, where power and authority are invested in those delegated to control the finances. When

Table 7.1   Sample Budget Table for Youth Leisure Project

	Task 1	*Task 2*	*Task 3*	*Task 4*	*Item Totals*
Salaries and consultants					
Materials and equipment					
Travel					
Telephone					
Total					Grand Total

decisions must be made about funding priorities, they should be made at meetings of stakeholders. In working through these controversial issues and the negotiation of sometimes conflicting demands, a group can establish purpose and unity. When people in positions of power make forced decisions, divisions and antagonism often result.

My high school history teacher constantly emphasized, "He who holds the purse strings holds the power!" Research participants should keep this in mind when pursuing empowering, community-based processes.

Decisions must also be made about where funds are to be held. Public finances are usually held within some incorporated body (e.g., the Gleneagle Youth Association) that has the facility to dispense and account for monies. The problem here is that the incorporated body itself has restrictions placed on the ways in which monies can be spent, with implications for the project. As a project increases in size, the group responsible for initiating activities may need to be formally incorporated to acquire and disburse funds. These are contingencies that project facilitators should take into account as they lead people through a research process.

People sometimes are tempted to develop projects or programs because grant monies are available. They either launch into projects that are only peripherally relevant to their purposes or find themselves striving valiantly to fulfill the conflicting demands of the grant and the research project. In the process, the focus of their activities moves away from the issues and concerns that provide the energy for the formation of community, and participants risk burnout, disillusionment, or loss of direction.

Participants in action research projects should formulate specific plans to ensure that they have adequate funding for the period of the project. In many instances, people set up programs, services, or facilities with seed grants (grants given one time only, for specific purposes) only to find that they have no continuing funding. However, people should not restrict themselves to action for which funding is available. Research facilitators need to do a delicate dance to enable participants to actualize their dreams through their own efforts without leading them into situations of failure by focusing on priorities that come from funding agencies rather than their own analyses.

A good friend of mine used to view government funding with suspicion. "Stay away from government funding," he would say. "You'll kill yourself. Do what you can with your own resources."

Certainly, the situation of the Aboriginal community school I described in Chapter 1 is testimony to this counsel. Most of the initial work for the school came from the community's own funds, and only later did they acquire funds from other sources. The teacher who assisted the community in its formation admitted to me in conversation that she doubts whether the school would have been so successful if the people hadn't had to struggle, with meager resources, to get it going.

GUIDING THE RESEARCH PROCESS

Principles in Operation

The literature of management is replete with concepts such as supervision, leadership, and control, which are antithetical to the principles of community-based research. Hierarchical styles of management embody processes that engage centralized decision making, in which people in superior positions define courses of action to be taken, and relationships of dominance and subordination, in which obedience to authority is assumed to provide the best way to get things done.

Management of a community-based process, however, requires a different approach to operation and organization. As facilitators assist participants in organizing and implementing activities, they should consciously enact the key concepts and principles of action research, constantly providing participants with information about what is happening, maintaining positive working relationships, and including all stakeholders as active participants in planning and decision-making activities.

All participants should be aware of meeting times, places, and agendas, and facilitators should clearly articulate procedures for dealing with people's issues or concerns. Coordinators should have clearly defined procedures for passing on the outcomes of coordination meetings to their team members, and all stakeholders should be regularly informed about activities and events. All participants should be able to take advantage of opportunities to engage other stakeholders in activities and events related to the processes of inquiry.

Appropriate Language

When talking with others, people provide not only direct information but also many subtle, powerful messages that signify an orientation to the listener. The way we speak and the words we use carry implicit messages about the relative status and worth of the speaker and listener and the nature of their interaction. In general terms, therefore, it is better for research facilitators to use inclusive forms of language that have a connotation of togetherness—the first-person plural *we* rather than the first-person singular *I* or the third-person *you* or *they.* Facilitators who ask, "How do you want to do this?" subtly alienate themselves from the process. "How can we do this?" is a more inclusive form of the same question that implies the facilitator is an equal member of the team.

For the same reason, one should designate tasks using language that signals roles rather than status. Use terms such as *teams* or *groups* rather than *departments* or *divisions* (note the images those words evoke). It is better to have "convenors" or "coordinators" than "directors," "supervisors," or "heads." Both researchers' behavior and the symbolic universe within which it is encompassed should enhance the empowering intent of research activities. The language we use has an impact on the way we work.

Examine the following questions and statements for the implicit messages embedded in them:

- How can we make kids stop wearing that sort of clothing?
- How can we get parents to become more involved in the school?
- I think that you need to develop an antismoking campaign.
- I don't like the way you've done this.

Each of these implies relationships of control, authority, and exclusion that are all the more powerful because we usually accept the form of the message as we concentrate on its content. Language orients us to our world and to each other; appropriate language thus becomes a fundamental cornerstone of action research.

Making Decisions

Significant decisions about policies, purposes, objectives, tasks, organizational structure, general procedures, and the allocation of funds and resources should be made at meetings attended by all stakeholders or their spokespersons. All stakeholders should know what is happening and have the opportunity to contribute to discussions about issues. This process sometimes can be tedious as stakeholders are brought up to speed on the organizational limitations within which many of their activities are bounded. Equality of worth, however, is bound up with equality of knowledge. If parents, clients, and other community members do not understand the circumstances under which they are working, they are not in a position to become fully active participants in the research process.

This approach may seem a time-consuming and sometimes inefficient way to go about decision making, but the investment can pay off bountifully in the long run. On the one hand, people clearly informed about purposes and procedures are more likely to invest themselves energetically in activities and to work tenaciously to maintain their ownership of the research process. Decisions made by an inner circle of experts, administrators, or "loaded" committees, on the other hand, are apt to be viewed with suspicion and to achieve only low levels of support.

I once attended a meeting at which 3 days of intensive work were required to articulate a plan for a regional organization that had become so inefficient it could no longer operate effectively. Representatives from the different stakeholding groups in the region attended this meeting and worked through the issues meticulously and deliberately.

Because extensive preparatory work had been conducted with all stakeholding groups, there was considerable agreement on most issues.

Nevertheless, many details had to be worked through carefully to ensure that the functions and operations of the regional body did not interfere with the work of local groups. At each stage of the proceedings, time was allocated to allow participants, as individuals or as representatives of their groups, to voice concerns or bring forward issues that needed to be addressed.

After 3 days, consensus was reached about the basic constitution of the regional body, and representatives elected interim officeholders who would initiate the new body. Years later, that organization is still operating effectively, although it deals with contentious matters among groups of people often in conflict. The time taken to work through the issues with all stakeholders has been repaid many times over.

Research facilitators and other participants should make decisions by consensus, following procedures that ensure everyone is clear on what is planned and how it will work. Resolutions made on the basis of a vote often leave the agendas of marginal groups neglected and sap the energy of a community. Although major decisions about policy, purpose, and objectives are made corporately by stakeholders, detailed planning of tasks and activities should be left to the people responsible for carrying them out. This provides a sense of responsibility, competence, and autonomy that heightens people's feelings of ownership of the research process.

Support and Monitoring

Chapter 6 emphasized the need to provide participants with support as they enact their action plans. This is an important function for facilitators or team coordinators, whose task is to assist participants in marshaling their energies, monitoring their activities, and maintaining a focus on their purposes. Facilitators and team coordinators should talk regularly with project members, giving them opportunities to reflect on their activities and provide feedback. Their role is not to supervise, evaluate, or judge participants' performance but to act as consultants, providing information, advice, or assistance to team members. The demeanor and behavior of facilitators and coordinators always should imply that they are resource or support persons, rather than bosses or organizational superiors.

EVALUATING

As stakeholders work through the recursive processes of observation, reflection, planning, and review, they are involved in a constant process of evaluation that enables them to monitor their activities and progress. There may be times, however, when a formal review of a project or program is either required by a funding agency or perceived as necessary to the project. When people take the time to stand back from their day-to-day activities to explore and reflect on the processes in which they have been engaged and to share perceptions and interpretations, they gain greater clarity about the direction of their work and efficacy of their activities.

Evaluation needs to be clearly focused to achieve its desired purposes. If evaluation includes a mass of detail that is only peripherally relevant and fails to capture the crucial elements at the core of the project, then it may be counterproductive, directing attention to the wrong areas of activity and distorting the research process.

Steps to Evaluation

Purpose: Assessing the Worth and Effectiveness of Activities

Evaluation should, ultimately, assess the worth and effectiveness of a set of activities or a project according to its impact on the primary stakeholders. Many evaluations focus on the activities in which project members engage but fail to provide any indication of the extent of their impact on the lives of the people for whom the project was formulated.

I once helped a group of community workers in reviewing a program that engaged them in a diverse array of activities with many community groups. They enjoyed the work they were doing, and their efforts appeared to be appreciated by the people with whom they worked, but such was the extent of their activities that some of them were feeling stressed and overworked.

When I asked the community workers to estimate the extent to which their activities contributed to the purposes of the program—an increase in work opportunities for unemployed youth—they were silent. Although they had engaged in many activities with youth in the community, none could make any connection between the activities in which they were engaged and the specific purposes of their program. Young people, it seemed, did not have increased work opportunities as a result of their enterprise. The activities were pleasurable but unproductive in terms of the ostensive purposes of the program.

Audience: Who Will Read the Evaluation Report?

Prior to commencing an evaluation, the research facilitator should define the groups to whom the results of the evaluation will be reported. The processes and products will differ depending on the audiences. Is the evaluation being conducted for those who provide funds, those who control the organization, those who are the recipients of services, those for whom the project was initiated, those who provide the services, or any other stakeholder group? Answers to these questions will help the facilitator formulate a suitable evaluation process and present the resulting report in an appropriate form.

Procedures: How Is the Evaluation Carried Out?

Evaluation is an intrinsic part of the action research cycle. The period of evaluation is a time when researchers formally examine or review the processes in which they have been engaged—another cycle in the Look, Think, Act process. In evaluation, the processes are as follows:

- Look: Describe all that the participants have been doing.
- Think: Reflect on what the participants have been doing. Note areas of success and any deficiencies, issues, or problems.
- Act: Judge the worth, effectiveness, appropriateness, and outcomes of those activities.

In keeping with the principles of action research, however, evaluation is not carried out by an outside evaluator to make judgments about the worth, effectiveness, success, or failure of a project. It is a process that enables those engaged in the research project to learn from their own experience. In Chapter 6, I provided some detail on the constructivist approach to evaluation advocated by Guba and Lincoln (1989), an orientation to evaluation in harmony with the philosophical principles of action research. Another example is provided by Wadsworth's *Everyday Evaluation on the Run* (2011).

In some instances, funding agencies require a more direct form of evaluation to assess the extent to which project activities have attained their purposes or objectives. It requires participants to do the following:

- Define the purposes and audiences of the evaluation.
- Determine the goals of the project. What is the purpose? What is to be achieved? For whom? What are the intended outcomes and for whom (e.g., to increase the rate of employment of youth in Queenstown)?
- Set the objectives. What will be done to achieve the purposes (e.g., to initiate a youth employment program in Queenstown)?
- Describe activities related to the objectives (e.g., "The Youth Employment Program will increase employment opportunities for youth in Queenstown. . . .").
- Gather information indicating the activities in which participants have actually engaged.
- Gather information that enables people to judge the extent to which the activities were successful in achieving the purposes of the project or, when purposes have not been achieved or have been poorly achieved, what might account for that poor achievement.
- Engage in processes that enable participants to make judgments about the effectiveness and worth of their activities.

Careful initial planning facilitates the evaluation process because participants have clearly defined their activities and the relationship between these activities and the purposes of the project. Evaluation can sometimes highlight the lack of correspondence between purposes and activities. In the youth employment example given earlier, for instance, project workers had failed to articulate the relationship between their purposes and the activities in which they had engaged. They rationalized their activities as "providing good role models for unemployed youth," "improving the self-concepts of unemployed youth," and so on. Their activities may or may not have accomplished these objectives, but it is clear that they did little, if anything, to ensure that youth were actually employed. Sometimes theories—the explanations we give for events and phenomena—are inadequate because they do not fit the reality of people's lives. In this example, the participants may have improved their project by engaging unemployed youth in the process of defining the problem—that is, the reasons they were unemployed—and in finding ways they could gain employment. Careful processes of evaluation can sometimes reveal the inadequacies of a research project's initial framing activities.

CELEBRATING

A good action research project often has no well-defined ending. As people explore their lifeworlds together and work toward solutions to their common problems, new realities emerge that extend the processes of inquiry. Problems merge, submerge, or become incorporated into larger projects. Still, there is usually a time when it is possible to stand back, metaphorically speaking, and recognize significant accomplishments. The time for celebrating has arrived.

Celebration is an important part of community-based work. It not only satisfies the human, emotional elements of the experience but also enhances participants' feelings of solidarity, competence, and general well-being. It is a time when the emotional energy expended in particularly difficult activity can be recharged and when any residual antagonisms developed during the project can be defused and relationships among stakeholders enhanced.

Celebrations should reflect the principles of action research as participants get to mingle, talk, and eat and drink together. Music or dance will assist the air of celebration, if the context allows it. Formal, sit-down dinners are usually not a good way of celebrating because they anchor people to tables, inhibit interaction, and usually are costly. Buffet lunches or potluck dinners are better, but barbecues, brunches, and other types of parties are equally appropriate ways of celebrating. Any celebration should be held at a time that will maximize the opportunity for all stakeholders, especially those who performed activities, to attend, and in a place where the members of the least powerful groups will feel comfortable.

Speeches should be kept to a minimum, as the purpose of the gathering is to allow participants to celebrate their accomplishments *together.* There should be a time, however, when "significant people" provide a ritualized and formal benediction to the project. Key people from within the process may speak to emphasize the collective accomplishment of all stakeholders and participants.

It may also be appropriate for other significant figures, such as the mayor or other politicians, church leaders, senior managers in government departments and community agencies, local sports heroes, or other important community figures to contribute. The message from such people should be that the broader community or organization recognizes the participants' accomplishments and contributions.

Speeches that highlight the accomplishments of single individuals and the giving of awards to limited numbers of participants are anathema to community-based processes. When the efforts of a few individuals are recognized, those who have made "less significant" contributions may feel that their work has been inferior. In some way, all should be recognized for the contributions they have made to the success of the project. Celebration is a time when all participants congregate to acknowledge their collective achievement and say, in one form or another, "Look what we have accomplished together."

REFLECTION AND ACTION

Most organizations, agencies, and institutions have a strategic plan, though they may not always define it as such. If you work in a school, for instance, your school may have a school improvement plan.

1. Read the strategic plan.

2. Reflect on the plan and discuss each aspect with a group of colleagues or classmates.

3. Evaluate the plan.
   - Is each section clear? Comprehensible?
   - How do you think and feel about the concepts and language within the plan?
   - Can you follow the steps in the plan? Can you understand the goal(s) of the plan?
   - Do you think the actions or steps in the plan are clear and achievable?

4. Using information within this chapter, describe what needs to be done by those in leadership positions to ensure the objectives of the plan are achieved.

5. Describe other factors that might threaten the viability or effectiveness of the strategic plan.

6. Plan a process for reviewing or evaluating the implementation of the strategic plan.

7. How could people in the organization celebrate their accomplishments in an authentic and effective way?

Box 7.1   Strategic Planning

Purpose

To enact procedures for organizing and managing large-scale or long-term change and development processes.

Process

Strategic Planning

Develop a vision statement: What is to be achieved?
Develop an operational plan: How will that vision be attained?
Develop action plans: Describe tasks and activities to be accomplished.
Review the action plans: Examine strengths, weaknesses, opportunities, and threats.
Political processes: Build cooperative links within and between stake-holding groups.
Financial plan: Construct budgets to provide for developmental and recurrent costs.

Guiding the Research Process

Leadership: Enact the principles of action research—provide information and maintain participatory, supportive relationships.
Language: Use clear language that reflects the values of community-based research.
Decision making: Engage participatory decision-making processes.
Support: Act as a resource to monitor and support people's activities.

Evaluating

Purposes: Assess the worth and effectiveness of research activities.
Audience: Decide which people will be informed of results of the evaluation.
Procedures: Describe procedures for evaluating activities.
Evaluation: Describe what has been done, what has been achieved, what is still to be done, and issues or agendas to be resolved.

Celebrating

Celebrate people's collective accomplishments.

8

REPORTS

Informing Stakeholders

THE PURPOSE OF REPORTING

Research participants need to ensure that all stakeholders are informed of ongoing developments in their investigations. These may take the form of informal conversations, in which people provide information about the activities in which they are engaged and developments that are emerging. From time to time they may prepare a short report, possibly in the form of meeting minutes, that reviews their progress. They may also be required to provide progress, evaluation, or final reports to funding agencies or organizational superiors to ensure continuing ownership by those who have participated in earlier developments of the investigation. Reports need not be dry, mechanical texts but are better presented in ways that enable readers to understand the visceral realities of the context and activities engaged. For these purposes reports may not only be rendered as written text but in forms that include visual materials such as photographs, videos, or PowerPoint slides. They may be artistically rendered in creative styles and include humorous pieces that capture the spirit of the events depicted. The style of the report will depend on the audience, as a report to a group of teenagers is likely to be different from that presented to a department head.

CONSTRUCTING GENERAL REPORTS

Reports should be precise, informative, and interesting, information artfully selected to ensure it is sufficient for the purposes required, but not overly long, including material peripheral to the matters engaged. Reports may be based on analysis of data identifying key features and significant elements of events recorded, and these may be used as headings of the report (see Chapter 5). Steps for preparing reports include the following:

- Define the audiences and purposes of the report.

  Who will read the report?

  Why has the report been written?

- Briefly preview previous reports to provide context for the current report, including a brief description of the purpose of the project, previous activities engaged, and outcomes achieved.
- Briefly describe current activities by those responsible to actions incorporated in the action plan.
- Provide an account of what has emerged thus far, using information obtained from analysis of data (i.e., key features and significant elements).
- Evaluate the progress made, including activities engaged and outcomes achieved.
- Provide a conclusion that comments on progress and describes further steps to be taken, as appropriate.

Incorporate visual materials, including photographs, graphs, flow charts, and so on to enhance the impact of the written report. Visuals may also include charts, PowerPoint slides, or videos depicting aspects of the research project.

FORMAL REPORTS

Stakeholders who operate from within institutional or organizational contexts often require formally structured reports presenting technical features of the research process and detailed descriptions and analyses of the outcomes of an investigation. Government departments, funding organizations, and universities are examples of institutions likely to require such reports. Because continuing funding of projects, programs, and services often rests on the power of reports, this chapter presents a framework for constructing formal reports that do justice to the rigor and efficacy of action research.

The purpose of formal reports, theses, and dissertations is to communicate the outcomes of inquiry to major institutional stakeholding groups. They speak specifically to an academic or bureaucratic audience and must therefore be presented in forms acceptable within these contexts. Because of the status enjoyed by science in the modern world, many organizations, institutions, universities, schools, government departments, and business corporations try to replicate the formats required of experimental scientific research in their reporting procedures. In doing so, however, they often lose significant information or present it in a form that fails to adequately represent the complexity and significance of events or to capture the agonies, achievements, tragedies, and triumphs that constitute the reality of people's lives.

Recent developments in interpretive, action-oriented research differ in significant ways from experimental scientific investigation (see, e.g., Denzin, 1989, 1997; Guba, 1990; Lincoln & Guba, 1985) and therefore require somewhat different reporting procedures. This chapter thus suggests a framework for presenting formal reports that not only is true to the principles of action research but also enables individuals, organizations, and community groups to communicate effectively the processes and outcomes of their research and development work to bureaucratic and academic audiences.

I have seen many cases in which community groups engaged in effective developmental work constantly face withdrawal of their funding. These groups lack the skills or resources to construct reports that enable those who fund their activities to understand what they have achieved or to write proposals that clearly articulate their potential. I have been guilty of failing to provide reports that clearly described my activities in terms meaningful to departmental officers and the guidelines within which they necessarily worked. Although I complained bitterly when funding for my activities was withdrawn, I can see in retrospect that I had failed to keep one of our principal stakeholders clearly informed about my activities.

I have also listened to the agonized accounts of students and colleagues who felt assaulted by comments such as "That's not [real] research!" from people who did not understand interpretive or action research processes and the associated procedures and types of outcome. This chapter speaks to people in these situations.

GIVING VOICE: REPORTING IN ACTION RESEARCH

The approach to action research presented in this book is derived from interpretive research processes suggested by Denzin (1989, 1997). It is based on the assumption that knowledge inherent in people's everyday, taken-for-granted lives has as much validity and utility as knowledge linked to the concepts and theories of the academic disciplines or bureaucratic policies and procedures. The intent is to concede the limitations of expert knowledge and to acknowledge the competence, experience, understanding, and wisdom of ordinary people. Action research therefore seeks to give voice to people who have previously been silent research subjects.

Like other forms of interpretive research, action research seeks to reveal and represent people's experience, providing accounts that enable others to interpret issues and events in their daily lives. In the process, researchers provide information that enables those responsible for making policy, managing programs, and delivering services to make more informed judgments about their activities, thus increasing the possibility that their policies, programs, and services might be more appropriate and effective for the people they serve. Action research reports consequently will differ significantly from those derived from prevailing studies because of the interpretive assumptions implicit in the approach to inquiry.

- Studies are usually limited in context, engaging processes of inquiry that focus on a specific issue or problem in a particular context.
- Researchers seek to empower principal stakeholders by engaging them as active participants in all phases of the research project, including the planning and implementing processes. It has been described as research *of, by,* and *for* the people.
- The principal purpose of the research is to extend people's understanding of an issue by providing detailed, richly described accounts that reveal the problematic, lived experience of stakeholders and their interpretations of the issue investigated.
- Stakeholder joint accounts, derived from creative processes of negotiation, provide the basis for therapeutic action that works toward resolution of the issue or problem investigated. These processes ensure tangible outcomes of direct benefit to the principal stakeholders.
- Stakeholder perspectives are placed alongside viewpoints found within the academic and bureaucratic literature.
- The outcomes of the research make the experience and perspectives of ordinary people directly available to stakeholders—professional practitioners, policy makers, managers, and administrators—so that more appropriate and effective programs and services can be formulated.

REPORTS, THESES, AND DISSERTATIONS

One of the problems of reporting is the extent to which formal reports silence the voices of those of whom they speak. For years now, I have been confounded, especially in my own work, by the inability of official reports to capture the sometimes excruciatingly damaging, damning, or disappointing features of people's lives—or the moments of triumph, small or large, that signal significant, life-changing events. The ponderous language of the reports often obscures the experiences of participants and the significance of events portrayed in the body of the text. As one report notes, the words of a government report indicating that "the sewage system in the community is inadequate" do not capture the same image as "children playing around raw sewage that flows past their houses."

Reports, theses, and dissertations derived from action research, therefore, have purposes that differ from those of the traditional objective accounts sanctioned by the scientific community. Recent developments suggest new ways of formulating written reports that more effectively represent people's experience and enable audiences to understand more clearly the impact of events on people's lives. Denzin (1997) points to the need to formulate more evocative accounts that provide empathetic understandings of events and experiences, research reports that look and sound more like fictional works—novels or short stories—than the impersonal, objective accounts common in many official reports.

New ways of writing, however, often are confined by traditional formats that structure reports in ways marginally compatible with the intent of the writer. Although traditional reporting structures associated with experimental science seem incompatible with the narrative forms suggested by experimental ethnographic writing, it is still possible to find ways to fulfill the needs of institutional and bureaucratic audiences while remaining true to the intent of action research.

Box 8.1 compares a framework for organizing experimental and survey research reports with a framework relevant to interpretive, action-oriented inquiry. The intent of the former is to provide concise descriptions of observed relationships between variables, often related to the testing of a null hypothesis. The latter provides the means to present narrative accounts derived from the processes of action research.

The remainder of this chapter presents ways of reporting interpretive, action-oriented research processes. The structure is not prescriptive but

Box 8.1 Ways of Organizing Experimental and Interpretive Research Reports

Experimental/Survey Research

Section 1: Introduction

The introduction identifies the problem, provides background information, presents the research question(s), and states the hypothesis to be tested.

Section 2: Literature Review

The literature review presents a summary of published research studies that have explored the problem. It identifies outcomes, gaps, and inconsistencies in the research.

Section 3: Methodology

The methodology section presents the research design and describes the operationalization of hypotheses, sampling procedures, instrumentation, and procedures for data collection and analysis.

Section 4: Results

The results section presents the outcomes of the study, revealing and interpreting the results of data analysis.

Section 5: Conclusion

The conclusion discusses the theoretical and practical implications of the study, sometimes also presenting recommendations for applying the results of the study.

Interpretive/Action Research

Section 1: Focus and Framing

This section identifies the problem or issue on which the research focuses and describes the context in which it occurs, the question requiring a solution, and the objective of the study.

Section 2: Preliminary Literature Review

This section summarizes published research related to the issue, identifying the outcomes, perspectives, theoretical assumptions, and gaps in the existing literature.

Section 3: Methodology

This section describes the processes and philosophical assumptions of action research. It provides details of research procedures, including choice of participants (sampling), data gathering, data analysis, and reporting processes. It also describes procedures for ensuring rigorous and ethical research practices.

Section 4: Outcomes or Findings

This section presents detailed accounts that provide an empathetic understanding of how participants experience and interpret the issue investigated. It also describes the steps taken by participants to resolve the problem studied and the outcomes of those activities and events.

Section 5: Conclusion

This section compares and contrasts the participant perspectives with those in the research literature. It also presents implications of the study for policies, professional practices, and future research.

suggests one way of organizing outcomes of inquiry acceptable to people working in institutional and organizational contexts. Researchers should feel free, therefore, to creatively play with the ideas presented, provided that they remain true to the principles of the interpretive processes presented in this book.

The frameworks in this chapter are derived from my attempts to assist graduate students in formulating dissertation reports within a large research-oriented university. Because most of the faculty had been trained in experimental and survey research and had little understanding of interpretive or naturalistic inquiry, they were puzzled by the students' apparent inability to formulate studies according to the dictums of hypothesis-testing research. The frameworks we designed together enabled university faculty to understand the equivalence of the research reporting procedures and thus to "make sense" of it within their own meaning structures.

I have presented this model in a number of university contexts and received positive feedback from many people, both faculty and students, who indicated that it provides a simple way of formulating a research report acceptable to the evaluative requirements of university life.

STRUCTURE OF A REPORT

This section presents a format commonly used to present the outcomes of a formal research project. Later sections of the chapter describe formats more appropriate to the purposes of action research processes involving community and lay audiences. The major purpose of reporting is to ensure that stakeholders are fully informed about the processes and outcomes of research activities, and the form of the report consequently depends on the needs of particular stakeholding groups. What is appropriate for funding authorities or agency management will be different from reports required for young people, parents, or community members. A typical report uses the following format:

1. *Introduction.* Presents the problem and purpose on which the research focuses.

2. *Review of the literature.* Provides an overview of current understandings or explanations of the issue investigated.

3. *Methodology.* Incorporates a rationale for the approach to research and describes the research procedures used.

4. *Research outcomes or findings.* Provides a narrative account of the processes and outcomes of the research—in effect, the story of participant experiences and perspectives.

5. *Conclusion.* Compares and contrasts findings in the study to those presented in the literature and discusses their implications.

Section 1: Introduction—Focus and Framing

This section of a report presents an overview that enables readers to understand why the study was instituted and the issue on which it focuses. It frames the study by locating it within the boundaries of a particular social context—for example, classroom, home, community, or office—and describes the people involved—for example, students, teachers, young people, parents, and so on. The following information is presented:

- The problem or issue on which the research focuses
- The context in which that issue or problem is played out
- The question that requires an answer or solution—that asks, in effect, "Why is it so?"
- The purpose of the research—generally, to seek an answer to the research question
- The significance of the study—why the issue is important or why the problem needs to be resolved

Section 2: Review of the Literature

This section describes what has been learned about the issue from previous studies reported in the research and professional literature. It presents the outcomes of studies that have investigated the issue on which the current study is focused. These studies are also subject to critical analysis to reveal the concepts, theories, and underlying assumptions on which their claims and viewpoints are based. This process digs below the surface of the reports to reveal the implicit systems of knowledge (discourses) and cultural practices embedded in the theoretical literature and the programs and services on which they report.

The literature review includes studies reported in literature derived from

- *The academic disciplines:* academic texts, research reports, and academic journals
- *The professions:* publications and journals of professional bodies, such as teachers' unions, social worker associations, public service journals, and so on
- *Government agency policies and programs:* government records, legislation, departmental documents, policy papers, annual reports, research reports, sectional reports, client service literature, reviews, evaluations, procedural manuals, and so on

The review and analysis of this literature sets the stage for a later process (see Section 5) in which official and academic viewpoints are compared and contrasted with research participant perspectives. The review also points to gaps or inadequacies in the literature, thus revealing the need for the current study.

Section 3: Methodology

Introduction

The third section of a report presents a rationale for the approach to research used in the study (philosophical assumptions) and describes in detail the people involved (sample), the context in which it takes place (site), and the procedures used to conduct the research (research methods). It informs readers why this approach to research is appropriate to the issue investigated and indicates steps taken to ensure that the study was rigorous and ethical.

Methodological Assumptions: Philosophical Rationale

Because interpretive, action-oriented approaches to inquiry have been accepted only recently as legitimate in academic and official settings, the first subsection may require a more extended treatment than is expected of experimental or survey research reports. It provides information that identifies the research paradigm and provides readers with details of the purposes, processes, and outcomes of naturalistic or interpretive research. In doing so, it is useful to cite sources that enable readers to extend their understanding of the paradigm (e.g., Denzin & Lincoln, 2005; Lincoln & Guba, 1985; Reason & Bradbury, 2007).

This subsection should implicitly answer the following questions: "Why have we used this approach to research?" and "Is it a valid and rigorous research process?" It may be helpful to clarify the nature of the research process by comparing and contrasting naturalistic or interpretive inquiry with the experimental and survey research often presented in academic and bureaucratic reports. It is useful to know the extent to which intended readers value and have experience with interpretive action research.

> Some years ago, I presented to a government department a report that evaluated one of its programs. When I formally presented the report, the head of the department informed me rather frostily that "this is not an evaluation!" Although I thought I had negotiated details of the evaluation prior to accepting the contract, the departmental officers responsible had moved on to other positions. Their replacements did not understand the nature of the report I had written, in part because of my own failure to describe the nature of my approach to inquiry in my report. I now know that my report should have clearly articulated what readers could expect as outcomes of the research process.

Research Methods

The third subsection details the way the study was carried out. It enables readers to clearly understand how researchers went about the work of investigating the issue, including who was involved, what information was collected, and how the information was analyzed. This section is called the research design in experimental and survey research.

Position of the Researcher

It is especially important to describe and explain the role of the research facilitator. Readers should understand how the relationship between the research facilitator and other participants helped shape the processes and outcomes of the investigation. The researcher may be described as a consultant, resource person, scribe, or coparticipant whose role is to assist people rather than control them. The research is done *with* the people, not *on* or *about* them. This section is relevant to the general interpretive purpose of representing the experience and perspective of participants and to the values inherent in action research. The term *participant* is a departure from the term *subject* normally used in experimental and survey research and reflects a change in the status and role of people involved. Participants in action research actively engage in monitoring and directing the processes of inquiry.

Participants

Readers should be informed of the number and type of people who participated in the investigation (called "the sample" in quantitative studies) and the way the participants were chosen (sampling procedures) so they will clearly understand the sources of information. Researchers particularly need to identify the principal stakeholders—those most affected by the issue—and other important groups who have contributed to the study.

> In a school-related project, students and parents were identified as the principal stakeholders. Other significant stakeholders included the principal of the school and other principals in the district, teachers, and the district superintendent. Information from these sources enabled research facilitators to build an understanding of how the issue affected the lives of the students and their parents and how the issue fit into the local school context.

Information (Data) Gathering Techniques

As discussed in Chapter 4, this subsection describes the type of information acquired and how it was recorded. It is sometimes useful to cite authors who have suggested those procedures—for example, "This study used interviewing, data collection, and data analysis procedures suggested by Spradley

(1979). Initial open-ended questions that enabled participants to describe and interpret experiences in their own terms were complemented by. . . . " The following types of detail may be included:

- *Interviews:* the type of interviewing procedures used, with whom, number and duration of interviews, during what period, and where and when interviews occurred
- *Observations:* activities, events, or locations observed, related to which people, how, at what time, for how long (or actors, acts, activities, events, objects, places, and times)
- *Documents, media, and artifacts:* documents, official reports, minutes, procedures, materials, policies, letters, records scrutinized; films, videos, and media reports reviewed; artwork, working papers, and other objects produced by participants; samples; and so on
- *Recording:* how information was recorded—field notes, audio- and videotapes, photographs, photocopies, and so on

Analysis: Procedures for Distilling and Interpreting Information

This subsection of the report provides readers with an understanding of the ways that research participants analyzed or interpreted information. It describes details of procedures used for selecting, categorizing, and labeling information (see Chapter 5). Readers need to clearly understand how interpretive procedures (data analysis) relate to the processes and products of investigation—that is, how analytic procedures provided the material on which the report is based.

Rigor

This section provides readers with evidence that the research has been carried out rigorously, that the procedures and processes of inquiry have minimized the possibility that the investigation was superficial, biased, or insubstantial. Because traditional criteria for evaluating the rigor of experimental and survey research are inappropriate, action researchers report on the set of issues that establish the study's trustworthiness (see Chapter 3)—credibility, transferability, dependability, and confirmability.

Limitations

Researchers should indicate any limitations that arose from the pragmatic realities of investigation. It is not usually possible to include all the people who should be included, to interview them for the extended periods warranted by interpretive inquiry, to follow up on all relevant issues, and to deal with all the contingencies that arise. Human inquiry, like any other human activity, is both complex and always incomplete. We need to acknowledge the extent of that incompleteness in our written accounts of the work.

Ethical Issues

This section of the report describes steps taken by research facilitators to maintain the rights and privacy of research participants, including procedures that guard against unwarranted intrusion into their lives, maintain their privacy, and establish appropriate ownership and uses of the products of investigation. It may also describe how research processes were enacted in ways sensitive to the cultural values and protocols of research participants (see Chapter 3).

Section 4: Research Outcomes or Findings

Section 4 is sometimes described as the "results" section of the report, enabling researchers to present what they have discovered in their investigation. Unlike experimental research that usually reports on observed relationships between variables, interpretive research presents narrative accounts that reveal the ways people experience the issue investigated and the context within which it is held. This section presents richly detailed, thickly described accounts that enable readers to empathetically understand the lived reality of research participants. These accounts are constructed from information collected and analyzed during the study (see Chapter 5). They should include the perspectives of people from all major stakeholding groups.

Interpretive procedures described in Chapter 5 present features and elements that provide the basis for detailed, coherent accounts that

- *Describe* events, activities, and contexts from the perspective of the participants (This may include sequential accounts of events and acts, activities, objects, times, places, purposes, and emotions relevant to the issue investigated.)

- Present the way participants *interpret* events, activities, and so on, including how things occur and explanations for those occurrences (why they occurred as they did)
- Describe the *actions* taken by participants to resolve the issue or problem

These accounts may incorporate aspects of the study described in the following sections.

Setting the Scene: Describing the Context

As with any story, readers need to understand where the story is set, the people involved, and other relevant background information. One way of organizing this section of the account is to first set the scene and then tell the stories that have emerged. Another method is to begin with individual stories, weaving in descriptions of the setting as the person's story emerges. The purpose at this stage is to present a more detailed account extending the general information provided in Section 1. Descriptions should reflect participant views of the setting, rather than the "objective" voice of the researcher, so that accounts ring with participant voices, using their concepts and language to describe the people and the setting. Any of the following descriptive features might be included:

- *Actors:* people significant or relevant to the story
- *Acts and activities:* the things people do, activities in which they engage
- *Events:* significant events or incidents that take place
- *Place:* where those activities or events take place
- *Time:* when they occur and for how long
- *Purpose:* what people are trying to accomplish, why they do what they do
- *Emotion:* how they feel about what happens, what they do
- *Objects:* buildings, goods, materials, clothes, cars, books, reports, and so on

In setting the scene, writers should focus on those features of the situation that appear important from the participants' perspectives. This enables readers to see the context through the eyes of the participants and to understand their perspective. In some instances, large chunks of data may be included in the text to strengthen this process.

Constructing Accounts: Telling People's Stories

Common reporting practice formulates generalized accounts by combining information acquired from a number of individuals or groups. The problem with generalized accounts is that they fail to capture the lived reality, the actual on-the-ground experience of the people whose lives they are reporting. By aggregating the data, report writers risk losing those significant events or features of experience that really make a difference in participants' lives. A method more appropriate to an action-oriented, interpretive approach to research commences with stories of individuals.

As the story emerges, use descriptive features (e.g., actors, acts, and activities; see earlier list) that seem most suited to illuminating the person's experience. Focus on those aspects of the context that are significant from the person's perspective, rather than on commentary derived from others. Narrate a story that the person would recognize as his or her experience told from his or her perspective.

Accounts should provide sufficient material to enable intended audiences to understand the experience and perspectives of key people in the primary stakeholding group. The stories that emerge in the report should also provide understandings of the ways that other significant stakeholders experience the issue investigated. A report of an investigation of school dropouts not only would focus on the perspectives and experiences of students who left school early but also should provide an understanding of the perspectives of peers, teachers, parents, school administrators, and others having a stake in the issue.

Constructing a General Account

Most reports contain a section that summarizes what has been discovered during the processes of investigation. This section provides an opportunity to understand the issue in ways that enable participants to work toward a resolution of the problem(s) on which the research has focused.

Once individual accounts have been formulated, list the key features that formed the basis for each account and review them. Categorize the features according to previously described procedures, that is, identify features or themes common to all or a number of the stories. Names or headings may differ but refer to similar features; for example, "arguing," "fighting," and "criticizing" might be incorporated within a category labeled "conflict." Extended descriptions of this process are provided in Chapter 4 and Chapter 5.

After those features or themes are identified, organize them into headings and subheadings that provide the framework for a narrative that tells how groups of people experience the issue being investigated. Accounts will focus on experiences and perspectives that people have in common but may also refer to the different perspectives people have of events. At this time, do not explore, analyze, critique, or otherwise comment on their experience. The intent at this stage is to reveal and accept nonjudgmentally and uncritically the ways people describe and interpret their experience.

Section 5: Conclusion—Discussion of Findings

Whereas the previous section presented accounts of participants' experiences and perspectives, the final section places those experiences and perspectives in a broader context. This is the "so what" section of a formal report or dissertation that enables writers to articulate newly emerging understandings of the issue and to compare and contrast them with perspectives from academic literature or bureaucratic documentation. In effect, it presents succinctly what has been discovered and explores the implications of those findings. This section does the following:

- Summarizes the outcomes of the study
- Places stakeholder viewpoints in the broader social context of the issue by comparing and contrasting their perspectives with those presented within the literature
- Explores the implications of the study for policies, programs, services, and practices related to the people and issue investigated
- Suggests actions that may be initiated or extended or modifications of activities or procedures that will improve existing programs or services
- Suggests the need for further research to enhance or extend the outcomes of the current study

Its purpose is to show clearly how stakeholder perspectives illuminate the issue investigated and to suggest changes in organizational or programmatic practices implied by the outcomes of the research. In the academic world, it may also propose ways in which existing theoretical perspectives are enhanced or challenged by the new understandings emerging from the research process.

I was involved in a project that investigated the training needs of workers in a human services agency. The research clearly revealed the types of skills and knowledge required and suggested ways that skills development training could be organized. A review of existing literature on adult education and the human resources procedures of the agency augmented this information. It was creative work, requiring careful planning that encompassed the training needs revealed in the research process within the human resource development procedures of the agency. This resulted in a powerful training program that in the long term significantly enhanced the capabilities of the agency.

GIVING VOICE: ALTERNATIVE REPORT STRUCTURES

I have previously alluded to the need to develop more effective means for communicating the outcomes of research and development work. I have suggested ways in which the knowledge, understanding, and more pragmatic outcomes of our research efforts might be represented, including poems, dramas, narratives, fiction, memoirs, autobiographies, autoethnographies, films, and so on. This requires us as writer–researchers to draw on and develop literary devices able to evoke more clearly the deeply felt and experienced realities of people's day-to-day lives.

Apart from the style and nature of the language used in reports, however, their very structure often inhibits the clear and adequate representation of people's experiences and perspectives. This has recently become clear to me as I have helped people write formal dissertations. The report structure presented earlier engages both author and reader in an extensive discussion, first of the study itself, then of the literature related to the issue, and finally of the methodology and research processes. By the time readers arrive at the heart of the report, they have waded through many pages of writing that provide essentially background information. The voices of the principal stakeholders have become muted and sometimes lost in the academic or bureaucratic issues that tend to predominate in reports of this variety.

With my colleagues, I have recently commenced to creatively modify the structure of formal reports so that the experience and the voice of research participants remain clearly in the forefront of the document. The frameworks in Box 8.2 are adapted from those presented in the first sections of this chapter. Although they require some modifications and adaptations to the content of some sections, the rearrangement seems more clearly suited to an approach to research seeking to give voice to those it studies.

The objective of these report structures is to provide ways of reporting that focus on the central objective of a report—the perspective of the principal stakeholders. The intent is to ensure that the most important information derived from the processes of inquiry—the perspectives, agendas, experiences, interests, and ideas of research participants—are given greatest prominence.

Structure 1 removes the methodological section from its prominent place in the report and places it as an appendix in the rear of the report. This change removes a potentially lengthy technical discussion from the body of the report, placing it in a less intrusive position in the text, while still providing that information for audiences who may be concerned about the technical features of the research process.

When Structure 1 is used, the report needs to expand the first section a little to include basic information about the nature of the report. This informs readers of the nature of research carried out and the results they might expect in the report. If people read this type of report expecting to see results in the form of causes and effects depicted as variables accompanied by tables of frequencies, they may not orient their reading to the type of text presented or realize the consequence of the report.

Structure 2 takes this process a step further, removing the sometimes intrusive voices of bureaucratic and academic research reports as the frame for research participant perspectives. Thus the outcomes of the research process are reported in Section 2, leaving discussion of the literature for the following section. This enables the literature to be reviewed in light of the perspectives emerging from the research process, thus conceding the limitations of expert knowledge and emphasizing the primary relevance of the experience and know-how of people in their everyday lives.

Box 8.2   Alternative Research Report Structure

Report Structure 1

Section 1: Introduction

Research purpose, focus, context, and participants; brief synopsis of the methodology; the nature and structure of the report, including a brief synopsis of each chapter

Section 2: Deconstruction/Literature Review

Description and critique of existing perspectives from academic and bureaucratic literature

Section 3: Results/Accounts

Accounts that reveal ways stakeholding participants describe and interpret their experiences of the issue studied

Section 4: Contextualization

Contrasts and comments on the differing perspectives presented in the results section and the literature review; suggests implications for policies, programs, and professional practices

Appendix: Methodology and Research Process

Describes the research paradigm and gives details of the research processes

Report Structure 2

Section 1: Introduction

Same as Structure 1

Section 2: Results/Accounts

Accounts that reveal ways stakeholding participants describe and interpret their experiences of the issue studied

Section 3: Deconstruction/Literature Review

Description and critique of existing perspectives from academic and bureaucratic literature

Section 4: Contextualization

Same as Structure 1

Appendix: Methodology and Research Process

Same as Structure 1

The commonalities and differences between participant perspectives emerging in the study and the perspectives on the issue reported in the literature become one of the focal points of Section 4. We are, in effect, exploring the implications of the outcomes of the study. Where the outcomes concur with perspectives in the literature, we are able to validate, to some degree, our findings; where research outcomes are at odds with perspectives within the literature, we can explore the implications of the situation. Some people suggest that the literature review section of the report be deleted altogether, introducing perspectives from the research literature only in the final section in counterpoint to the major findings of the research and as a point of discussion for its implications.

REFLECTION AND ACTION

1. Using a framework presented in this chapter, write a report about the people you interviewed or the setting you observed.

2. Give a draft of your report to the person you interviewed or the people you observed. Ask them to comment on the report's accuracy or fidelity—whether it faithfully represents their reality or perspective.

3. Using the report as a base, prepare and present a presentation for a group of your colleagues or classmates. Use some of the creative techniques for presentation suggested in this chapter.

4. Alternatively, if you are reading this text as part of a class:

   Prepare a report about your experience of the class, using techniques and processes learned in the class.

   Using some of the creative techniques suggested in this chapter, prepare a presentation for your classmates.

5. Within your work group, reflect on and discuss the reports and presentations.

6. Summarize what you have learned from the experience.

9

ACTION RESEARCH AND
THE INTERNET

Ernest Stringer and Michael Kent

Talking about the Internet as a separate part of research or indeed everyday life seems almost redundant as the network becomes an increasingly integrated part of our lives. However, in this section a number of online services useful for action research are outlined.

The Internet provides the opportunity to quickly and inexpensively gain access to information and to disseminate our own research findings. It allows for resources to be shared and identified and for rapid and easy communication between individuals and groups. It is particularly significant that collaboration and discussion is now easily facilitated by people who would otherwise be geographically dispersed. The asynchronous nature of much of this communication also allows for collaboration and communication by people who are separated by time as well as space.

What follows are some of the more popular collaborative tools for information sharing and communication, followed by some Internet-based action research resources. These are just a sample of the tools and resources available and are subject to change over time as URLs move and the Internet continues to evolve.

SOCIAL MEDIA AND ONLINE COLLABORATIVE TOOLS

Blogs

Blogs take their name from the shortened version of the original *web log.* Robert Runtè from the University of Lethbridge has an excellent presentation

on the use of blogs in action research that can be found at www.slideshare.net/
Runte/blogs-in-action-research. He notes that blogs can be used for a variety
of purposes, including the following:

- As project management tools
- As alternatives to project management software
- To establish and maintain virtual communities of practitioners in a
  particular area of specialization
- As a way of people finding and joining virtual communities
- As places where developments in a particular field can be tracked by
  virtual communities
- As places where reactions to these developments can be posted
- As places to manage data
- As places to disseminate results

Carroll, Jenkins, Woodward, Kop, and Jenkins (2012) provide an interesting
account of the way they used blogs as a tool for reflection and feedback in
teaching action research. They used blogs to enable students to maintain a
private journal and as a discussion forum for groups of students. Students
were encouraged to reflect on what they were learning and experiencing in
the course and were provided with supportive and encouraging feedback by
instructors, as part of the development of iterative cycles of reflection, planning, and critically informed action. Students were thus able to share
thoughts and ideas, and the forum also encouraged them to build relationships with each other, so that this network of interactions encouraged students to make immediate connections, ask questions, and exchange points
of view.

How to Use Blogs

There are a number of blogging programs and packages available online,
including blogger.com and wordpress.com. These sites make it easy to start
and customize a blog and walk a new user through the process. Blogs also
provide the facility for other people to comment on what you have written and
to provide links to other material and resources online. Depending on the purpose of your blog and on how often and how much material you want to post,
there are a number of approaches to updating and maintaining it. It can be an

ongoing journal of activities that you share or a more dedicated place to disseminate information about a specific research project.

Some Blogs on Action Research

Brian Holmes' Research Blog

http://holmesbrian.blogspot.com.au/2010/08/action-research.html

This blog reports on the research activity of Brian Holmes at the University of Lancaster and the European Commission.

Action Research Journal

http://arj-journal.blogspot.com.au

This is the blog of the *Action Research* journal. The editors invite comments on all articles on action research posted there.

Action Research Ireland

http://actionresearchireland.blogspot.com.au

This is a blog by the Participant Action Research Programme at the Sociology Department NUI Maynooth.

eLearning Island

http://donalomahony.edublogs.org/tag/action-research

This is a blog by Dónal O' Mahony that approaches action research with a focus on education.

Twitter

Twitter is a microblogging site with many properties of a social networking site. It is an excellent tool for keeping up with current events through crowdsourcing—gathering lots of information from accounts that you have no connection to by following a particular hashtag. In the context of action research, like blogs it allows a researcher to network and communicate with fellow researchers, through sharing links to their own work and that of others that is available online. There are a number of researchers who actively tweet about action research, such as Alana James, who tweets from the account @AR4Everything, or Simon Haslett, @ProfSHaslett, as well as Twitter accounts linked to broader research groups such as @sdara_network, an account that provides information about action research at the University of

San Diego. The use of hashtags, such as *#actionresearch*, allows conversations on the same topic to be tracked across the network.

How to Use Twitter

To create a Twitter account, go to the Twitter webpage at www.twitter.com. There is also software available to access Twitter that often builds in more functionality than the Twitter website, such as Tweetdeck (www.tweetdeck .com). This software is easy to download and install on your computer. A more accessible web-based interface for people with disabilities can be found at Easychirp (www.easychirp.com). There are also numerous apps that allow you to access Twitter through smartphones and tablets.

Unlike some other online tools, Twitter doesn't make it immediately obvious what the value of the network is. Each tweet can be up to 140 characters long, limiting what can be said with each entry. The value is in the network, which requires you to "follow" other accounts. What these people tweet is then collated in your Twitter feed. You can also follow and engage with Twitter comments on a particular topic by searching for a particular hashtag. You can include this type of "tag" in your own posts on the topic by adding the # symbol to the start of the word you want to be searchable, such as *#actionresearch,* and can add a number of hashtags to the same post. Popular topics using these hashtags are listed by Twitter as trending. Twitter is often used from mobile devices, and in general all tweets are publicly available.

Facebook

Facebook is the current dominant social network, with half of all Internet users having an account. It can also be a useful research tool. Facebook groups, much like a more traditional blog, can form a venue for both collaboration and organization and as a place to disseminate ideas without having to provide "friends" access to people's personal profiles and information. There is also the facility within these groups to share documents and work on those documents collaboratively. There are a number of action research–related communities that make use of this platform. Facebook also has its own search function to help locate both people and information on different topics. For example, searching for "action research" provides a list of the communities with this focus. Some consideration however might want to be given to what intellectual property rights might be transferred to Facebook when using these venues and the potential exclusion of people who do not have a Facebook account. For Facebook users, there is a risk of collision between people's personal and professional lives.

How to Use Facebook

To sign up to Facebook go to www.facebook.com and the site will walk you through the process. As with all social network tools, the value is in the network. Like Twitter, this is accessed by finding your "friends," people you know who have a Facebook account. When these friends post to their own account it appears in a news stream to your account. Facebook's policy is that people's accounts should be personal, so you should use your actual name and details; however, in practice it is possible to set up multiple accounts for different purposes. Facebook allows you to post updates, similar to a blog; upload photos and videos; and share links you find on other people's accounts. Facebook also enables people to create groups. These groups allow the use of Facebook as a venue for communicating and sharing information without having to be friends with each other, thus avoiding privacy concerns that may arise from having full access to each other's accounts.

Second Life

Second Life is a three-dimensional online virtual world. It has an appearance similar to a number of online games, but rather than being a game itself, it provides a venue for a variety of activities. Second Life has hosted a number of action research studies. It can also be a good venue to communicate synchronously with a geographically separate group. Each person is represented in virtual space by an avatar, giving a greater sense of virtual presence, and the network provides both real-time speech and text-based communication.

How to Use Second Life

To create a Second Life account go to www.secondlife.com and download the Second Life software. Be aware that this software requires a computer with sufficient processing and graphics capabilities, often not found in smaller netbooks and laptops. Setting up a Second Life account takes considerably more time than many of the social networks mentioned in this section, as you need to create an avatar. Similarly Second Life, like many online games, can take some time to master, as within the virtual world you need to be able to move around and communicate, and these skills take a short while to develop. This is also significant in that this process will have to be undertaken by others that you may want to interact with on this platform.

Skype

Skype is the most popular of a number of voice over Internet protocol (VoIP) networks. At its most basic it allows people to engage in voice communication through the Internet and thus at a greatly reduced cost than by traditional telephone. It importantly also allows for video communication and conferencing. Skype also offers facilities for file transfers between users. Although Skype is predominantly free, it also offers some paid services, such as the ability to divert Skype calls to one's traditional telephone and also to set up a traditional phone number in a particular region that diverts to a Skype account. This technology has been used in a number of action research projects and is a useful collaborative tool.

> The editorial board of the *Action Research* journal uses Skype and ooVoo (described shortly) for board meetings and planning meetings. By these means board members from around the globe are able to participate in quarterly meetings or to engage in planning meetings for particular projects. The ability to see each other provides a dimension of collaborative communication difficult to achieve in purely voice-driven interactions.

How to Use Skype

Go to www.skype.com to set up an account. To use Skype you will then need to download additional software onto your computer. There are also apps for smartphones and tablets to access this technology. A computer needs to have a microphone and speakers to use the voice functions and a video camera for video calls. Most laptops and netbooks come with these features already built in. All people using the service need to have the software running in order to communicate with Skype.

ooVoo

This is a popular alternative to Skype for video conferencing and offers similar functionality. It also has a range of free features, as well as some additional paid options, including calls to landlines, the option of sharing what is on the computer screen during a call, and recording video calls. Currently ooVoo provides videoconference facilities for up to six people at no cost, though additional participants can be added through a paid upgrade.

How to Use ooVoo

This service works very similar to Skype. You can set up an account at www.oovoo.com. To use the service, simply download and install the ooVoo software on your computer. There are also apps that run this service on smartphones and tablets.

Google Docs

Google Docs and other similar services allow a group of people to work collaboratively on the same document. This can be done both in real time, with two or more people working on the same document at the same time, and also asynchronously with people editing the same document at different times. The system supports offer word processing, spreadsheets, photograph editing, and slide presentations, among other options.

How to Use Google Docs

Visit Google at www.google.com and select "Drive" from the options at the top of the screen. If you don't have a Google account, you will need to create one. Once you are logged in you can start a new document and then invite others to collaborate with you via their e-mail address.

Dropbox

Dropbox provides a similar way to share files or folders and is ideal for groups of people who wish to work on the same files together. It provides 2 GB of free storage, though this can be upgraded for a fee. When you create a shared folder, add others to the folder and its files will appear in their Dropbox just as they do in yours. Go to www.dropbox.com for a free download and instructions for use.

How to Use Dropbox

Visit the Dropbox website at www.dropbox.com to set up a free account. Your account and files can be accessed through this website. The Dropbox software automatically updates and synchs your files on all computers, say between a desktop and a laptop, on which it is installed. There are also apps that run this service on smartphones and tablets.

Wiki

Another useful online collaborative tool is a wiki. The most famous of these is the online encyclopedia Wikipedia that by allowing almost open access to contributors has built a huge resource for researchers and field workers. However, smaller versions of wikis can be a useful online collaborative research tool. A number of places host these, such as Wikispaces (www.wiki spaces.com). These sites allow people to come together to create collaborative documents. Each collaborator can edit and update any page of the document, and each of these pages can be linked to others to make it easy to track ideas and information. Documents can contain text, images, video, and other media.

How to Use a Wiki

This will depend on which hosting service you choose, but most will have a clear explanation for how to set up a wiki and invite collaborators.

Carroll, Jenkins, Woodward, Kop, and Jenkins (2012) describe a wiki as a cross between a website and a Word document that can be used to facilitate group collaboration. Participants are able to read and reflect on information on the website, add more information, modify other people's contributions, and edit the work. They suggest that as more people become involved, the wiki increases in interest and becomes more comprehensive. They were able to use wikis in their course to encourage students to work together to create definitions, explore complex issues, and to tease out answers to questions. As they worked on the wiki, students had the power to remove or change existing contributions and thus exercise and develop their democratic and collaborative values.

Cloud Storage

Another useful method for sharing information and collaborating online is through one of the many cloud storage services. Documents can be stored both on a computer's hard drive and also "in the cloud" on an Internet accessed storage space. Sites like Dropbox (www.dropbox.com) offer services that offer file sharing between collaborators. Each person can edit a document, although not the same document at the same time. Both Apple and Google now offer similar shared storage space online.

How to Use Cloud Storage

The setup procedure will vary depending on the service. Some, such as Dropbox, require you to download and install software on your computer. Anyone who wants to collaborate on a particular file must do the same.

PhotoVoice

As indicated on its website, PhotoVoice is used to build skills within disadvantaged and marginalized communities using innovative participatory photography and digital storytelling methods so that they have the opportunity to represent themselves and create tools for advocacy and communications to achieve positive social change. Used in a wide range of fields, it often combines photography with grassroots social action, allowing participants to represent their own community or individual point of view. Through discussion of photos relevant to their own experience, people are able to better conceptualize and develop narratives—stories—giving insight into their circumstances. The following website provides useful information about the use of photography as a tool for action research.

www.photovoice.org

A useful collection of photos and images relevant to action research is also available on the following website. This is particularly useful when people wish to describe their action research processes.

www.123rf.com/stock-photo/action_research.html

ACTION RESEARCH WEBSITES

The following websites are a small sample of those that provide resources for people involved in action research activities and projects. Websites continue to evolve, and some either disappear or are not updated, though the better sources provide ongoing access to useful information. To find websites with a particular focus, action researchers may use any of the popular search engines, entering key descriptors that will identify potentially relevant sources.

Community Development and Community Organizations

Asset-Based Community Development Institute
Hosted by Northwestern University, this site presents a strength-based model of community development.
www.abcdinstitute.org

Informal Adult and Community Education
This site presents an annotated bibliography about the nature and use of action research in informal education, adult education, and community education.
www.infed.org/research/b-actres.htm

Landcare Research/Manaaki Whenua
This site provides a summary of action research goals, differences between action research and mainstream science, and how reflection in action research is used to support change.
www.landcareresearch.co.nz/research/sustainablesoc/social/ar_working.asp

Poverty & Race Research Action Council
This nonprofit national organization links social science research to advocacy work to address problems at the intersection of race and poverty. The site incorporates links related to health, housing, urban renewal, education,

and human rights and provides information about relevant articles, literature, and grants.

www.prrac.org

Research for Action

This is a nonprofit organization engaged in educational research and reform to improve educational opportunities and outcomes for students. The site provides an extensive range of resources.

www.researchforaction.org

Disabilities

Careers & the disABLED Magazine

This is a career guidance and recruitment magazine for people with disabilities.

www.eop.com/mags-CD.php

Disabled People's International

This is a network of international organizations or assemblies of disabled people concerned with promoting the human rights of disabled people through full participation, equalization of opportunity, and development.

www.dpi.org

Disabilities-R-Us Chat Network

This is an Internet chat site for people with physical disabilities. It provides a number of resources, including a chat room, community message board, online disability meetings, disability links, and FAQs.

www.disabilities-r-us.com

disABILITY Information and Resources

This site lists online resources available to disabled people.

www.makoa.org

Education

An Action Research Approach to Curriculum Development

Action research has been used in many areas where an understanding of complex social situations has been sought in order to improve the quality of life.

http://informationr.net/ir/1-1/paper2.html

Action Research in Education

This site offers a comprehensive program on action research that includes an introduction, a theoretical underpinning for action research in education, doing action research, limitations and criticisms of action research, learning tasks, and further reading.

www.edu.plymouth.ac.uk/resined/actionresearch/arhome.htm

Action Research Special Interest Group of AERA

This is the home page of the Action Research Special Interest Group of the American Educational Research Association.

http://coe.westga.edu/arsig

RFA: Research for Action

RFA is a Philadelphia-based nonprofit organization engaged in educational research and reform to improve educational opportunities and outcomes for all students. A rich range of resources includes those associated with school improvement civic engagement, building literacies, community and youth organizing, teacher quality and effectiveness, and policy research.

www.researchforaction.org

Teacher Action Research—EdChange Multicultural Pavilion

This site provides practical information to assist educational practitioners in improving their own practice. These resources are especially relevant to equity and multicultural education.

www.edchange.org/multicultural/tar.html

Themes in Education

This site hosted by Brown University describes the use of action research in schools.

www.lab.brown.edu/pubs/themes_ed/act_research.pdf

Gender Issues

Feminist.com

This site includes resources and links to other related sites, resources, articles, and speeches.

www.feminist.com

General

Action Research & Data
This site provides links to action research resources on the web. It is maintained by COMM-ORG.
http://comm-org.wisc.edu/?q=node/20

Action Research at Queens University
An excellent resource, the site lists many links to action research websites providing information about action research programs, courses conferences, publications, and student and faculty reports.
http://resources.educ.queensu.ca/ar

Action Research Net
This site, maintained by Jack Whitehead from Liverpool Hope University, offers a variety of action research resources, including theses and links to other sites.
www.actionresearch.net

Action Research Resources
This is collection of links and resources for action research compiled and maintained by Bob Dick.
www.aral.com.au/resources/index.html

ALARA: Action Learning, Action Research Association
This site provides information about upcoming conferences and events linked to action research. Once you sign up to the site it also provides links to recent publications and resources.
www.alara.net.au/public/home

Canadian Journal of Action Research
The site provides full access to all the articles published in this online journal on action research. Also provides an excellent set of links and other online resources.
http://cjar.nipissingu.ca/index.php/cjar/index

CARE: Centre for Applied Research in Education
This important UK action research site located at the University of East Anglia offers resources and links to other websites.
www.uea.ac.uk/edu/research/care

CARN: Collaborative Action Research Network
CARN is a professional development network, focusing particularly on education.
www.esri.mmu.ac.uk/carnnew

EmTech Action Research
Action research resources are offered here—papers, link to other sites, and more.
www.emtech.net/actionresearch.htm

Health

British Columbia Centre of Excellence for Women's Health
This site provides information about resources, publications, and grants related to women's health.
www.bccewh.bc.ca

CARAMAsia
This is the home page of the Coordination of Action Research on AIDS and Mobility.
www.caramasia.org

Ethnographic Action Research UNESCO-CI
Ethnographic action research is an innovative research approach to poverty reduction.
http://portal.unesco.org/ci/en/ev.php-URL_ID=18401&URL_DO=DO_TOPIC&URL_SECTION=201.html

HELP: Health Education Library for the People
This site provides health education resources for people in India, including resources for action research in holistic health.
www.healthlibrary.com

HIV InSite
This site provides a comprehensive resource for information on HIV/AIDS treatment and prevention.
http://hivinsite.ucsf.edu

Office of Women's Health

This site empowers women to live healthier lives and offers research, information, and services.

www.womenshealth.gov

Poverty and Race Research Action Council

This organization seeks to link social science research to advocacy work to address problems of race and poverty. Health-related links focus on diet and nutrition, women, and families and children. It provides access to relevant articles, literature, and grants.

www.prrac.org

SAMHSA: Substance Abuse and Mental Health
Services Administration

This site presents research briefs about the use of community action research in the prevention of alcohol and other drug problems.

www.samhsa.gov

SHARP: Sustainable Health Action Research Programme

This website provides information about the Sustainable Health Action Research Programme (SHARP), an action research initiative focusing on community health development.

http://wales.gov.uk/topics/health/research/research/sharp/?lang=en

Social Action for Health

This is a community-based organization that facilitates solution-focused changes in practice that lead to increased equity and better health for local people.

www.safh.org.uk

U.S. National Institute of Mental Health

This site provides resources for practitioners, researchers, and the public. It includes information and research fact sheets, conference reports, research reports, funding opportunities, and patient education materials.

www.nimh.nih.gov

WHARC: Women's Health Action Research Centre

This site promotes women's reproductive health in sub-Saharan Africa, conducting multidisiplinary and collaborative research, advocacy, and training on this issue. WHARC is a nongovernment organization based in Benin City.

http://wharc-online.org

World Health Organization

The World Health Organization site provides links to publications, programs and projects, and data and statistics.

www.who.int

Project Management and Evaluation

International Development Research Centre

The evaluation theme of this site presents processes of evaluation for hard-to-measure projects, for example, community development. It includes sections on theory, frameworks, examples, projects, and publications.

www.idrc.ca/EN/Programs/Evaluation/Pages/default.aspx

Project Management Institute—Knowledge Centre

This site provides links to a number of useful resources and publications related to project management.

www.pmi.org/Knowledge-Center.aspx

Youth

Institute for Community Research

The Youth Action Research Institute (YARI, formerly the National Teen Action Research Institute) promotes the use of action research for personal, group, and community development.

www.incommunityresearch.org/research/yari.htm

Reconnect Action Research Kit

This kit shows how action research is applied to a youth program designed to reconnect at-risk young people to their families, schools, and the community.

www.fahcsia.gov.au/our-responsibilities/housing-support/publications-articles/homelessness-youth/reconnect-action-research-kit

Youth Worker Resources

This site offers tools for youth work.

www.youthworker.org.uk

Youthwork Links and Ideas

This site provides links to youth work resources, including advocacy, prevention, health, stories, programs, issues, and numerous other sites.

www.youthwork.com

REFLECTION AND ACTION

Social media provide resources to assist researchers in communicating and sharing information.

1. With a group of colleagues discuss ways in which you use the Internet and social media—Facebook, blogs, and so on.

2. Extend your discussion to explore the use of other social media presented in this chapter.

3. Discuss ways social media might be used to enhance action research processes. Focus on ways participants might use social media to communicate, share information, or enhance presentations.

4. Practice different ways of searching for information—e.g., web search, Wikipedia.

5. Set up and practice using social media sites that will enhance your work or study.

APPENDIX

Case Examples of Formal Reports

Transitions—The Experiences of Older Women From Hospital to Home[1]

Deborah Rae

INTRODUCTION

This report[2] outlines an action research process conducted with women from the Older Women's Network in Mackay. Action research is a methodology that recognizes the researcher, as a fellow human being interacting with others within a social context, as necessarily an implicit part of the research. It is also a cyclical, reflexive process that advocates continued learning and development. I have prepared this report in the first person, which illustrates the transparency of my subjectivity in this process and the benefits of this subjectivity and also allows for my ongoing reflection on my actions throughout the action research process.

1. PURPOSE OF THE REPORT AND THE INTENDED AUDIENCE(S)

This Report Has a Dual Purpose

One of the purposes of the report is as an assessment item for SWSP7348 Community Based Action Research as a course in my study of a master of social administration at University of Queensland. It is intended to demonstrate my use of a participatory action research process in an activity within the particular community in the Mackay (north Queensland) district. As such, its intended audience is the lecturer for this course, Dr. Ernie Stringer.

Within this report is another report, which details the progress of this action research to date. As such, its intended audience is the primary stakeholders and their identified community for this research. At this stage, this includes older women who have had experiences in transitioning from a hospital stay to home (primary stakeholders) and the Older Women's Network, of which these women are all members (identified community).

2. ISSUE INVESTIGATED

After a preliminary inquiry of possible issues or problems was conducted in late August 2005, the following issue was raised, with the understanding that it could possibly change after further investigation and clarification with a broader range of stakeholders.

Issue: Older women are experiencing problems when they return home following a stay in hospital, such as not having the capacity to cook meals, perform routine household tasks, or care for other family members (e.g., an older spouse).

Problem: There are no transition services from hospital to home for older women.

Question: How do older women experience the transition period from hospital to home?

Objective: To understand what this experience of the transition from hospital to home means for older women.

While this report is based on the previously described issue and objective, following the focus group meeting on October 20, modifications were made to these. These modifications are detailed in the following section titled "Outcomes of the Study."

3. CONTEXT OF THE STUDY

Mackay is located on the Queensland coast, 1,000 km north of Brisbane, and covers an area of more than 90,000 km², equivalent to about 5.2% of the total area of Queensland (Mackay City Council, 2005). In 2001 it had an estimated population of more than 143,578 permanent residents, of which approximately 69,800 are females. More than half of the total population (78,401) live within the jurisdiction of the Mackay City Council, while others live in outlying districts. Approximately 11,935 people in Mackay are over the age of 65, which means that Mackay's population is younger than that of the rest of Queensland. However, this does represent an increase of 12% in the Mackay elder population from 1996 to 2001 (MWREDC, 2003).

The region is serviced by the Mackay Base Hospital and Mater Misericordiae Hospital and to a lesser extent by the smaller Pioneer Valley Private Hospital. The Mackay Base Hospital, which is publicly funded, provides a range of medical facilities and services, with other services provided by visiting specialists from Townsville or Brisbane. This hospital has recently been the subject of media reports concerning a lack of human resources, especially a lack of appropriately trained medical specialists, a lack of community confidence in its services, declining workplace morale, and workplace bullying.

Other key community health services in the Mackay region include Blue Care (in-home nursing care), Meals on Wheels, Golden Doves (care for people with disabilities), Home Assist (general handyman services), and Home and Community Health Assistance, including a local bus service for older and/or disabled people.

Researcher/Historical Perspective

Because I have no previous professional experience in community development and have been a member of the Mackay community for only a short time, the context of my research has included

(a) Making initial contact with an appropriate organization and key people within the organization

(b) Negotiating entry into the organization

(c) Identifying further opportunities for other individuals to enter the research group to participate in a possible research project

(d) Making contact and negotiating with key stakeholders external to this organization to initiate a research project

Stakeholders, Sites of Action, and Time Frames

Primary Stakeholders

Originally, older women who have had experiences in the transition from a hospital stay to home were the primary stakeholders in this action research project. These stakeholders were initially drawn from the Older Women's Network (OWN), which is "an independent forum in which the special needs of older women could be specifically addressed" (OWN, 2004).

At the focus group meeting on October 20, these primary stakeholders decided to modify the context of this action research to include both women and men. They also decided that being identified as "older" is not a numerical representation but subject to self-identification by the person. For example, more explicit self-identification as an older person is represented by a decision to participate in social groups such as OWN, 50 and Better, Independent Retirees, the Senior Citizens Association, or National Seniors. They also decided that the context would include older people who have had an experience in any of the private or public hospitals in the region and that the project would not be limited to Mackay city limits but also its immediate regional districts. This involves western, northern, and southern districts within approximately 50 km from Mackay city limits.

Other Stakeholders

During interviews with individual primary stakeholders, when the project was focused on the experiences of older women, other possible stakeholders for this action research were identified. During the October 20 focus group meeting, however, these stakeholders were further clarified by the primary stakeholders and divided into separate groups. They now included

(a) Other primary stakeholders
- Men and women from organizations such as Independent Retirees, Older Women's Network, 50 and Better, the Senior Citizens Association, National Seniors, and Australian Pensioners League
- Friends and acquaintances of current primary stakeholders

(b) Hospital representatives
- Representatives of Continuum of Hospital Extended Care (CHEC), which "provides care and support for discharge from hospital"
- Social workers

(c) Community service providers

- Home and Community Care (HACC) transport services
- Blue Nurses in Mackay
- Meals on Wheels in Mackay
- Home Assist in Mackay
- Dial an Angel (based in Southeast Queensland)
- RSL Home Care in Mackay

(d) Other community members

- President of the Mackay Regional Council of Social Development (MRCSD), who is also a local member of Queensland Council of Social Services (QCOSS)
- Member of the Mackay and District Health Council
- President of National Seniors, who is also on the State Council for Seniors

Sites of Action

The project has essentially been situated in locations that were preferred by the primary stakeholders. Specifically,

- Meeting with OWN at their usual venue (Blue Nurses function room)
- Meeting with primary stakeholders in their homes (except for one who chose to meet at a coffee shop)
- Focus group meeting at a primary stakeholder's home, as decided by the stakeholders themselves

Because the primary stakeholders are expecting the size of the meeting group to expand, they have commenced inquiries into accessing an alternative meeting venue. Options they are currently considering include the MRCSD's meeting room, the Mackay Neighborhood Centre, or the Mackay City Council library.

4. PROCEDURES USED TO CARRY OUT THE STUDY

(a) Data gathering

Data gathering has been accomplished by

- Participation in OWN meetings to gain access to potential primary stakeholders

- Identifying people I could approach to participate in the action research project, as this group is comprised of many primary stakeholders. This included identifying people with particularly tragic experiences (extreme case sampling), usually reported experiences (typical sampling), particular knowledge of this issue (concept sampling), and divergent experiences (maximal variation sampling; Stringer, 2004).

Comments by individuals at this meeting seemed to suggest that they are particularly interested in achieving a specific tangible outcome that they have already thought about. I attempted to be mindful of this when I met individuals and heard their stories, so that

- They had an opportunity to fully explore their own experiences and possibly come to realize a range of issues and possible options.
- They had an opportunity to benefit from the process, not just the outcome.

This required me to use grand and minitour questions effectively, make full use of stakeholders' opportunity to review and clarify their words, and give stakeholders plenty of time to reflect on their actions and statements.

Data-gathering activities will ensure that primary participants remain included in, and the focus of, the process, as well as the determining elements of the "substance of our research." Participants' involvement in contacting other stakeholders and arranging and chairing future focus group meetings is an initial step toward guarding against the dangers of excessive networking, neglect of primary stakeholders, and the predominance of the "agendas and perspectives of organizational people."

Clarifying My Role

Even though I explained that it is not my role or intention to lead the project, or do all the work, it appeared that OWN members were still assuming that this was indeed the case. For example, an individual asked if I expected the outcome would be something that would be government or privately funded. I therefore think that, although I may have initially explained my role in the process, it will require further clarification, probably on a few occasions. Also, I think my actions may not have been consistent with my words. For example, I was introduced by the president while standing in front of a seated group. I believe this created an impression that I had some sort of authority over the process. It would therefore have been better for me to initially meet the participants individually, rather than in this group forum. This could have been achieved during informal chats during the morning tea break (which was my original intention).

Note Taking

Note taking initially proved to be difficult because of my focus on verbatim recording of each participant's words. This detracted from my ability to keep eye contact and maintain some degree of natural conversation with the participant. This proved to be less of a problem in later interviews, however, when I changed my physical position so it was easier to maintain eye contact, and my note-taking skills began to improve, so that I could relax a little and give more attention to the participant. I also found that in the pauses while I was writing, the participant had an opportunity to contemplate what she had been saying, which was reflected in her subsequent comments.

Participant Reactions

Judging by the passion and intensity with which these stories were told, it would appear that participants generally appeared to appreciate the opportunity to be heard and to tell their story. I attempted to ascertain their perceptions of the process by inviting comments about the interview or directly asking them for their comments.

Focus Group

I conducted a focus group with the primary stakeholders. The preparation, structure, and format were as follows:

The meeting time and date were scheduled by two of the participants, who then telephoned me and some of the other participants, while I contacted two others.

The meeting was held in the home of one of the research participants.

The meeting was attended by six primary stakeholders, three of whom have been interviewed once; the other three have been interviewed twice.

All participants were provided with transcribed copies of their interview(s).

The meeting duration was 2.5 hours. Participants requested that I chair the meeting, "since it's the first one."

Focus Group Outcomes

The meeting was, from my perspective, very successful. This was evident from the outset, when the passion and depth of these women's concerns became evident before the meeting started. This suggests that the timing of the group meeting was appropriate, as they are all currently keen to share their stories and make this issue public. The tone of the meeting was informal and friendly but also focused on a particular objective. It was lively, enjoyable, and very active but also primarily concerned with the issue at hand. The meeting provided an ideal forum for these women to express their passion about this issue and also actively work toward realistic options for resolution. Similarities can be seen with Stringer's description of a workshop, where "the level of animation in their discussions and the extensive lists of useful information emerging from their discussions were testament to their enthusiasm and the extent to which they appreciated opportunities to learn from each other" (2004, p. 123).

Artifacts

A range of brochures and pamphlets were reviewed by other participants and me throughout the interview and focus group process. These were pre-dominantly documents related to hospital preadmission and discharge pro-cesses and services, medication sheets, and newspaper clippings about community services related to transition from hospital to home. The data within these documents were useful in developing the knowledge of participants regarding this issue, particularly in enlightening us about the range of services available. A critique of this data also revealed how its stated intentions did not match reality, which was emphasized by participants in their interviews.

(b) Data Analysis

Data analysis in this action research project has been conducted according to the interpretive interactionist methodology of identifying and analyzing epiphanies and illuminative experiences. As Denzin (2001, p. 158) defines it, an epiphany is a "moment of problematic experience that illuminates personal character and often signifies a turning point in a person's life." It is within the research participants' epiphanies that the researcher may "capture the concepts, meanings, emotions and agendas that can be applied to problems affecting their personal, institutional, and professional lives" (Stringer, 2004, p. 99). Data analysis processes therefore include

Identification of epiphanies in data collected in the first interview with individuals

Deconstruction of these epiphanies to reveal their features and elements

Preparation of accounts and narratives of these epiphanies for the individuals

Preparation of a joint account, via the focus group meeting of primary stakeholders

Interpreting the participant's world

I had significant concerns about using the data gathered from participants in any way, as I feared that I could distort their perspectives. I considered it more important to keep their words and concepts intact, without any interference on my part. However, after reading Denzin's (2001, p. 133) explanations of the "thick, contextual, interactional, multivoiced interpretation," it became evident that this actually provides the reader with an opportunity to extend his or her understanding of the issue being investigated.

(c) Report Construction

Following the focus group meeting, it was agreed that I would prepare a written account from the meeting minutes of the project to date, including the issues raised by participants. Participants also agreed that they would prepare a verbal account to present to OWN members. My written account, which served as a progress report for OWN members, is provided in the later section titled "Outcomes of the Study."

(d) Ethical Procedures

At the commencement of the project, ethical issues to be addressed included

Maintaining ethical principles of MRCSD

Maintaining the confidentiality of interactions with participants, particularly with respect to any comments they provide about local services

Ensuring appropriate storage of confidential information at MRCSD

Obtaining permission from participants to share with others information they provide and how it will be shared (e.g., verbally in general references, in written brochures)

(e) Checks for Rigor

Checks for rigor within this action research project include the following:

- Prolonged engagement

Individual interviews with participants (either one or two) were each at least 2 hours in length, and this prolonged engagement enabled sufficient exploration of the issue at hand. This was coupled with the initial interaction with primary participants at the OWN meeting.

- Persistent observation

The initial meeting, first and second rounds of interviews, and the focus group meeting took place over a period of approximately 10 weeks. This element also included sending e-mails and making telephone calls throughout this period.

- Triangulation

I used a range of sources, including individual interviews, focus groups, participation in a group meeting, observation of interactions between participants, literature review, and a review of artifacts, including brochures and other documents.

- Transferability, dependability, and confirmability

The thickness of the detail of each individual interview is evident in the transcribed documents, and its applicability to this whole group was confirmed in the focus group meeting. That is, issues of each person are clearly identifiable in her accounts, due to the level of detail, passion, and intensity in participants' stories. The primary participants seem assured of the dependability of this data, which has been fully transparent and provided to them at every opportunity. This dependability will be assessed more rigorously with the production and distribution of the progress report to the OWN meeting. The confirmability of the data is clearly apparent even within this report, as all data, including electronic and paper meeting minutes, learnings reports, brochures, and other documents have been filed and stored.

- Philosophical rationale

Action research is a form of naturalistic inquiry with the purpose of studying people's subjective experience and "explor[ing] perspectives on an issue or problem" (Stringer, 2004, p. 16). Thus it is a form of "transformational learning" (p. 3), which provides research participants with the opportunity to gain enhanced clarity and realizations of their own situations within a social context. Action research processes therefore include a progressive development of events, through continuous cycles of looking, thinking, and acting. Simply, it is research conducted by, with, and for people (Reason & Bradbury, 2001, p. 2). Reason and Bradbury (2001, p. 1) emphasize the democratic nature of action research that is concerned with "developing practical knowing in the pursuit of worthwhile human purposes" with a view to "the flourishing of individual persons and their communities." This occurs within the realm of the interconnected complexity of people and their cultural worlds and the expectation of outcomes perceived as worthwhile by these people in their everyday lives. Action research is therefore concerned with "a more equitable and sustainable relationship with the wider ecology of the planet of which we are an intrinsic part" (Reason & Bradbury, 2001, p. 2).

OUTCOMES OF THE STUDY

The outcomes of this study are represented in the following progress report that will be forwarded to OWN membership. While this report provides them with a written record, the research participants will also make a verbal presentation to the OWN meeting of research outcomes. This report has been prepared by me at the request of the research participants and is, in essence, the minutes of the focus group meeting of the primary stakeholders. Its framework has been constructed according to the key elements identified by the research participants' joint account of this issue.

Transitions: Experiences of Older People From Hospital to Home—Progress Report

INTRODUCTION

This is a report to the members of the Older Women's Network about the progress of an action research project being conducted by some OWN members with Deborah Rae, a volunteer worker with the Mackay Regional Council for Social and Regional Development (MRCSD).

This progress report includes

- A brief description of the background of the action research project
- The project's objective
- A summary of the key issues that OWN members identified
- A conclusion
- Background

The OWN members who have been a part of this research have

- Met with Deborah for an individual interview, where they talked about their experiences when they went from hospital to home
- Met with Deborah again (some but not all participants) so she could verify what they told her and so that they could explain their story further
- Met together as a focus group to share their stories and decide what to do next

OBJECTIVE

The issue that OWN members have been talking to Deborah about is that older people, especially those who live alone, experience problems when they return home after a stay in a hospital, such as not being able to cook meals, do housework, or care for other family members (e.g., an older spouse). The problem is that there are no transition services for older people from hospital to home.

The OWN members' objective is to find ways to improve the experience of the transition from hospital to home for older people.

SUMMARY OF THE KEY ISSUES

It Could Be Anyone—It's a Community Issue

The participants feel that they shouldn't just do this for women. It should be "across the board, not just channelling down one lane to one sort of people." It's a community issue and "should be available for anyone that requires it." One woman explained, "The community as a whole needs to say, we gotta put something in place. Everyone needs to know they've got someone to fall back on, if they need it. It's about that support. It's not a luxury. It's a basic need for the community. It should be there for people of any status."

Infections

Participants talked about how you can become very sick from infections after you get out of the hospital. One woman explained, "If you're lucky, you don't get an infection. The infection actually caused more hassle. The infection part is one of the really major problems that the hospital has got. And the patient has got. The hospital just can't fight these germs anymore."

Another very independent woman had a major operation that was very successful. She didn't know that she had an infection until her daughter found her collapsed in her bedroom. She said that infections "take over you—you have no control. It just knocks you for six. If you don't have a positive attitude, the infection can just take control. You're not aware of it yourself. You don't realize you're getting sicker. Then you're unable to get up. You just collapse and stay there. Somebody on their own wouldn't have someone to push them."

Who's Responsible for Telling You This Information?

Many women talked about problems with the information they get from the hospital and from other places. They also talked about how "you've got to make people aware, educate them." They said that you "find things out when you don't need it anymore," or "they give you information but then you can't access it," and "you hear people talking about these things [services]. That doesn't mean that when you come to need it, you get it right." Even during the focus group meeting, some women found out about some services for the first time, exclaiming, "I didn't know you could do that!" "Yeah, I just found out too."

One woman talked about how she saw her friends struggling to cope with finding information. She said, "I've seen women who are so depressed. You say hello and they fall to pieces. They're lost as to who can help them and who can't. They suffer with depression. They don't know what to do in this situation. They can't help themselves. They don't know how to get *into* these services. I know that I've had to resource things myself to find out what is available."

One woman was given information in a brochure about a service that would come to her house to help her. But later she was told that they wouldn't do it. She says, "It's about having things at your fingertips when you need it. They should be saying, 'This is what we can offer you now.' It could have happened at preadmission. It's all about the timing. You need appropriate information that can be followed through. My life could've been made so much easier."

How Am I Going to Get There?

Some women talked about the problems with public transport in Mackay, which is a "problem when you come out of hospital, and have to go back a few days later." Many women don't drive: "Public transport is almost nonexistent, depending on the area," and "taxi transit is such a hassle. If you're sick you can't be bothered with all that."

One woman said that after a successful operation on her neck, her main distress was when she was told to go to her doctor to get the staples out. She explains, "I was feeling exceedingly unwell. I had to get the staples out. I had nine of them in my neck. It's hard to get to a doctor. I rang all day. I was exhausted. I just kept thinking 'Where in hell am I going to get these staples out of my neck? How can I *get* there?'"

You Need Someone to Call on You

Several women said that they were most concerned about women who are living on their own. One woman, who lives alone herself, explained that "if you're living on your own, you need to know how to arrange tradesmen, pay rates. But if you lose your husband in your 60s, you're thrown in the deep end. You have to learn all these things, especially if they have no children who have time to help them out."

Another woman, who lives in a group of units, has seen many friends and neighbors struggling to manage alone. She says, "The Blue Nurses get sent out, just to redress the wound. They're not there all the time. Even Meals on Wheels don't have time to stop and chat. They rush in, drop the meal and go. They have to struggle to get around at home, even to make a cuppa. For dinner they just have a packet of biscuits and a cup of tea. It's not enough. Some people wouldn't even bother with that. They just sit."

I'm Happy to Be Home, but Is It Practical?

One woman, who has lived at home alone for many years and enjoys her independence, explains, "There are a lot of hazards when living alone at home, and you do things you shouldn't do. Old people and children don't know their limitations. I think I can do that—then find you can't." The group talked about the dangers of having an accident and how it changes your life. As one woman who lives alone explains, "At our age, if you get a fractured hip, half your life is over. It takes a long while to heal, if it heals, and your whole life is altered. Its structure is altered. I'm scared as hell of slipping over."

They also talked about the ability to plan ahead if you live at home. For example, as one woman says, "If you have an accident at home, then you're in an ambulance, in old clothes, they've ripped the leg of your pants to look at your knee. . . . You haven't had a chance to put anything in an overnight bag. . . . How do you handle that? You have to ring a friend and explain where everything is in your house. In the end of my wardrobe, I have an overnight bag with nightie, slippers. . . . You have to be prepared. You have to realize these things."

FAMILY AND FRIENDS

Many women talked about having family and friends who would "put themselves out for me" but were not keen on "family having to interrupt their lives." One woman who developed an infection and suddenly became very ill explains, "When I came home I was sicker than when I was in hospital. My daughter had to leave her two children and come down from Townsville to look after me. It was very, very inconvenient. I was lucky that I had that option. Not everybody has that."

They also talked about feeling pressured to get support from friends. One exasperated woman exclaimed, "Friends, friends, friends, friends! Well if I kept asking friends, I won't have any left. I didn't feel comfortable asking for help. Yeah, I felt *really* uncomfortable with it. I had to do what was asked of me [in preadmission]. I was totally pressured. I absolutely had no choice—you were pushed onto your friends. I think there should be an alternative."

All the women said they would help their friends and family, but some admitted that they preferred to manage alone when needing help themselves. One woman reveals, "I should've [called someone to help] but . . . a neighbor came over to see if there's anything I needed, but I said, 'Oh I'm alright.' Getting around I could manage it, it just took a long time. I didn't want anyone to take me to the loo. I'm one of those silly ones—too independent. I've been living on my own a long time."

CONCLUSION

The OWN members participating in this research have identified several key issues for older women in their transition from hospital to home. They have also started to find some ways to improve this transition and have an action plan in place to continue researching this issue and working toward possible improvements. They have decided to meet again in November and will keep OWN informed of their future actions.

LITERATURE REVIEW

Research participants have not expressed an interest in reviewing literature related to this project. They are aware that similar research has been conducted by OWN members in other states (although not based on action research methodology), but at this stage they have made the decision to continue gathering data from older women within their own organization, as well as to broaden their data gathering to women and men from similar organizations in Mackay. Simultaneously, they have requested that I commence gathering data from other stakeholders, including community service providers and hospital personnel.

The data in this review is derived from three sources:

A health and aging submission to the federal budget, prepared by the Council of the Ageing (Australia)

A survey on experiences of care after hospital, conducted by the Older Women's Network (Action) group in Canberra

A research activity describing the "reported experiences of elderly patients regarding their transition from an acute hospital to independent community living," as reported in the *International Journal for Quality in Health Care.*

REFERENCES

Denzin, N. (2001). *Interpretive interactionism* (2nd ed.). Thousand Oaks, CA: Sage.

Mackay Whitsunday Regional Economic Development Council (MWREDC). (2003). *Mackay Whitsunday regional statistical profile.* Retrieved from www.mwredc .org.au

Older Women's Network, Mackay. (2004). *About the Older Women's Network.* Unpublished brochure.

Reason, P., & Bradbury, H. (2001). *Handbook of action research.* Thousand Oaks, CA: Sage.

Stringer, E. (2004). *Action research in education.* Upper Saddle River, NJ: Pearson Education.

A New Mathematics Curriculum[3]

Karen Swift

THE ISSUE TO BE RESEARCHED

At Blacksmith Primary School I am a member of the mathematics curriculum team and have a real interest in this subject area. Over the past 2 years, this team has been looking at the Curriculum Frameworks in the mathematics area. We have been investigating and identifying the key points and strategies of the learning area outcomes. We have inserviced our teachers and informed them of the information we have learned from our investigations. We have also discussed with teachers new strategies and techniques they should be using in their classrooms to achieve the outcomes stated in the Curriculum Framework document.

As it has been more than a year since the changes have been implemented, I was keen to see how teachers, parents, and students of the school were experiencing the new changes. I had intended to complete this research project on the whole school, but due to my inexperience as a researcher, the short allocation of time to conduct the research, and my determination to start small, I decided to complete my research project just on the five junior primary classes (Year 1 to Year 3) within the school.

STATING THE RESEARCH QUESTION

How are teachers, parents, and students in the junior primary classes (Year 1 to Year 3) experiencing the new mathematics curriculum?

METHOD

After deciding on the research problem I discussed with the school principal my research proposal. She thought it sounded very interesting and was keen to see the results in the final report and presentation at the completion of the project.

I began this research project by purposively selecting a sample of participants from each of the groups significantly affected by the issue being studied—achieving mathematics outcomes—taking into account sex, age of participants, academic ability, and ethnic backgrounds. The participants who were included consisted of three teachers, three students, and three parents from all of the junior primary grades. Once the students had been selected, I wrote letters to the children's parents explaining the project and asking for their permission for their child to be included in the project. I also gained informed consent from the other participants involved.

All the participants were interviewed individually. The teachers and parents were interviewed over a 2-week period in my classroom before school or straight after school. The children were interviewed in their own classroom so they could give a grand tour and explain their own classroom procedures. I used ethnographic interview questions (Spradley, 1979), and I recorded the participants' responses using field notes. I then spent a week analyzing the data from each individual interview. I decided to use the categorizing and coding method of data analysis. I photocopied my field notes and then cut up all the words into little units of meaning. I then placed the units of meaning into categories, thus enabling the participants to interpret and have a better understanding of the data collected.

Once I completed all the initial interviews with participants, I decided to have a focus group meeting with the three different groups. These were short meetings during the last week of the school term. The aim of these meetings was for all the members involved to get to know each other, to be informed about the next procedure, and to decide on a convenient time to meet each week to work collaboratively to investigate how we could achieve mathematics outcomes in the school. The teachers decided to meet on Tuesday afternoons, the children at Wednesday lunch times, and the parents on Thursday afternoons.

When I completed my data analysis from the individual interviews I returned the analyzed data to the participants for member checking. For the students, I individually read their report with them.

The participants then gathered together for another focus group meeting. During these focus group meetings the participants created joint written accounts that gave a clear understanding of how all the participants in their group were experiencing and perceiving the issue.

After all the focus groups had created their group reports, a meeting was held where all the participants attended. At this meeting each focus group presented its report. The teachers used a PowerPoint presentation, the parents wrote a letter addressed to the teachers, and the students created a poster that expressed their likes and dislikes for math. The teachers also presented the information they had discovered during their literature study. After the students presented their report they left, and the teachers and parents worked collaboratively to create a narrative report to present to the principal and teaching staff. To create this report, they broke up into pairs of a teacher and a parent working together to identify common themes from the three reports. Each of the pairs reported back their findings, and then a group report was constructed.

During the next meeting the parent and teacher participants created a plan of action. The group identified the key issues to be addressed and suggested solutions to accomplish the desired outcome. An action agenda plan was then established using a planning chart. Next, the action agenda plan was added to the narrative report that was presented to the principal and teachers at a staff meeting.

The teacher and parent focus groups continued to gather once a week during the fourth term to continue to supervise and monitor the progress of the actions being implemented during that term.

MY PHILOSOPHICAL RATIONALE

An experimental style of research is not appropriate for my research issue, as I am looking at the behaviors and attitudes of teachers, students, and parents in relation to the mathematics curriculum. According to Stringer, "The social and behavioral worlds cannot be operationalized in scientific terms because the phenomena to be tested lack the stability required by traditional scientific method" (1999, p. 192).

The naturalistic inquiry approach studies people's subjective experiences and explores their perspective and views of a particular issue or problem. By using this approach, researchers "gain greater insight into the ways people interpret events from their own perspective, providing culturally and contextually appropriate information assisting them to more effectively manage problems they confront" (Stringer, 2004, p. 15). Once the researcher gathers the information from the people's experiences, he or she uses interpretive methods to analyze the data before producing reports that give detailed descriptions of the people's understandings of events and their behaviors. The researchers' reports and presentations can vary depending on the purpose and audience involved in the research.

Action research is at the center of the naturalistic qualitative research approach, as there is a "need to understand how people experience and make meaning of events and phenomena" (Stringer, 2004, p. 26). Action research "is a cyclical, dynamic and collaborative process in which people address social issues affecting their lives" (p. 4).

Action research uses a number of cycles of the Look-Think-Act sequence. During the Look or Observation stage the researcher gathers the information from a variety of sources and builds a picture to clarify the nature of the research problem or issue. The main information is gathered through interviews with stakeholders, where each stakeholder gives meaningful accounts of their personal experiences and perspectives of the research topic. Researchers also use participant observation, surveys, artifacts, and literature reviews to gain a clearer understanding of the problem or issue. Artifacts can include documents, records, student work samples, materials, equipment, and facilities.

The second part of the cycle, the Think or Reflection stage, is where the researcher analyzes large amounts of data to reduce the quantity of information and to gain a clearer understanding of what is happening and how it is happening for each stakeholder in relation to the problem or issue being investigated. According to Stringer (2004), there are two ways of analyzing the data: analyzing epiphanies and categorizing and coding.

Analyzing epiphanies involves the researcher identifying the epiphanies from each individual interview with the participants. An epiphany is an "illuminative or significant experience" (Stringer, 2004, p. 97) in a person's life. Once the epiphanies are identified, the researcher distinguishes the detailed features and then the elements associated with each epiphany. Each participant's experiences are then consolidated into a framework that shows his or her own personal perspectives and experiences in relation to the issue or problem. Once all of the individual reports have been completed, connections of similarities and differences are identified between the stakeholders (Stringer, 2004).

The categorizing and coding method is a traditional process where the large amount of data from each stakeholder's interview is divided into units of meaning. These units of meaning are then placed into the appropriate categories, subcategories, and themes that have been established by the researcher or participants involved. Organizing the information into a system of categories allows the participants to understand and interpret all the information and explains the significant features of the experiences appearing from the investigation (Stringer, 2004).

Analyzing the noninterview data is also an important part of the Think stage. Even though action research is mainly based on the participants' personal perspectives and experiences, noninterview data can present an extra resource to assist the participants in clarifying, supporting, and understanding the problem or issue being investigated (Stringer, 2004). Analyzing all the data then provides the background information necessary for effective action to be taken.

The final part of the cycle, the Act or Action stage, is divided into two processes. The first process is to inform all participants and stakeholders of the data analyzed and the outcomes established. This information can be presented in written reports, presentations, or performances. The research participants need to think carefully about how they present their information so it is communicated effectively to the appropriate audiences and represents understanding of their personal experiences and perspectives. Before any report, presentation, or performance is presented to an audience or focus group, member checking needs to be completed to ensure that the participants' experiences and perspectives are being presented accurately (Stringer, 2004).

The second part of this stage involves creating solutions to solve the problem or issue being investigated. All research participants need to be involved in the solution-solving process. The participants need to review all the information that has been presented to them in the reports, presentations, and performances, and they need to select the most important issues they would like to solve. The participants create a schedule outlining the action and order of events to be taken for each of the issues identified. This information is best recorded in a chart or table so it can be clearly read and reviewed by all participants. Once the action plan has been established and the tasks and steps are being implemented, each action needs to be assigned a supervisor. The role of this supervisor is to assist and support the people involved and monitor and communicate the progress to other participants. Regular meetings with the research participants should still occur at this stage so that the participants can report on their tasks and make any necessary changes and review the overall plan (Stringer, 2004).

Action research is powerful because of "its ability to allow researchers to tentatively state the problem, then refine and reframe the study by continuing iterations of the Look-Think-Act research cycle" (Stringer, 2004, p. 46). This means that the research can change as needed to meet the needs of the individual participants involved. It also allows the researcher to continue using these cycles until the problem or issue is completely solved. According to Johnson and Christensen, "Action Research is a cyclical process because problems are rarely solved through one research study" (2000, p. 7).

OUTCOMES OF THE STUDY

Context of the Study

Blacksmith Primary is a double-stream school located in Hurstenville, Western Australia. It employs teachers with varying degrees of experience and understanding of the Curriculum Framework document. A new principal was appointed in Term 2 this year, so many changes are beginning to occur throughout the school.

This school has a strong community base with good relationships among the teachers, parents, and students of the school. The parents openly volunteer their assistance in all aspects of the school and often help out in many classrooms on a regular basis, and parents are always welcomed into the school environment.

Over the past 2 years at Blacksmith Primary there have been many changes implemented into the teaching of the new mathematics curriculum. During this time, the mathematics curriculum team has been investigating and identifying the key points and strategies needed to implement the new curriculum into the classrooms. This information has been taught to the classroom teachers through regular inservicing and collaborative learning sessions held during school staff meetings.

After a year of teachers' inservicing on the new curriculum, the mathematics team became interested in seeing how the classroom teachers, students, and parents were experiencing the new curriculum and how they felt it was working in each individual classroom. This came about after listening to many teachers talking to colleagues in the staff room. One teacher made the comment that "there is not enough time to fit the entire new mathematics curriculum into the school year." Another teacher said, "It is great how you can now integrate your math lessons into the themes that you are teaching." The mathematics team decided to start their investigation with the junior primary section of the school.

Student Experiences

Most of the students in the junior primary grades expressed a positive attitude to math in their classroom. Only one little boy had some concerns: "I don't always like math as sometimes it is too hard." All the students responded with answers that stated they loved their teachers and were always able to gain assistance and help from their teachers when they required it.

During the individual interviews, each student gave a grand tour of his or her classroom, which they seemed to enjoy. They showed their workbooks, textbooks, the whiteboard ("this is where the teacher writes lots of sums," one student said), mathematics resources, and work hanging up around the room.

Most of the students did not make any comments about the textbook, but one girl said, "We don't use this book very much, I don't know why we even have it." When the students were showing the activities completed in their workbooks—most work was on worksheets that had been stuck into their book—one student said in a moaning voice, "We do lots of these worksheets, and they are so boring and easy. I complete them really quickly."

When the students came to the point in their tour that demonstrated the mathematics resources in their classrooms, most of the students started to play with the equipment. They displayed some of the things they liked to do with it. All the students' responses were positive, and they expressed enjoyment with using the equipment, but they said they wished they could use it more, as "it is great fun playing with it, with my friends."

During the first focus group meeting, the students drew pictures of their favorite math lesson or activity that they really liked. All of the pictures drawn by the students involved using concrete material and working collaboratively with their friends. One girl drew herself and her friend playing on the computer, another drew herself playing with a group of children with the MAB blocks, and a boy drew himself and his friend measuring objects in the classroom.

At the second focus group meeting, the children created a poster with pictures of their likes and dislikes of mathematics. On the likes side, the children drew pictures of themselves playing games, using the mathematics equipment, using a calculator, working with their friends, and working on the computer. On the dislikes side, the children drew pictures of themselves sitting at their desks, the whiteboard, the mathematics textbook, and a math worksheet. When students were asked why they disliked these things, they said, "They're boring and no fun because we can't play or talk to our friends."

Overall most students had a positive attitude to math but would like to see some changes so they can enjoy math more by regularly using concrete materials and learning collaboratively with their friends rather than working individually at their desks to complete worksheets or sums from the whiteboard.

Teacher Experiences

The teachers' responses all showed enthusiasm and enjoyment regarding teaching mathematics. All of the teachers had made some changes to the strategies and techniques they were using, but they still felt like they "have a lot more to learn." The teachers made many comments about their strong feelings about the use of textbooks, the mathematics resources, the children's attitudes, the need for continual inservicing, and time to share great ideas with their colleagues.

The teachers had both negative and positive responses to the use of the textbook. Some teachers liked "the textbook, as it makes for easy programming, and there is not much preparation for math lessons." However, the opinion of most teachers was that the textbooks were "repetitive and boring, and they don't allow for real-life problem solving." One teacher even stated, "The textbook is stopping me from completing creative and integrated lessons, and I hope we don't have to use them next year."

According to all the junior primary teachers there is a real concern with the mathematics resources in the school. All the teachers stressed the importance of using math equipment, "as it enhances the children's learning during a math lesson." However, all the teachers' responses stated that integrating math equipment into their lessons was difficult, as "the school is really lacking in resources" and "the resources are stored all over the school and you spend half your day trying to find them, and teachers don't have time for that." All the teachers would like to see more resources purchased. Some teachers felt that "more teacher reference books which show how to teach real-life problem-solving skills to the students need to be purchased." Other teachers believed that "having a collection of websites that both the teachers and students could use would be very beneficial."

All of the teachers enjoyed seeing students' enthusiasm for math lessons. Every teacher gave an example of a successful math lesson that he or she felt students enjoyed and with which he or she believed they had real success. One teacher explained, "The children cheer every time I ask them to collect a calculator from the shelf." Another teacher explained how her class loved playing the Buzz game and asked if they could play it every day. All the teachers agreed that most math lessons could be "fun and enjoyable if they offered variety, interaction, and the use of resources and equipment."

All of the teachers felt that they still required further inservicing with the mathematics curriculum. Many teachers felt that problem-solving skills and the Working Mathematically outcomes were two strong areas of concern. One teacher said, "I find it very difficult to assess the children in the Working Mathematically area as the pointers are not clear to me." Some teachers also stated that it would "be nice to take the time out to meet informally with other teachers and discuss different matters that arise in our classrooms or share successful math lessons with others."

Parent Experiences

All the parents expressed very strong and positive feelings toward the teachers at this school, and they congratulated them on the wonderful job they do. The parents believed that the teachers were "dedicated and enthusiastic teachers who showed love and kindness to all children in their classes." The parents felt the teachers explained new topics to the children clearly and concisely, and this was reflected in the children's being "able to complete their math homework independently, which is great for us."

The parents were very appreciative of the teachers for keeping them informed about their children's progress. One parent said, "It is great the way we receive feedback every term as you can always see how your children are doing." Another said, "I would like to see the school have parent-teacher interviews at the end of Term 1 so we can see early on if our children are having any problems." The parents also found teachers very approachable, and they liked how teachers gave up their time whenever a parent requested it to discuss any concerns or questions they had regarding their children. One parent explained, "I have never had a teacher tell me they were too busy to see me; they always saw me that afternoon or the very next day."

All of the parents' school experiences were very different from what their children are experiencing today. One parent stated, "It is very different from when I went to school; we didn't play games or use equipment. The teacher just wrote on the blackboard and we copied it down." Another parent said, "All I remember is the constant math tests every Friday." The parents expressed concerns about their understanding of the teaching and assessing techniques being used in the classroom today. One parent said, "When the children bring home their portfolios there are all these tables on their work with ticks all over it. I don't read any of the writing, because I don't understand it. I just look at the marks to make sure that they are satisfactory or above." One parent suggested "holding information sessions to inform parents about the new teaching and assessing techniques."

Parent involvement and inclusion during math lessons in the classrooms was a strong point made by many of the parents. One parent believed "the children would learn better if there were more adults in the room," and another said, "More group work could be completed and the children could be grouped in ability like with reading." One parent expressed strongly that "having parents in the room is a great idea, but there has to be some time for the teacher to teach these children independently. Children also need breaks from their parents and time to spend with just their peers."

Students' Results From Standardized Tests

During one of the teacher focus group meetings, the teachers decided to review how students were performing in the mathematics area. The teachers felt that this would give an extra perspective to the investigation. The students completed the standardized tests during Term 4 every year. The results from these tests show each child's strengths and weaknesses in the different mathematical strands. They also give individual class profiles that show the class's strengths and areas of concern. From the results, the teachers discovered that, since the last year, the students had really improved in the number and space strands. The Working Mathematically strand had not changed in most of the classes over the past 2 years, and in one class the results were very low.

Literature Study on Working Mathematically

Because there was a strong focus coming through from the participants' responses about needing to implement and come to a better understanding of problem-solving skills and the Working Mathematically outcomes, the teacher focus group decided to investigate what the literature had to say about these ideas. All the literature researched discusses the idea that the "process of Working Mathematically is learning to work like a mathematician." This involves providing the children with problems to which they don't know the answers, and they have to play around and use a variety of strategies to solve them.

The teacher focus group also discovered a variety of schools around Australia that have changed their teaching styles and approaches to teaching mathematics to incorporate this new concept of working mathematically. The teacher focus group contacted these schools for advice and information to assist them in implementing new ideas into the Blacksmith Primary School community as part of the Action Agenda for 2005.

Action Agenda

After the three focus groups presented their group reports to each other, parents and teachers gathered together to form a new focus group. This larger group reviewed all the data collected in the group reports, the results from the standardized testing, and the information from the literature study. They used this information to identify the issues of concern and suggested solutions to accomplish the group's desired outcomes.

The group prioritized the issues and the areas of concern into the following categories: the school mathematical resources, the use of mathematics textbooks, parent involvement in the classrooms, teacher collaborative learning meetings, and inservicing teachers on using real-life problem-solving techniques in their classrooms and gaining a better understanding of the Working Mathematically outcomes. The group decided that with Term 4 being such a short one, only some of the issues would be able to be addressed in this term and some would have to wait until Term 1, 2005.

Term 4, 2004

The teachers and parents felt that the school mathematical resources and the use of mathematics textbooks in the school required priority in Term 4. Throughout the reports, there was a strong emphasis on the importance of using resources and equipment in the teaching of the new mathematics curriculum. The school mathematical resources needed attention both with the reviewing of equipment in the school and with the purchasing of new equipment and teacher reference books. The teachers and students would also like to see the Internet being used more as a tool for teachers to gain ideas about teaching mathematics and for students to improve their mathematical skills.

To achieve these results the teacher and parent groups suggested the following action plan:

Complete a stock take of all the mathematics equipment in the school.

Discuss with the principal and the P&F Committee about including funds in next year's budget to purchase new mathematical resources and equipment next year.

Contact mathematical sales consultants for advice and samples of new resources and materials available to be purchased.

Create a property box on the school webpage for great mathematical webpages to be included for easy access for all members of the school community.

Regarding the use of mathematics textbooks for next year, a meeting has been scheduled for November 15, 2004. At this meeting the principal and the junior primary teachers will discuss the positives and the negatives of using the textbooks and will then come to a decision about the approach for next year.

Term 1, 2005

In Term 1, 2005, teachers will provide parents with information and exploration sessions. These sessions will help parents come to a clearer understanding of the teaching and assessing of mathematics today. At these sessions parents will be given the opportunity to experience some hands-on problem-solving math lessons as well as gain greater understanding of the use of outcomes to teach and assess students.

As all the participants expressed the belief that math lessons should be fun, a small committee of teachers, parents, and students will be established to create fun math sessions in which all junior primary students can participate. The aim of these sessions is to expose children to activities where they can work collaboratively to solve real-life problems and to include parents in the classroom activities as requested.

Many teachers believed that they could learn a great deal from each other by just sitting and communicating together. This belief encouraged teachers to look into having regular collaborative learning meetings for the junior primary teachers. At these meetings teachers would gather together to gain advice and ideas from their colleagues as well as share successful math lessons.

As most of the teachers still feel they lack expertise in the teaching of the new mathematics curriculum, a proposal will be put forward to the administration team of the school for a math consultant to come and inservice the teachers as part of the professional development plan for 2005. The information gathered from the literature study by the teacher focus group will assist in this area. The math consultant will inform teachers of new strategies and techniques they will be able to use for teaching real-life problem-solving skills and the Working Mathematically outcomes to the students. The mathematics curriculum team would also investigate the purchasing of new teacher reference books with problem-solving and Working Mathematically teaching ideas.

CONCLUSION

I received the approval for the research project from the principal on August 24, 2004, and I presented the results to the principal and the teaching staff on Monday, November 22, 2004. The report was presented in the form of a big book that told the story of how the project was completed, the participants' experiences, and the actions that needed to be implemented. Even though the project was completed, there were still some areas of the action plan that will continue to be implemented this term and during Term 1, 2005. Now that I have completed a successful project, I feel more confident about completing action research projects in the future.

REFERENCES

Johnson, B., & Christensen, L. (2000). *Educational research: Quantitative and qualitative approaches.* Boston: Allyn & Bacon.

Spradley, J. (1979). *The ethnographic interview.* New York: Holt, Rinehart and Winston.

Stringer, E. (1999). *Action research* (2nd ed.). Thousand Oaks, CA: Sage.

Stringer, E. (2004). *Action research in education.* Upper Saddle River, NJ: Pearson.

Understanding the "Understanding": Preliminary Findings on Aboriginal Perspectives on Engagement With Governments

Annie Kennedy

1. INTRODUCTION

Engagement has become an all-embracing term these days for anything from opinion seeking to the development of joint partnerships and establishment of national indigenous representative bodies.[4] In this presentation today I am not seeking to present a typology of engagement or to talk about indigenous governance structures. Rather I am hoping to reflect my preliminary findings regarding Aboriginal perspectives from a very remote part of the Central Desert and their experience of their relationship with government around key services and reforms designed to improve Aboriginal well-being. How have the people I have worked with experienced and interpreted these events in their lives? How do they *engage* in the programs and services meant to benefit them?

Although my work originally focused on Aboriginal engagement in housing, the topic and approach to the research changed as a consequence of a number of events—primarily the introduction of 5-year leases introduced under the federal government's emergency response in the NT, the changes to CDEP, and the NT government's Shire reforms and draft outstation policy. It was these events, which Denzin (1989) calls *epiphanies,* that provided a unique opportunity for people to express how they understood what was taking place in the context of their daily lives. This was the background against which I began to understand how we might better engage and partner with Aboriginal people in remote, desert settlements.

2. THE RESEARCH METHODOLOGY

I will just touch briefly on my research methodology, which emerged out of indigenous concerns regarding the aims, methods, and construction of knowledge by researchers engaging with indigenous peoples around the world.

Central to indigenous concerns around the world is how research has been used, and continues to be used, to construct indigenous identity &

nonindigenous understanding of indigenous peoples. Indigenous researchers challenge the rules applied to what can be determined as knowledge. They also claim that researchers use objectivity and neutrality to remove themselves from being accountable to indigenous people for knowledge derived from their research (Bishop, 1998; Marker, 2003; Martin, 2003; Nakata, 1998; Rigney, 1999; Smith, 1999; Wilson, 2004).

Research with indigenous peoples is therefore underscored by some important principles.

- Its aim is to enable indigenous people to have control over their lives.
- It sees knowledge as constructed through relationship and cultural practice.
- In the research, indigenous voices are privileged.
- Researchers speak with and not for indigenous people.
- The researcher is accountable to indigenous people. This has implications for permissions, informed consent, and people's engagement in discussion and analysis of findings.

I also drew on critical epistemologies, particularly theorists' writing about how truth and fact are socially constructed through gender, race, power, and culture. In addition, I brought to the research values and experience from my own background, which has been influenced by social justice movements in South America and South East Asia. As I saw it, my job through the study was to facilitate an understanding on the part of the reader, the listener, government, and policy makers of what events *mean* to the people involved so that programs and services can be made more relevant (Denzin, 1989, 1997; Denzin & Lincoln, 2008a, 2008b).

The study was undertaken in collaboration with Aboriginal outstation residents in the Central Desert. Things never ever went the way that I planned or intended in the field. Many were the times when I had to let go and let events take their course. However, this form of naturalistic inquiry, which required immersion in the field over a period of some 3 years, led to unexpected opportunities, "ah-ha" insights that I could never have predicted, and the beginnings of relationships that I treasure deeply. It involved many opportunistic conversations, shared encounters with the labyrinth of government reforms, and a learning on both sides as people in the field engaged in review of my findings. While it is not possible today to do justice to the voices that have been part of this journey, I am drawing today on some of the key people that eventually trusted me enough to tell me their thoughts. I use their words to tell their stories.

3. SO WHAT DO ABORIGINAL PEOPLE IN THE BUSH HAVE TO SAY ABOUT THE FACTORS AND CONDITIONS WITHIN WHICH THEY ENGAGE?

> We just gotta really try to understand it—what they're saying. Some people don't understand what you are asking or telling them about. This is like a question to them . . . gotta come up with an answer to explain . . . what meanings. . . . See even for lease and permits on Aboriginal lands.
>
> Some people can understand English, the easy part, but not the one down under. Otherwise you gotta come out with the dictionary. You might have an educated person, but they still don't understand what's happening. See, it's just that you gotta understand the understanding!

This comment came from Solomon, a man in his 40s, as he struggled to understand what it was that he was being asked to agree to under changes to the Aboriginal Lands Rights Act and Emergency Response legislation. These reforms promised Aboriginal people greater wealth, better housing, and protection for their families. Solomon has worked at the Resource Centre for many years. He is a grandfather, father, and uncle to many; connected to most of the families that occupy the Aboriginal Land Trusts that make up the region serviced by the Outstation Resource Centre. With this status comes enormous responsibility to maintain and foster the links to the land of his ancestors and, through this, to ensure his family's welfare and identity.

Solomon's statement encapsulates the difficulties for Aboriginal people as they struggle not only to understand what is being said but also to grasp how the government reforms and initiatives they are expected to agree to will impact their lives.

4. WHAT IS ENGAGEMENT?

In the Australian policy arena, engagement has as its essence a desire to work with, to partner with, or to capture the interest and involvement of Aboriginal people. Understanding what is proposed and having the proposal accord with one's priorities, responsibilities, and circumstances is therefore a prerequisite to being able to reach an "understanding"—or agreement. Understanding is therefore both the capacity to comprehend and make sense of what is taking place, as well as agreement making through which one accords with decisions being made. It is agreement making underpinned by informed decision making.

Along this continuum a number of assumptions are made.

- The first assumption is that people understand what it is they are being asked to participate in. This requires not only being able to hear, access, and understand communications but also implies the ability to seek information or clarification and the right to communicate one's thoughts and ideas.
- Understanding also assumes comprehension of, or familiarity, with the concepts that sit behind the language. People interpret events in the light of their own experience and local conditions, so a shared under-standing of the concept or proposal being conveyed is an essential prerequisite to agreement making.
- And to fully engage, there is an assumption that people will agree—or reach an understanding about what is to take place. This in turn implies that people understand or can assess the implications of what they are agreeing to. It also assumes that what is proposed fits with what people feel is important in their lives as in making an agreement there is an assumption of shared purpose.

Understanding and agreement making necessarily take place in a context. In very remote Aboriginal Australia this centers on people's responsibilities to and nurturing by family and country.

5. UNDERSTANDING THROUGH COMMUNICATING

English Language Capacity

For outstation families a significant issue in engaging with governments is understanding language. Apart from a handful of people, most outstation residents speak Western Aranda, with English spoken as a second or third language. Language difference brings with it a range of difficulties when governments seek to reach an understanding with desert people about what is taking place.

The first and not least of these is that people understand the words being spoken. From the time that the Howard government first announced its Intervention into Aboriginal communities in the Northern Territory on June 21 2007, a plethora of new words and acronyms entered the bush. Under the *Intervention* people heard that jobs would be *normalized* and *mainstreamed*; there would be *compulsory acquisition* of Aboriginal land; people would be *transitioned* off CDEP; *income management* would replace CDEP wages; and Centrelink benefits would be *quarantined.* In the middle of this something called a *Shire* was coming.

As the Intervention proceeded, one of the key events that brought this issue to light at the Resource Centre was the transfer of 170 CDEP participants onto the Centrelink system and the introduction of income management. Marie and Ruby talk about how residents emerged bewildered from interviews with Centrelink or a Job Network Provider to seek their advice about what it was that they had just been told by the visiting teams.

Marie: They don't have the English!

Ruby: Lot of them don't know how to read and write. That's the main one.

Marie: 'Cause you've got Abstudy, youth allowance, new start allowance, pension payments, disability support pensions and carers pensions . . . and all those things, and there are a lot of forms, and they ask a lot of questions . . . questions people don't understand, or they can't answer those questions.

Ruby: That's what I'm sayin' . . . to explain. That's the main thing. The job of dealing with all these changes will fall on the interpreters . . . so all of the complainin' will come to me. It's gonna fall back on us 'cause they'll (Centrelink) still be reliant on us for help, because the government won't understand what the Aboriginal person is talkin' about, and the Aboriginal person won't understand what the government wants.

Understanding what was happening with the introduction of the Shires was also problematic. Even though Thatha had been to an English-language school in Alice Springs until she was 16, she still struggled to understand a lot of what was being said in government meetings. Following a local government–initiated meeting at a nearby township, which sought to explain the structure of the Shire, she came home frustrated.

That's how people get mixed up. It's alright for some . . . but old people don't understand. Like old J. They should explain properly. And instead a explainin' in plain English they just use the hard words. Plain English instead of hard words! They should use simple words n' go back n' explain. Like some words I can't understand myself. Try to explain it slowly, and see if you can get the right word to explain instead of just rushin' it. That's how people get confused.

Throughout my time in the field, people's understanding of what was said by visiting teams was complicated by the fact that in order to accommodate "avoidance" relationships, meetings were held outside. As a result many people sat on the ground some distance from the presenters. As there was no amplification provided by the visiting teams, only those nearest the government presenters could hear the proceedings.

[Other elements included Access to Information and Interpreters sections.]

6. FEELING COMFORTABLE AND SAFE

These comments indicate that misunderstandings arise from mixed-language encounters, and these encounters may bring with them emotions that impact the quality of local relationships. Feelings, however, also impact profoundly people's decisions about participating in direct encounters with strangers as well as their engagement in employment and training opportunities. Shame, trust, feeling safe, and feeling comfortable are dominant themes that emerge from the study.

Shame

In an Aboriginal context, shame acts as a substantial barrier to effective communications and compromises people's ability to speak and to participate in many programs. Even when people understand the language used, there can be a reluctance to offer an opinion or seek clarification as this would involve shame.

My discussions with people show that shame colors many aspects of Aboriginal interface with non-Aranda speakers. Shame may be felt when a person is afraid of making a mistake or when he or she feels likely to be embarrassed. Phone conversations are often extremely challenging for people who are afraid of not being understood or of not comprehending the English speaker's response. In the office Ruby faced these realities daily as people sought to deal with myriad dealings with Centrelink, banks, Job Network Providers, and vehicle repair shops.

> Like we tryin' to tell them to . . . you know, sign up for themselves. Teach them how to make . . . you know, call Centrelink and do things for themselves for a change. That's why we're there for. I tell them, "You have to give them a call . . . and make them fax it for you." But I dunno, everybody is too shame . . . too shy. Hmmm . . .
> . . . and most of 'em don't understand. I just tell 'em . . . "Just talk and just say, 'I want the agency to talk on behalf of me.'" . . . I tell 'em, "Just have a little talk, and if you don't understand, just say, 'I want the Centrelink agent to talk up on behalf of me.'" . . . So I'm slowly trying to tell them to, you know, do it themselves.

Dealing with official correspondence can also lead to feelings of shame and efforts to cover this up. As Ruby says,

> They act like they're readin' it, but they're not.

Shame may be a normal response to being with strangers, particularly for those who have difficulties with English, with people often avoiding these situations. Orgki talks with some of the women about how she or her son always gets pushed in front in these situations.

> C and P, they can speak English, but . . . same like what we were talkin' about earlier. Shame job. They get shame to talk to strangers. Like with our younger generations, they *been* with European people in schooling you know. And they got better English, more understanding, so they put them in front. "You talk, you talk, you talk!"

[Other sections included Comfort and Safety and Looking for Meanings Underneath. The following material included Understanding Priorities, Conceptual Understanding, Understanding Implications, and "Gettin' in the Middle" sections.]

7. FINAL REMARKS

Understanding the "understanding" is about the need to create a level playing field within which the Aboriginal participants in this study can meaningfully contribute to and participate in the programs and services that are meant to benefit them. Not only does it require conditions that enable Aboriginal people to understand and make sense of government initiatives but also that governments reach a more informed understanding of Aboriginal aspirations and realities. Can this be done?

These preliminary findings suggest that resetting the relationship and reengaging with indigenous peoples will require a strategic restructuring of government service delivery models. New ways need to be forged that value time and relationships as critical elements required to negotiate services and programs that reflect local realities and accord with Aboriginal responsibilities for country and family. These models necessitate more participatory modes of program development and delivery, flexible contracting strategies, new ways of partnering with civil society, and innovations in monitoring and evaluation systems.

The significance of this research and its call to work differently with Aboriginal people in remote communities to address the issue of understanding is much more than touchy-feely nonsense. After reading the recent Rudd government discussion paper on the future of the Northern Territory Emergency Response (Department of Families Housing Community Services and Indigenous Affairs, 2009), what is of concern is the positioning of indigenous policy initiatives in the Northern Territory as Special Measures under the Racial Discrimination Act. While there is debate as to whether the act requires the consent of those affected by the Special Measures, the emphasis given to consultations with NT communities indicates that the government is hoping at least to get positive feedback on what is proposed as Special Measures. If this is used as a precursor to arguing that existing provisions under the legislation are indeed Special Measures—in that they positively discriminate in favor of Aboriginal people in the Northern Territory, my concern is whether people are likely to understand what is at stake here and how their responses may be used. My preliminary findings suggest that current government systems, capacities, communications patterns, and time lines will do little to close the gap for Aboriginal people in understanding that particular understanding.

There are real dilemmas for the Aboriginal people who participated in my research concerning the way forward. Solomon sums it up:

> There is a solution there, but before that to come out it will be pretty hard for people to say it. They gotta think *how* they gonna say it! But you still gotta

come back to that wall. There is a solution, but it's gotta pass through to that man (in government), and we don't know what he's gonna say.

Each individual people they got their own solution, but sometimes they shy to say in public. If they are in a smaller group might say something. Sometimes it's hard to talk to these people to get that solution outta them. Sometimes they say in language, but they . . . you gotta translated it back into English and then you get it wrong. People got the solution, but do we get it out of them? Gotta have a real good translator to make you (the outsider) understand. See the solution they gonna give you is a solution and a problem (at the same time) . . . like they gonna say, "Why did the government change all them things?" Then it comes up, and you gotta have answers there too. You know, people got the solution there, but they don't say it.

REFERENCES

Bishop, R. (1998). Freeing ourselves from neo-colonial domination in research: A Maori approach to creating knowledge. *Qualitative Studies in Education, 11*(2), 199–219.

Denzin, N. K. (1989). *Interpretive interactionism* (vol. 16, 17). Applied social research methods series. London: Sage.

Denzin, N. K. (1997). *Interpretive ethnography.* Thousand Oaks, CA: Sage.

Denzin, N. K., & Lincoln, Y. (2008a). *Handbook of critical indigenous methodologies.* Thousand Oaks, CA: Sage.

Denzin, N. K., & Lincoln, Y. (Eds.). (2008b). *Collecting and interpreting qualitative materials* (3rd ed.). Thousand Oaks, CA: Sage.

Department of Families Housing Community Services and Indigenous Affairs. (2009). *Future directions for the Northern Territory emergency response: Discussion paper.* Canberra: Australian government.

Marker, M. (2003). Indigenous voice, community, and epistemic violence: The ethnographer's "interests" and what "interests" the ethnographer. *Qualitative Studies in Education, 16*(3), 361–375.

Martin, K. (2003). Ways of knowing, being and doing: A theoretical framework and methods for Indigenous and Indigenist research. *Journal of Australian Studies, 76,* 203–214.

Morgan Disney & Associates, Tracey Whetnall Consulting, & Wis-Wei Consulting. (2006). *Synapsis review of the COAG Trial Evaluations.* Commonwealth of Australia. oipc.gov.au/publications/PDF/COAG_Trials_Synopsis_Review .PDF.

Nakata, M. (1998). Anthropological texts and indigenous standpoints. *Australian Aboriginal Studies, 2,* 3–11.

Rigney, L. (1999, Fall). Internationalisation of an indigenous anti-colonial cultural critique of research methodologies: A guide to indigenist research methodology and its principles. *Journal for Native American Studies, 14*(2), 109–121.

Smith, L. T. (1999). *Decolonizing methodologies: Research and indigenous people.* Dunedin, NZ: University of Otago Press.

Wilson, S. S. (2004). Research as ceremony: Articulating an indigenous research paradigm. Unpublished PhD thesis, Monash University.

Milyirrtjarra Kuurl Mirrka Palyalpayi (Making Good Food at Warburton School)

Ros Beadle

EARLY DAYS

The *Milyirrtjarra Kuurl Mirrka Palyalpayi* (Making Good Food at Warburton School) Program commenced as a school breakfast program in November 2008.[5] It was initiated by community concerns regarding low school attendance. With the support of the school principal, four local grandmothers commenced a daily school breakfast program with resources provided by FoodBank WA and the Warburton Community Office. As described by one of the breakfast ladies, "Kids go to school every day when they have that good healthy breakfast, so they can stay in school and be good kids."[6]

The program rapidly expanded as the older women sought help from their younger relatives. They trained the "young girls" (daughters, nieces, and granddaughters) to work on the program and organized themselves as a "pool" of workers to allow for pressures of family and community life that might prohibit them from attending work every day. As described by one of the grandmothers, sharing the load had further benefits: "It was good for them to have a job, and we learned them how to do the *mai* (food) for the kids."[7]

The women also used their networking skills to liaise between themselves and ensure that if they are not available on any particular day, someone can work in their place. New women are constantly recruited to the program and to date, nearly 4 years later, over 35 women from different generations and families have participated. Once recruited, the women train each other "on the job," and within a few days there is a new Warburton Breakfast *Minyma* (woman).

At the same time as the Breakfast Minyma (women) began operating, several other initiatives were also taking place, meaning school attendance was being addressed from different angles. These other simultaneous efforts included the employment of a school attendance officer (who worked alongside the women) and also various rewards attached to improving attendance.

During the early stages of the program, the women and wider school community noted an improvement in attendance, and the principals have commented on the positive benefits the breakfast program had in encouraging kids to come to school and stay in class as well as increasing community engagement in school activities.

Although attendance was the original focus of the program, as the governance capacity of the Breakfast Minyma strengthened, the program took on more holistic approach.

BEYOND BREAKFAST

Despite continuing to proudly call themselves the Warburton Breakfast Minyma, the women soon identified other catering activities to which to apply their skills. At the school's request, the women started catering for school Open Days and Theme Days each term.

In mid-2010, the Home and Community Care (HACC) coordinator working for Ngaanyatjarra Health Service struck up conversations with the Breakfast Minyma about the possibility of the women providing HACC meals (meals on wheels), which were at the time being prepared by the Warburton Community Store, to the elderly in the community. The Breakfast Minyma eased their way into the service, first by doing weekly cooking sessions of healthy meals focused around stews, curries, pastas, and bakes, complemented with desserts of rice cream, custard, and fruit. Initially, the meals were picked up by the HACC worker, but over time the women took this activity on themselves, mobilized by learning to drive and acquiring driving licenses and having a vehicle donated to the program by the Ngaanyatjarra Council.

Before, those meals came from the store, but they wanted us to make them. We were happy, you know, and make all the old people happy, all the breakfast ladies cooking them HACC meals. So they pukurlpa (happy).[8]

Today, following the establishment of a memorandum of understanding with the Department of Corrections, the women cook the bulk of their meals in the commercial kitchen at the Warburton Work Camp (a low-security, Department of Corrections facility)—an excellent well-appointed work space they very much enjoy having the opportunity to access.

It's a lovely big kitchen, and it feel likes our own while we are there. We enjoy learning how to use all the new equipment, especially that big oven.[9]

Formally accredited training undertaken by the women assisted their access to the commercial kitchen space. Early in the history of the Breakfast Minyma, it became apparent that the women were keen to formalize their skills in a nationally accredited training program, a step that would assist them with further employment and create further meaning to their work. In April 2012 seven of the women completed their qualification (Certificate One in Kitchen Operations) and were presented with their certification at Polytechnic West.

At the beginning of this year, the high school teachers consulted with the Breakfast Minyma about the possibility of the high school girls coming to do some cooking with the women in the Family Place (a portable building with a meeting room and a small kitchen space run by the Minyma). Once a week the high school girls visit to make school lunches for the kids with the guidance of the Breakfast Minyma, another of their important contributions to the community.

> *When the girls come all the ladies help them, show them how to cook. Then sometimes when the ladies are cooking, like at BBQs and things, the young girls can help us. It makes us feel happy when they come in and help the workers. We teach the girls how to use knives. When we go for training we come back and then learn these other little girls, yeah, it's a really lovely way to teach them.[10]*

In 2010 the women published a storybook about the breakfast program that was launched by the WA Minister for Education and is used as a language resource in the local Warburton school classrooms. For the last 12 months the women have used photographic and video material from their activities in the Parent and Community Engagement (PACE) program, funded by DEEWR, to tell the kids at Warburton school about what they do. On the visuals the kids proudly point out their family members working in the kitchen and marvel at the wonderful facilities their mums, aunties, and grandmothers have access to.

> *It's good for the kids to see the photos, watch the ladies. Like they want to learn, when they grow older, they see the family working there, they get happy the kids, and when they must finish school, get a job you know, like the ladies too.[11]*

> *It makes them feel proud looking at the pictures of what their families are doing. The kids say, "Oh that's my mum working."[12]*

EXTERNAL SUPPORT

Since its conception the Milyirrtjarra Kuurl Mirrka Palyalpayi program has been supported by a diverse array of agencies both financially and in kind. These include the Ngaanyatjarra Council, the Warburton Community Office, WA Department for Child Protection, Community Development Foundation, FoodBank WA, LinkWest, the WA Department of Education, and many more.

However, as programs develop and enterprise skills evolve, the program is becoming increasingly financially independent with income arriving from catering events, small grants, fundraisers (BBQs and discos) and earring making. These funds are used for cooking equipment, other requirements such as crafts and makeup materials for the *Kungka* (Girls) Nights, a television for the Family Place, the installation of a washing machine, and to partially cover the costs of training trips to Perth. The finances are managed by LinkWest (an NGO in Perth), and at the weekly meetings discussions are had about the existing finances and decisions are made about outgoing costs.

GOVERNANCE PROCESSES AND PARTNERSHIPS

Each week on Monday mornings the women have a meeting at the Family Place to evaluate the different aspects of their program, make plans for upcoming events, and address current issues. The meetings usually last for 1 to 1.5 hours in which the women address the agenda items, raise issues, discuss issues with each other, and arrive at solutions. They gently guide the program in direction so that it suits their lives and the lives of their families while at the same time building capacity to enhance the well-being of them and their families. Over time as the women's confidence has risen, the chairing of the meeting has rolled from the support staff to the most senior member of the program, Olive Lawson. For the most part the meetings are conducted in the local language, with translation where support from support staff is necessary.

Over time, the women have also played a role as consultants for visiting staff and agencies who want to know their perspective on community issues. The women too have become regular attendees at the monthly Warburton Interagency Meeting, as well as representing the Ngaanyatjarra Lands

School on the Goldfields Aboriginal Education Advisory Group that meets in Kalgoorlie.

> *Some visitors go round there (Family Place), some big people go round, come see us, come talk to us, stay there a bit and have a yarn. Boss people, government ladies, DCP, staff, and all. They come and see us when we are working. They come and praising the workers. They just say, "Oh, it's really wonderful job that you are doing ladies."[13]*

The role of support worker within the program, which continues to be essential, has rapidly evolved as the women gain capacity and confidence. Support includes staff from the Department for Child Protection, a Youth and Family Support worker, the Parent and Community Engagement (PACE) coordinator, and the Ngaanyatjarra Council community project officer.

The women have played a major part in shaping the role of the support workers. The critical requirement is for the staff to act as a catalyst to assist the women in bridging barriers between themselves and mainstream systems in areas where they are not already competent. As autonomy and skills increase, it requires the role of support staff to shift and, in some cases, cease.

After 4 years of engagement in self-initiated activities, the Breakfast Minyma have created a program that suits the interests and agendas of them, their families, and their community. There have been constraints along the way, but together the women have worked to overcome them. They have successfully designed an organization upon frameworks that were not prede-termined nor had any external expectations.

The program continues to evolve, governed by the Breakfast Minyma, and demonstrates that remote communities have the strength, power, and resil-ience to provide their own services rather than being dependent on outside resources.

NOTES

1. Used with permission of Deborah Rae.

2. The reports in this appendix are different in style but follow the basic proce-dures for formulating a report outlined in Chapter 8. Note that the first report, "Transitions," contains a report within a report. Part of the formal report is a report presented by the author to the women with whom she had been working. They repre-sent reports that emerged from action research projects.

3. Used with permission of Karen Swift.

4. This example is excerpted from a larger paper presented by Annie Kennedy at the Centre for Remote Health Seminar Series, Alice Springs, 2009.

5. This paper is excerpted from a report by the Aboriginal and Torres Strait Islander Commission Report (2012), Sydney, Australia.

6. Quote from a Warburton community member.

7. Breakfast Minyma (woman) 1.

8. Breakfast Minyma 1.

9. Breakfast Minyma 2.

10. Breakfast Minyma 3.

11. Breakfast Minyma 4.

12. Breakfast Minyma 5.

13. Breakfast Minyma 1.

REFERENCES

Alinsky, S. (1989). *Rules for radicals.* London: Vintage/Random House.

Anderson, G., Herr, K., & Nihlen, A. (2007). *Studying your own school: An educator's guide to qualitative practitioner research* (2nd ed.). Thousand Oaks, CA: Corwin.

Atweh, B., Weeks, P., & Kemmis, S. (Eds.). (1998). *Action research in practice: Partnerships for social justice in education.* New York: Routledge.

Bellman, L. (2003). *Nurse led change and development in clinical practice.* London: Whurr.

Bellman, L., Bywood, C., & Dale, S. (2003). Action research to improve clinical practice. *Nurse Education in Practice, 3*(4).

Benner, P. (1994). *Interpretive phenomenology: Embodiment, caring, and ethics in health and illness.* Thousand Oaks, CA: Sage.

Berger Gluck, S., & Patai, D. (Eds.). (1991). *Women's words: The feminist practice of oral history.* New York: Routledge.

Black, J. K. (1991). *Development in theory and practice: Bridging the gap.* Boulder, CO: Westview.

Block, P. (1990). *The empowered manager: Positive political skills at work.* San Francisco: Jossey-Bass.

Brown, D. (1970). *Bury my heart at Wounded Knee: An Indian history of the American west.* London: Vintage.

Bruner, J. (1990). *Acts of meaning.* Cambridge, MA: Harvard University Press.

Brydon-Miller, M., & Greenwood, D. (2006, March). A re-examination of the relationship between action research and human subjects review processes. *Action Research, 4*(1), 117–128.

Burnaford, G., Fischer, J., & Hobson, D. (Eds.). (1996). *Teachers doing research: Practical possibilities.* Mahwah, NJ: Lawrence Erlbaum.

Calhoun, E. (1993, October). Action research: Three approaches. *Educational Leadership, 51*(2), 62–65.

Carroll, F., Jenkins, A., Woodward, C., Kop, R., & Jenkins, E. (2012, June). Exploring how social media can enhance the teaching of action research. *Action Research, 10, 170–188.*

Christians, C., Ferre, J., & Fackler, M. (1993). *Good news: Social ethics and the press.* New York: Oxford University Press.

Coghlan, D., & Brannick, T. (2004). *Doing action research in your own organization* (2nd ed.). Thousand Oaks, CA: Sage.

Coghlan, D., & Brannick, T. (2009). *Doing action research in your own organization* (3rd ed.). Thousand Oaks, CA: Sage.

Coghlan, D., & Brydon-Miller, M. (in press). *Encyclopedia of action research.* Thousand Oaks, CA: Sage.

Collins, P. (1991). *Black feminist thought.* New York: Routledge.

Coover, V., Deacon, E., Esser, C., & Moore, C. (1985). *Resource manual for a living revolution.* Philadelphia: New Society.

Denzin, N. K. (1989). *Interpretive interactionism.* Newbury Park, CA: Sage.

Denzin, N. K. (1997). *Interpretive ethnography.* Thousand Oaks, CA: Sage.

Denzin, N. K., & Lincoln, Y. S. (Eds.). (1994). *Sage handbook of qualitative research.* Thousand Oaks, CA: Sage.

Denzin, N. K., & Lincoln, Y. S. (Eds.). (2005). *Sage handbook of qualitative research* (3rd ed.). Thousand Oaks, CA: Sage.

Denzin, N. K., & Lincoln, Y. S. (Eds.). (2011). *Sage handbook of qualitative research* (4th ed.). Thousand Oaks, CA: Sage.

Derrida, J. (1976). *Of grammatology.* Baltimore: Johns Hopkins University Press.

Deshler, D. (1990). Conceptual mapping: Drawing charts of the mind. In J. Mezirow & Associates (Eds.), *Fostering critical reflection in adulthood* (pp. 336–353). San Francisco: Jossey-Bass.

Dick, B. (2012). Action research literature 2008–2010: Themes and trends. *Action Research, 10*(3), 122–143.

Fals-Borda, O., & Rahman, M. (Eds.). (1991). *Action and knowledge: Breaking the monopoly with participatory action-research.* New York: Apex.

Fish, S. (1980). *Is there a text in this class? The authority of interpretive communities.* Cambridge, MA: Harvard University Press.

Fortune, A., McCallion, P., & Briar-Lawson, K. (2010). *Social work practice for the twenty-first century.* New York: Columbia University Press.

Foucault, M. (1972). *The archaeology of knowledge.* New York: Random House.

Foucault, M. (1984). *The Foucault reader* (P. Rabinow, Ed.). Harmondsworth, UK: Penguin.

French, S., Reynolds, F., & Swan, J. (2001). *Practical research: A guide for therapists* (2nd ed.). London: Butterworth Heinemann.

Goodenough, W. (1963). *Cooperation in change: An anthropological approach to community development.* New York: Russell Sage.

Greenwood, D., & Levin, M. (2006). *Introduction to action research: Social research for social change* (2nd ed.). Thousand Oaks, CA: Sage.

Guba, E. G. (1990). *The paradigm dialogue.* Newbury Park, CA: Sage.

Guba, E. G., & Lincoln, Y. S. (1989). *Fourth generation evaluation.* Newbury Park, CA: Sage.

Gustavsen, B. (2001). Theory and practice: The mediating discourse. In P. Reason & H. Bradbury (Eds.), *Handbook of action research* (pp. 17–26). Thousand Oaks, CA: Sage.

Habermas, J. (1979). *Communication and the evolution of society* (T. McCarthy, Trans.). Boston: Beacon Press.

Habermas, J. (1984). *The theory of communicative action: Reason and the rationality of society.* Boston: Beacon Press.

Haebich, A. (1988). *For their own good.* Perth: University of Western Australia Press.

Hart, E., & Bond, M. (1995). *Action research for health and social care: A guide to practice.* London: Open University Press.

Hendricks, C. (2011). *Improving schools through action research: A reflective practice approach* (3rd ed.). Upper Saddle River, NJ: Pearson.

Heron, J. (1997). *Co-operative inquiry: Research into the human condition.* Thousand Oaks, CA: Sage.

Hickman, G. (2009). *Leading organizations: Perspectives for a new era* (2nd ed.). Thousand Oaks, CA: Sage.

Hinkin, T. (2005). *Cases in hospitality management: A critical incident approach.* Hoboken, NJ: Wiley.

Holly, M. L., Arhar, J., & Kasten, W. (2008). *Action research for teachers: Travelling the yellow brick road* (3rd ed.). Upper Saddle River, NJ: Prentice Hall.

Huyssens, A. (1986). *After the great divide: Modernism, mass culture, postmodernism.* Bloomington: Indiana University Press.

Juhnke, G., & Kelly, V. (2005). *Critical incidents in addictions counseling.* Alexandria, VA: American Counseling Association.

Kagan, C., Burton, M., & Siddiquee, A. (2008). Action research. In C. Willig & W. Stainton,-Rogers (Eds.), *Sage handbook of qualitative research in health.* Thousand Oaks, CA: Sage.

Kelly, A., & Gluck, R. (1979). *Northern Territory community development.* Unpublished manuscript, University of Queensland, St. Lucia, Australia.

Kelly, A., & Sewell, S. (1988). *With head, heart, and hand.* Brisbane, Queensland, Australia: Boolarong.

Kemmis, S., & McTaggart, R. (1999). *The action research planner* (3rd ed.). Geelong, Australia: Deakin University Press.

Kickett, D., McCauley, D., & Stringer, E. (1986). *Community development processes: An introductory handbook.* Perth, Western Australia: Curtin University of Technology.

Kincheloe, J. (1991). *Teachers as researchers: Qualitative inquiry as a path to empowerment.* London: Falmer.

Koch, T., & Kralich, D. (2006). *Participatory action research in healthcare.* London: Blackwell.

Koshy, E., Koshy, V., & Waterman, H. (2011). *Action research in healthcare.* Thousand Oaks, CA: Sage.

Kretzmann, J., & McKnight, J. (1993). *Building communities from the inside out.* Chicago: ACTA.

Levin, M., & Greenwood, D. (2001). Action research and the struggle to transform universities into learning communities. In P. Reason & H. Bradbury (Eds.), *Handbook of action research: Participative inquiry and practice* (pp. 103–113). Thousand Oaks, CA: Sage.

Levin, M., & Greenwood, D. (2011). Revitalizing universities by reinventing the social sciences. In N. Denzin & Y. Lincoln (Eds.), *Sage handbook of qualitative research* (pp. 27–42). Thousand Oaks, CA: Sage.

Lewin, K. (1946). Action research and minority problems. *Journal of Social Issues, 2,* 34–46.

Lincoln, Y. S. (1995). Emerging criteria for quality in qualitative and interpretive inquiry. *Qualitative Inquiry, 1,* 275–289.

Lincoln, Y. S., & Guba, E. G. (1985). *Naturalistic inquiry.* Beverly Hills, CA: Sage.

Lincoln, Y. S., & Tierney, W. (1996). *Representation and the text: Reframing the narrative voice.* Albany: SUNY Press.

Lyotard, J.-F. (1984). *The postmodern condition: A report on knowledge.* Minneapolis: University of Minnesota Press.

Malinowski, B. (1961). *Argonauts of the western Pacific: An account of native enterprise and adventure in the archipelagoes of Melanesian New Guinea.* New York: E. P. Dutton. (Original work published 1922)

McCauley, D. (1985). *Community development.* Unpublished manuscript, Perth, Western Australia.

McMurray, A., & Pace, R. W. (2006). *Action research in learning organizations.* Thousand Oaks, CA: Sage.

McNiff, J., Lomax, P., & Whitehead, J. (2003). *You and your action research project* (2nd ed.). New York: Routedge.

McNiff, J., & Whitehead, J. (2006). *Action research for teachers: A practical guide.* Abingdon, UK: David Fulton.

McNiff, J., & Whitehead, J. (2009). *Doing and writing action research.* Thousand Oaks, CA: Sage.

McNiff, J., & Whitehead, J. (2011). *All you need to know about action research* (2nd ed.). Thousand Oaks, CA: Sage.

McTaggart, R. (Ed.). (1997). *Participatory action research: International contexts and consequences.* Albany: SUNY Press.

Mead, G. H. (1934). *Mind, self, and society: From the standpoint of a social behaviorist.* Chicago: University of Chicago Press.

Milgram, S. (1963). Behavioral study of obedience. *Journal of Abnormal and Social Psychology, 67,* 371–378.

Mills, G. (2013). *Action research: A guide for the teacher researcher* (5th ed.). Columbus, OH: Merrill/Prentice Hall.

Minkler, M., & Wallerstein, N. (2008). *Community based participatory research for health* (2nd ed.). San Francisco: Jossey-Bass.

Morton-Cooper, A. (2000). *Action research in healthcare.* Oxford: Blackwell Publications.

Neumann, A., & Peterson, P. (1997). *Women, research, and autobiography in education.* New York: Teachers College Press.

Noffke, S. E., & Somekh, B. (Eds.). (2009). *Sage Handbook of educational action research.* Thousand Oaks, CA: Sage.

Noffke, S. E., & Stevenson, R. (Eds.). (1995). *Educational action research: Becoming practically critical.* New York: Teachers College Press.

Peck, M. S. (1993). *A world waiting to be born: Civility rediscovered.* New York: Bantam.

Reason, P. (Ed.). (1988). *Human inquiry in action: Developments in new paradigm research.* Newbury Park, CA: Sage.

Reason, P., & Bradbury, H. (Eds.). (2001). *Handbook of action research.* Thousand Oaks, CA: Sage.

Reason, P., & Bradbury, H. (Eds.). (2007). *Handbook of action research* (2nd ed.). Thousand Oaks, CA: Sage.

Reason, P., & Marshall, J. (1987). Research as personal process. In D. Boud & V. Griffin (Eds.), *Appreciating adult learning* (pp. 112–125). London: Kogan Page.

Reeb, R. (2007). *Community action research: Benefits to community members and service providers.* Binghamton, NY: Haworth Press.

Sagor, R. (2004). *The action research guidebook: A four-step process for educators and school teams.* Thousand Oaks, CA: Corwin Press.

Schmuck, R. (2006). *Practical action research for change* (2nd ed.). Boston: Allyn & Bacon.

Schouten, D., & Watling, R. (1997). *Media action projects: A model for integrating video in project-based education, training and community development.* Nottingham, UK: University of Nottingham Urban Programme Research Group.

Senge, P. (2006). *The fifth discipline.* New York: Crown Business.

Senge, P., Kleiner, A., Roberts, C., Ross, R., Roth, G., & Smith, B. (1999). *The dance of change: The challenges of sustaining momentum in learning organizations.* New York: Crown Business.

Smith, D. E. (1989). Sociological theory: Methods of writing patriarchy. In R. A. Wallace (Ed.), *Feminism and sociological theory* (pp. 34–64). Newbury Park, CA: Sage.

Spradley, J. P. (1979). *The ethnographic interview.* New York: Holt, Rinehart & Winston.

Spradley, J., & McCurdy, D. (1972). *The cultural experience: Ethnography in complex society.* Prospect Heights, IL: Waveland Press.

Stake, R. (2005). Case studies. In N. Denzin & Y. Lincoln (Eds.), *Sage handbook of qualitative inquiry* (pp. 236–247). Thousand Oaks, CA: Sage.

Stringer, E. (2002). *Parent-teacher associations in East Timor.* Dili, East Timor: Ministry for Education, Culture, Youth and Sports/UNICEF.

Stringer, E. (2004). *Action research in education.* Upper Saddle River, NJ: Pearson.

Stringer, E. (2007). "This is so democratic!" Action research and policy development in East Timor. In P. Reason & H. Bradbury (Eds.), *Handbook of action research.* Thousand Oaks, CA: Sage.

Stringer, E., & Dwyer, R. (2005). *Action research in human services.* Upper Saddle River, NJ: Pearson.

Stringer, E., & Genat, W. (2004). *Action research in health.* Upper Saddle River, NJ: Pearson.

Tillman, L. (2002). Culturally sensitive research approaches: An African American perspective. *Educational Researcher, 31*(9), 3–12.

Trinh, M.-H. (1992). *Framer framed.* New York: Routledge.

Tripp, D. (1993). *Critical incidents in teaching: Developing professional judgment.* London: Routledge.

Tyler, S. (2006). *Communities, livelihoods, and natural resources: Action research and policy change in Asia.* Rugby, UK: Intermediate Technology Development Group.

Tyson, L., Perusse, R., & Whitledge, J. (2004). *Critical incidents in group counseling.* Alexandria, VA: American Counseling Association.

Unger, R. (1987). *Social theory: Its situation and its task.* Cambridge: Cambridge University Press.

U.S. National Science Foundation. (2013). *Frequently asked questions and vignettes.* Retrieved from www.nsf.gov/bfa/dias/policy/hsfaqs.jsp

Van Willigen, J. (1993). *Applied anthropology.* South Hadley, MA: Bergin & Garvey.

Vlachos, E. (1975). *Social impact assessment: An overview.* Fort Belvoir, VA: Army Corps of Engineers, Institute of Water Resources.

Wadsworth, Y. (2011). *Everyday evaluation on the run* (3rd ed.). Walnut Creek, CA: Left Coast Press.

Warner Burke, W. (2010). *Organization change: Theory and practice* (3rd ed.). Thousand Oaks, CA: Sage.

West, C. (1989). *The American evasion of philosophy.* Madison: University of Wisconsin Press.

Whitehead, J., & McNiff, J. (2006). *Action research: A living theory.* Thousand Oaks, CA: Sage.

Whyte, W. F. (1984). *Learning from the field: A guide from experience.* Beverly Hills, CA: Sage.

Williamson, G., Bellman, L., & Webster, J. (2012). *Action research in nursing and healthcare.* Thousand Oaks, CA: Sage.

Winter, R., & Munn-Giddings, C. (2001). *A handbook for action research in health and social care.* London: Routledge.

Witherall, C., & Noddings, N. (Eds.). (1991). *Stories lives tell: Narrative and dialogue in education.* New York: Teachers College Press.

INDEX

Figures, boxes, and tables are indicated by *f*, *b*, or *t* following the page number.

Aboriginal people
  breakfast program, 117–118
  child protection manual and, 57
  experts failing to understand, 44–45
  judgmental attitude towards, 138
  statements of the problem, 99
  subgroups in, 78
  as teachers, 3–4
  as testing ground, xvi
  victim view of, 197
Aboriginal school, 11–12
Accounts, 116, 124, 224–225. *See also*
    Formal reports; Reports
Action plans
  overview, 166–168, 185–186b
  construction of, 169–173, 171f
  evaluation of, 182–183
  linking of support networks,
    179–180, 181f
  modeling, 178–179
  priority identification for, 168–169
  quality checks, 173–175
  results possible with, 166–167
  review of, 180–182, 196
  for strategic planning, 195–196
  supporting of, 175–178
Action research
  overview, 35b
  applications of, 11–13, 13–14b
  change as outcome of, 59, 62b, 63
  communication in, 26–28, 27b
  community basis of, xxi
  as community of inquiry, 23–24
  critque of, 63
  inclusion in, 31–33, 31b
  legitimacy issues, 41–45
  literature on, 64–68
  meaningfulness and, 54–57
  as participatory, 6–8, 14–20,
    28–31, 28b
  power differentials and, 68–69

purposes of, 1–5
relationships in, 24–26, 24b
scripts and, 59–64, 62b
social values of, 14–15
solutions as the focus of, 10–13
as systematic process of inquiry,
    5–10, 8–9b, 9f
traditional research compared, 5–6, 8,
    8–9b, 62b
websites for, 239–246
See also Action plans; Formal reports;
    Look phase; Planning stage;
    Reports; Theory; Think phase
Action Research & Data website, 241
Action Research Approach to
    Curriculum Development, 240
Action Research at Queens University
    website, 242
Action Research in Education
    website, 241
Action Research Ireland, 232
Action Research journal, 232, 235
Action Research Net website, 242
Action Research Resources website, 242
Action Research Special Interest Group
    of AERA website, 241
Act phase. *See* Action plans
Affirming statements, 176–177
Afrocentric feminist epistemology, 56
Agendas, 82, 84–85, 157
ALARA: Action Learning, Action
    Research Association website, 242
Analysis. *See* Think phase
Analysis enrichment
  overview, 147–148, 147f
  concept mapping, 152–155, 154f
  organizational reviews, 150–152
  six questions, 148–150
Antecedents, 155–156, 156f
Asset-Based Community Development
    Institute website, 239

Audit trails, 94
Authoritarian style, 21–23, 24–25, 73–74

Beadle, Ros, 287–291
Best practices, 45
Block, P., 190–191
Blogs, 230–232
Bracketing, 139–140
Bradbury, H., 37–38
Brannick, T., 65–66
Brian Holmes' Research Blog, 232
British Columbia Centre of Excellence
    for Women's Health website, 243
Budgets, 198–200, 199*t*
Bureaucratic organizations, 190

Calhoun, E., 64
Canadian Journal of Action Research
    website, 242
Capacity building, 16–17
CARAMAsia website, 243
CARE: Centre for Applied Research in
    Education website, 242
Careers & the disABLED Magazine, 240
CARN: Collaborative Action Research
    Network website, 242
Categorization of data, 139–144
Celebrations, 207–208
Centralized control, 29
Change
    as goal, 59, 62b, 63
    internal to facilitators, 65
    political issues of, 196–198
    as sustainable, 187–189
Cloud storage, 238
Coding of data, 139–144
Coghlan, D., 65–66
Collaboration. *See* Participation
Collaborative descriptive accounts, 124
Collaborative online tools. *See* Internet
Collins, Patricia Hill, 56
Communication
    about action plans, 176
    about meetings, 131–132
    about strategic planning, 200–201
    in action research, 26–28, 27b
    effectiveness, elements of, 26–27
    meaning-making dialogue, 19–20
    sociable participation and, 95
    See also Reports
Community consultation, 22
Community of inquiry, 23–24

Community profiles, 125–126
Concept mapping, 152–155, 154*f*
Confirmability, 94
Conflict, 15–16
Conflict resolution, 178
Consensus, 75–76, 131, 203
Consequences, 155–156, 156*f*
Constructions, 75–76
Context and history, 85–88, 223–224
Control. *See* Power and control
Cooperativeness in execution, xi–xii
Corporate mentality, 29–30
Credibility, 92–93
Critical incidents, 144–145
Critical reference groups, 79, 80*t*
Crowdsourcing, 232

Data gathering. *See* Look phase
Data types. *See* Look phase
Debriefing, 93
Decentralization, x–xi
Demographics, 125–126
Denzin, N. K., 53, 55, 58–59, 136–137
Dependability, 94
Deregulation, x–xii
Derrida, J., 50–51
Descriptive analysis, 123–126
Descriptive features, 223
Design. *See* Planning stage
Disabilities-R-Us Chat Network, 240
DisABILITY Information and
    Resources website, 240
Disabled People's International, 240
Discourses, 48–49
Dissertations and theses, 214–216, 215b
Diverse case analysis, 93
Documents, records and reports, 115–116
Dropbox, 236–237, 238
Duty of care, 89–90

East Timor, 138–139, 172–173, 187–188
Easychirp, 233
Education, 67–69
eLearning Island, 232
Emic knowledge, 106
Empowerment, 16–17
EmTech Action Research website, 243
Encouragement comments, 108
Engagement, 92
Enlightened self-interest, 191
Entrepreneurial organizations, 190–191
Epiphanic events, 144–145

Ethic of caring, 56
Ethics, 88–91, 117
Ethnocentrism, 44–45
Ethnographic Action Research
	UNESCO-CI website, 243
Etic constructs, 60–61, 106
Evaluation, 182–183, 204–206
Example questions, 108
Experience-near concepts, 137–138
Experimental method, 42–44
Experimental research. *See* Research
Experts, 21, 43
Extension questions, 108

Facebook, 233–234
Facilitators
	impacts of during research, 96
	leadership and, 30–31
	modeling by, 178–179
	power differentials and, 68–69
	practitioners as, 2–3
	in reports, 219–220
	role of, 15
	sociable participation by, 94–95
	stance and presentation, 82
	support of action plans by, 175–178
Feminist.com website, 243
Feminist theory, 56–57
Field notes, 110, 113, 114*b*
Filmer, Dick, 25–26
Financial planning, 198–200, 199*t*
First-person research, 65
Fish, S., 49–50
Focus groups, 111–113
Food, 207
Formal reports
	action research reports
		compared, 215*b*
	alternative structures for,
		226–229, 228*b*
	conclusion section, 225–226
	funding and, 212
	introduction section, 217
	literature reviews, 217–218
	methodology section, 218–222
	need for, 211–212
	outcomes and findings section,
		222–225
	purposes of, 216
	structure overview, 216–217
	theses and dissertations, 214–216, 215*b*
	voice of participants and, 214–216, 215*b*

See also A New Mathematics
	Curriculum (Swift); Transitions
	headings; Understanding the
	"Understanding": Preliminary
	Findings on Aboriginal
	Perspectives on Engagement
	With Governments (Kennedy)
Foucault, Michel, 48–49
Fourth Generation Evaluation (Guba &
	Lincoln), 19–20, 182–183
Frustration, 16–17
Funding, 198–200, 199*t*

Gatekeepers, 79–81
Gathering data. *See* Look phase
Goal identification, 169
Google Docs, 236
Grand tour questions, 107, 109*b*
Greenwood, D., 42, 66
Ground rules for meetings, 130
Group interviews, 111–113
Guba, Egon G., xiv, 19–20, 75, 92, 182–183
Guided reflection, 105–111, 109*b*
Guided tour questions, 108
Gustavsen, B., 38

Habermas, Jurgen, 26, 52
Handbook of Qualitative Research
	(Denzin & Lincoln), 53
Hashtags, 232–233
Health sciences, action research
	resources for, 67–68
HELP: Health Education Library for the
	People website, 243
Hermeneutic dialectic process, 19–20,
	75–76
History and context, 85–88
HIV InSite website, 243
Human service agencies. See Social
	programs and services
Huyssens, A., 51

Ideal speech situations, 26–27
Implementation. *See* Action plans
Incarceration, 32
Inclusion, 31–33, 31*b*
Informal Adult and Community
	Education website, 239
Information sources. *See* Look phase
Informed consent, 89–91
Institute for Community Research
	website, 245

Institutionalized practices, 40–41
Internal review boards (IRBs), 91
International Development Research
    Centre website, 245
Internet
    action research websites, 239–246
    blogs, 230–232
    cloud storage, 238
    Dropbox, 236–237, 238
    Facebook, 233–234
    Google Docs, 236
    literature reviews using, 121–122
    ooVoo, 236
    PhotoVoice, 238–239
    Second Life, 234–235
    Skype, 235
    Twitter, 232–233
    wikis, 237–238
Interpretive communities, 49–50
Interviews, 105–111, 109b, 124
IRBs (internal review boards), 91

Joint constructions, 75–76
Judgment, withholding of, 106–107,
    138, 177–178

Kennedy, Annie, 277–286
Key experiences, 144–145

Landcare Research/Manaaki Whenua
    website, 239
Language use, 201–202
Leadership, as facilitation, 30–31
Leading questions, 109–110
Legitimacy issues, 41–45
Levin, M., 42, 66
Lifestyle, 125
Lincoln, Yvonna, 19–20, 53, 75, 92,
    182–183
Linking, 179–180, 181f
Literature on action research, 64–68
Literature reviews, 120–122, 217–218
Location of meetings, 127–128, 131
Look phase
    overview, 133–134b
    acquiring information, 101–103
    descriptive analysis, 123–126
    documents, records and reports, 115–116
    focus groups, 111–113
    information sources generally, 103–105
    interviews, 105–111, 109b
    literature reviews, 120–122
    meetings, 127–132

participant observations, 113–115, 114b
purposes of, 101
statements of the problem, 99–101
statistical information gathering,
    122–123
surveys, 118–120
visual media, 116–118
Lyotard, J.-F., 50

Making Good Food at Warburton School.
    See Milyirrtjarra Kuurl Mirrka
    Palyalpayi (Making Good Food at
    Warburton School) (Beadle)
Marxist theory, 46
McNiff, J., 65
Meetings, 127–132, 157
Member checking, 93, 110
Milgram experiments, 89
Milyirrtjarra Kuurl Mirrka Palyalpayi
    (Making Good Food at Warburton
    School) (Beadle) beyond breakfast,
    288–289
    early days, 287–288
    external support, 290
    governance processes and
        partnerships, 290–291
Minitour questions, 108, 109b
Modeling, 178–179

Neutrality
    bracketing for, 139–140
    in interview questions, 106–107, 109
    in language use, 201–202
    withholding judgment, 106–107, 138,
        177–178
A New Mathematics Curriculum (Swift)
    agenda, 274
    conclusion, 276
    context, 269
    issue investigated, 264
    literature study, 273–274
    method, 264–266
    outcomes, 269–276
    parent experience, 272–273
    philosophical rationale, 266–268
    question statement, 264
    references, 276
    student experiences, 269–270
    student standardized test results, 273
    Term 4, 2004, 274–275
    Term 1, 2005, 275–276
    teacher experiences, 271–272
Nurturing, 176–177

Objectivity, 101–102
Observations, what constitutes, 92–93
Office of Women's Health website, 244
Online collaborative tools. *See* Internet
ooVoo, 236
Operational statements, 194–195
Opinion leaders, 79–81
Organizational procedures, 31–32
Organizational reviews, 150–152
Outcome statements, 169, 170–172
Ownership, 77

Participant observations, 113–115, 114*b*
Participants, in reports, 219–220
Participation
    as basis of action research, 6–8,
        14–20, 28–31, 28*b*
    benefits of, 16–17
    effects of, 18–19
    theory and, 40–41
Performances. *See* Reports
Personal nurturing, 176–177
Photo elicitation, 117
Photographs, as data source, 116–118
PhotoVoice, 238–239
Planning stage
    overview, 73–75, 97–98*b*
    agendas, 82, 84–85
    authoritarian style and, 73–74
    collaborative design and, 96
    consensus as goal, 75–76
    context and history and, 85–88
    establishing contact, 76–77
    ethical considerations, 88–91
    identifying key people, 79–81
    identifying stakeholders, 77–79, 80*t*
    positional awareness, 82–85
    purposes of, 73
    rigor and, 91–94
    role establishment, 81–82
    sociable participation and, 94–95
    stance and presentation, 82, 84–85
    See also Strategic planning
Policies, plans and procedures,
    59–64, 62*b*
Political issues, 196–198
Positions, 82–85
Positivistic research. *See* Research
Postmodernism, 46–54
Poverty & Race Research Action
    Council website, 239–240
Poverty and Race Research Action
    Council website, 244

Power and control
    centralization of, 29
    in corporate world, 29–30
    facilitator awareness of differences
        in, 68–69
    finances and, 198–199
    postmodern perspective and, 47–54
    sharing of, 69
    theory and, 45–47
Practice scripts, 61–64, 62*b*
Practitioners, 1–3, 20–23. *See also*
    Facilitators
Preliminary meetings, 127–128
Presentation of self, 82
Presentations. *See* Reports
Priority identification, 168–169
Problem analysis, 155–156, 156*f*
Problem statements, 99–101
Procedures, organizational, 59–64, 62*b*
Programs, social. *See* Social programs
    and services
Project Management Institute—
    Knowledge Centre website, 245
Prophetic pragmatism, 51–52
Public meetings, 127–128
Purposeful sampling, 77

Quality checks, 173–175
Quantitative research. *See* Research
Questionnaires, 118–120
Questions
    example questions, 108
    extension questions, 108
    grand tour questions, 107, 109*b*
    guided tour questions, 108
    leading questions, 109–110
    minitour questions, 108, 109*b*
    neutrality in, 106–107, 109
    six questions, 124, 148–150, 169–170
    task questions, 108

Rae, Deborah, 247–263
Reason, P., 37–38
Recipe-based solutions, 167–168
Reconnect Action Research Kit
    website, 245
Records, documents, and reports, 115–116
Referential adequacy, 93
Reflection, xv, 177–178, 231. *See also*
    Think phase
Relationships, 24–26, 24*b*
Reports
    alternative structures for, 226–229, 228*b*

audience for, 205
categorization of data and headings
     for, 143–144
collaborative writing of, 157–162, 160*f*
as data source, 115–116
inaccessibility to participants of, 60
journalistic style in, 58–59, 160
macrostructure focus of, 60–61
presentations and performances as,
     160–162
purposes of, 210
steps for, 210–211
strategic planning and, 204–206
visual media, 160–162, 211
voice of participants and, 212–213
See also Formal reports; Milyirrtjarra
     Kuurl Mirrka Palyalpayi
     (Making Good Food at
     Warburton School) (Beadle); A
     New Mathematics Curriculum
     (Swift); Transitions *headings*
Representatives, 21–22
Re-search. *See* Think phase
Research
action research compared, 5–6, 8,
     8–9*b*, 62*b*
defined, 5–6
informational significance and, 54
purposes of, 10
Researchers, role of, 20
Research facilitators. *See* Facilitators
Research for Action website, 240
Resistance, 73–74
Respect, 76
RFA: Research for Action website, 241
Rigor, 91–94
Runtè, Robert, 230–231

SAMHSA: Substance Abuse and
     Mental Health Services
     Administration website, 244
Scientific method, 42–44
Scripts, 59–64, 62*b*
Second Life, 234–235
Second-person research, 65
Semistructured questioning procedures,
     106–110, 109*b*
Services. *See* Social programs and services
SHARP: Sustainable Health Action
     Research Programme website, 244
Six questions, 124, 148–150, 169–170
Skype, 235
Small-group processes, 130–131
Snowballing, 81

Social Action for Health website, 244
Social analysis, 78
Social mapping, 79, 80t
Social media. *See* Internet
Social programs and services
best practices and, 45–47
collaboration as neccessary for
     success of, 17–19, 30–31
ineffectiveness of, 2
scientific method and, 44
Social sensitivity, 63–64
Speeches, 207–208
Spurious results, 133
Stakeholders. *See* Participation
Stance, 82, 84–85
Standpoint epistemologies, 56–57
Statements of the problem, 99–101
Statistical information, 122–123, 183
Strategic planning
overview, 209*b*
action plans for, 195–196
celebrations for, 207–208
decision making, 202–203
evaluation of, 204–206
finances, 198–200, 199*t*
language use, 201–202
managing change process, 189–191
monitoring of, 203
operational statements, 194–195
political issues and, 196–198
principles in operation, 200–201
supporting of, 203
sustainable change as goal, 187–189
vision statements for, 192–193
Stringer, E., 140
Support networks, 179–180, 181*f*
Survey research. *See* Research
Surveys, 118–120
Sustainable change, 187–189
Swift, Karen, 264–276
Symbolic territories, 82–85

Tape recorders, 110–111
Task questions, 108
Teacher Action Research—EdChange
     Multicultural Pavilion website, 241
Teaching, circumstances affecting, 3–4
Terminology, 201–202
Theme identification, 142–143
Themes in Education website, 241
Theory
overview, 36–37, 71–72*b*
feminist theory, 56–57
giving voice and, 57–59

legitimacy issues, 41–45
postmodernism, 46–54
power and control and, 45–47
practice and, 36–39
role of, 37–39
Theses and dissertations, 214–216, 215*b*
Think phase
overview, 164–165b
case example for, 145–147
distilling data, 139–147
interpretation generally, 136–139
key experiences, 144–145
problem analysis, 155–156, 156*f*
purposes of, 135–136
report writing, 157–162, 160*f*
See also Analysis enrichment
Third-person research, 65–66
Traditional research. *See* Research
Transferability, 93–94
Transitions - The Experiences of Older
People From Hospital to Home -
Progress Report (Rae)
conclusion, 262
family and friends, 261–262
introduction, 258
key issue summary, 259–261
literature reviews, 262–263
objective, 258
Transitions - The Experiences of
Older Women From Hospital to
Home (Rae)
artifacts, 254
audience for, 247–248
context, 248–251
data analysis, 254–255
data gathering, 251–254
ethical procedures, 256
focus group, 253–254
introduction, 247
issue investigated, 248
note taking, 253
outcomes, 257
participant reactions, 253
procedures used, 251–257
purposes of, 247–248
report construction, 255
researcher/historical perspective, 249
rigor checks, 256–257
role clarification, 252–253
sites, 251
stakeholders, 250–251
Triangulation, 93
Trust
balance among stakeholders and, 83–84

credibility and, 92–93
dependability and, 94
in entrepreneurial organizations, 191
importance of, 68–69
inclusion and, 31–32, 31*b*
personal nurturing to increase,
176–177
Tweetdeck, 233
Twitter, 232–233

Understanding the "Understanding":
Preliminary Findings on Aboriginal
Perspectives on Engagement With
Governments (Kennedy)
Aboriginal people's comments, 279
engagement, what is, 279–280
feeling comfortable and safe, 282–283
final remarks, 283–285
introduction, 277
methodology, 277–279
references, 285–286
understanding through
communicating, 280–282
Units of meaning, 141–142
Upstream work, 192
U.S. National Institute of Mental Health
website, 244
U.S. National Science Foundation, 91

Van Willigen, J., 125

Venue for meetings, 127–128, 131
Verbatim principle, 110, 140
Videoconferencing, 235–236
Videos, as data source, 116–118
Vision statements, 192–193
Visual media, 116–118, 160–162, 211,
238–239

Watson, Lilla, 45
Websites. *See* Internet; *Specific websites*
West, C., 51
WHARC: Women's Health Action
Research Centre website, 244
Whitehead, J., 65
Wikis, 237–238
Wikispaces, 237
Women's studies, 56–57
Workshop facilitation, 145–147
World Health Organization website, 245
Worldviews, 125

Youth Worker Resources website, 245
Youthwork Links and Ideas website, 246

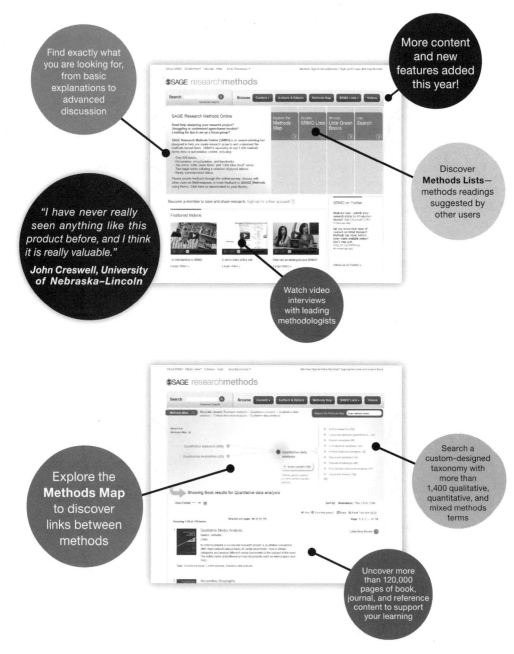

SAGE researchmethods

The essential online tool for researchers from the world's leading methods publisher

Find exactly what you are looking for, from basic explanations to advanced discussion

More content and new features added this year!

"I have never really seen anything like this product before, and I think it is really valuable."

John Creswell, University of Nebraska–Lincoln

Discover **Methods Lists**— methods readings suggested by other users

Watch video interviews with leading methodologists

Explore the **Methods Map** to discover links between methods

Search a custom-designed taxonomy with more than 1,400 qualitative, quantitative, and mixed methods terms

Uncover more than 120,000 pages of book, journal, and reference content to support your learning

Find out more at
www.sageresearchmethods.com